SOCIAL POLICY
OF THE AMERICAN
WELFARE STATE
An Introduction to
Policy Analysis

SECOND EDITION

Robert Morris
BRANDEIS UNIVERSITY

Longman

New York & London

To Sara

*For stimulating ideas
and constant encouragement.*

**Social Policy of the American Welfare State: An Introduction to
Policy Analysis, Second Edition**

Longman Inc., 1560 Broadway, New York, N.Y. 10036
Associated companies, branches, and representatives
throughout the world.

Developmental Editor: Irving E. Rockwood
Editorial and Design Supervisor: Barbara Lombardo
Production/Manufacturing Supervisor: Ferne Y. Kawahara
Composition: Pine Tree Composition, Inc.
Printing and Binding: The Alpine Press, Inc.

Library of Congress Cataloging in Publication Data

Morris, Robert, 1910–
    Social policy of the American welfare state.

    Includes bibliographies and index.
    1. United States—Social policy. 2. Housing policy—
United States. 3. Public welfare—United States.
I. Title.
HN65.M614 1985   361.6'1'0973   84–3955
ISBN 0–582–28539–9

Manufactured in the United States of America
Printing: 9 8 7 6 5 4 3 2 1   Year: 92 91 90 89 88 87 86 85

Contents

Preface to the Second Edition

Since the appearance of *Social Policy of the American Welfare State*, the election of a Republican administration has intervened to articulate strong opposition to the federal role in social welfare. While this event would seem to contradict the text's thesis of a steady evolution of public responsibility for human welfare, the early evidence, after 3 years of Republican and 4 years of conservative Democratic government, suggests that the thesis first advanced is still valid and defensible. The scale and scope of governmental responsibility has not been significantly altered despite the strong language calling for a rollback; the rate of increase has been slowed, and in marginal areas, responsibility has been shifted back to state government, but to government nonetheless. But the basic foundations of Social Security and food supplementation have not been altered, even when the benefits have been trimmed. Public expenditure for unemployment has increased, as has federal control over health costs. The weight of normative citizen convictions has supported continuity. The major change has been a shift in the ideology of the civil servants added to the federal system. The convictions of many of the new breed of civil servants are those of management of a system, not its development and growth. They bring skill in managing a crisis of resource constraint and in keeping a system going within both law and resource, but they do not bring enthusiasm for new frontiers or for further growth and development. It is too early to tell whether this shift will in time alter the direction of social policy, but there are very few signs that a major reversal is in the making. Evolution may be slowed down, but not reversed.

Special thanks are due Kathy King for research assistance in updating evidence about welfare activity and change since the appearance of the first edition and to the editors of Longman in encouraging the revision for a second edition.

ROBERT MORRIS

Preface to the First Edition

This volume was begun as an introduction to the general subject of so-cial policy as it is developing on the American scene, an introduction for students and citizens puzzled by the proliferation of welfare programs.

The rapid growth of United States governmental welfare programs is now a commonplace aspect of American life. In terms of simple dollar ex-penditure in relation to national income, American welfare has nearly reached the level achieved by those European states that were once consid-ered pioneers in decent dealing with human needs in an industrial age. In-stead of viewing this growth as a great achievement, many have strongly criticized it as a jerry-built hodgepodge of unconnected bits and pieces of social legislation that have not satisfactorily dealt with persistent human needs. This dissatisfaction is summed up in the complaint that the United States has no social policies or, if it has some, that they are regressive and punitive. While many needs that were ignored 40 years ago are now met by government programs, the criticisms stress the omissions, the gaps, the con-tradictions. To many it would appear that this growth has had a mindless quality about it, a blind and erratic and undirected groping out of a wilder-ness of human and national difficulties.

The intended introduction was soon enlarged to test whether the wel-fare evolution has in fact been as chaotic and thoughtless as it appears on the surface to be. I was early forced to ask whether it is possible that some pat-tern lay beneath the seeming confusion, a pattern that was not readily seen either in the rhetoric of political campaigning or in minutiae of program-matic detail. It soon became evident that any such search would have to con-sider a persisting reality in American life: that there are very few concrete or programmatic issues about which ordinary citizens have a widespread consensus. Rather, there are numerous and conflicting views about which issues are more rather than less urgently in need of attention, and there are as many differences about exactly how to handle those that are accepted as urgent. These differences of opinion are found among ordinary citizens, among experts, and among political leaders. There is also a conscious ambiguity about our national view as to the respective roles for the expert, the elected official, and the lay citizen in arriving at policy decisions. Often public views lag behind the understanding of leaders in any field, but we are reluctant to let such leadership act decisively in making decisions until widespread support in the general public can be generated. This wide consensus often emerges as slowly as public values shift. The margin between official leadership in guiding public thought and the tyranny of state manipulation of a passive electorate is very thin.

In much writing about social policy, two strands have evolved without effective synthesis. One has been concerned with the political dimension, analyzing the exchange between political forces and special-interest groups in maneuvering a decision through the processes of government and executive branch administration. The other has concentrated on the technical side of designing programs or policies in which the engineering or drawing-board aspect of planning is stressed. The relationship between the two can be described retrospectively, but a theoretical synthesis has not moved much beyond those that helped shape the American Revolution and the Constitution.

In trying to understand whether or not the evolution of welfare programs has proceeded by calculation or design, I have chosen to review the 40-year growth of federal programs in a few fields in order to seek out any patterns that may hold together the seemingly erratic bits and pieces of legislation and action. The approach is admittedly subjective. It is possible that a long involvement in social planning has produced a belief that a pattern *should* exist for planning purposes, and I may therefore be finding what I have wanted to find. In defense of the approach, I would offer the view that not all patterning in human affairs proceeds from a universal, comprehensive, and logical or engineering design that is introduced through conscious acts for which all consequences are calculated in advance. The social as well as the physical sciences have uncovered many examples of underlying coherence and continuity that frame seemingly isolated or random behaviors of human beings, of social organizations, and of atoms. Of course, this coherence is not complete, and much remains that is as yet unexplained, certainly in the behavior of individuals and of social organizations, because of emotional and other forces whose dynamics are only partly understood.

The empirical look, no matter how incomplete, can improve our understanding of how American society copes with its social problems, given the size and heterogeneity of both the people and the land. If an underlying pattern is discerned, this may help us cope with the admitted deficiencies of present arrangements to deal with poverty, mental and physical illness, deviance and delinquency, or criminal behavior. If no pattern is discerned at all, the argument for an increase in the mechanisms to introduce some more rational planning may be strengthened.

Some readers may see the conclusions of this exploration as constituting a defense of the status quo. This has certainly not been the intent. There are serious deficiencies in the ways we have chosen to handle grave personal difficulties. Certainly our mechanisms for conscious planning in the interest of both effectiveness and efficiency are primitive and incomplete. As a nation, we are still trying to improve the articulation of a few basic principles that both electorate and public officials can accept and count on over time. The more clear these principles become, the more they can serve as a guide for the development or improvement of social programs.

The arbitrary construct of underlying social values that both sustain and constrain governments' actions may seem like another case of blaming the victims (in this case the electorate) for the difficulties they experience. I believe the evidence is quite clear that our national experience is not one of denying the plight of the victims. Rather, it is one of steadily enlarging the range of plights to be attended to by government and, at the same time, shaping the *way* we allow our governments to help. It seems inescapable that either we must live with an ambiguity inherent in the symbiotic relationship between citizen and official or we must embrace some form of dictation. We can live with the fact that average citizens hold values shaped by their past, the kinds of information and stimuli to which they are exposed, and the knowledge that the past confers upon them. These views are changed, usually slowly, by the influence of leaders in thought and action. But elected officials are not free agents when it comes to changing public values; they are elected because they fit the electors' beliefs about who represents their views and who will express their values in action. Only a few values are so widely held that most citizens share them. Public officials can move beyond these few views only at their peril, unless they are so convinced of the rightness of their differing values that they are prepared to press their views and resist efforts to remove them from office. The rub, of course, comes in first identifying just what those key basic values are and then in selecting acts that do not do too much violence to them.

This set of dilemmas explains, at least in part, the surface untidiness that characterizes our welfare apparatus. I hope that our efforts to better serve humanity will be well served by an examination of underlying citizen attitudes that act as stabilizers and constrainers as much as they are stimulators of change. As a nation, we have changed much by creating a welfare state; we have changed less rapidly in the values that underly how we organize and express that state.

In this process, civil servants and elected officials come off not as badly as their sharpest critics believe. While there is no shortage of knaves and opportunists in public life, there are also many who are committed to civilized and humane efforts to improve the condition of the helpless. While political movements, pressure groups, and special interests have all played active roles in the past 40 years' evolution, civil servants and elected officials have also been just as active promoters of change and growth, albeit less recognized and much maligned. I suspect that many anonymous public servants have played important roles in advancing the responsibility of government for alleviating human distress. Whether this is good or bad is a matter of political philosophy about which people still differ.

There are certainly other ways of perceiving the underlying forces and processes of recent decades. Marxist and neo-Marxist analyses represent one of several alternative interpretations. In time, our study of the facts, as we can tease them out of organizational and personal behavior and out of history, will sharpen and improve our analysis. This will change the ways in which professionals, technicians, political figures, and concerned citizens go about the business of civilizing the world in which we live. One thing seems inescapable. It is not possible to peaceably reverse the tendency for government to play a greater and greater role in the lives of individuals. As this power increases, so may the power of the state apparatus increase to override or to ignore the underlying values of the governed. In this event, powerful interests will contend to guide government or to capture it. The power may then be used in the interest of the many or of the few. It is not at all clear that the power will inevitably be used to help the few who are likely to be helpless, which is, after all, the function of a welfare state.

I am indebted to many who have contributed to this effort: colleagues and pioneers in the search for systematic ways to approach policy questions, their writing and their conversations; the several editors at Harper & Row who helped so much to introduce more clarity and simplicity into the presentation; Sylvia Pendleton for research assistance; and Barbara Isaacson for careful preparation of an often messy manuscript.

ROBERT MORRIS

Acknowledgments

Excerpts from "R & D in the New Budget System," by W. D. Carey, *Science* Vol. 193, p. 103, 13 August 1976 Copyright © 1976 by the American Association for the Advancement of Science. Reprinted by permission of the author and the publisher.

Excerpts from "Science Values and Human Judgement," by K. R. Hammond and L. Adelman, *Science* Vol. 194, pp. 389–396, 22 October 1976, Copyright © 1976 by the American Association for the Advancement of Science. Reprinted by permission of the author and the publisher.

Excerpts from "Raising Children in Modern America: Problems and Prospective Solution," by W. Kessen, *Science* Vol. 193, pp. 310–311, 23 July 1976, Copyright © 1976 by the American Association for the Advancement of Science. Reprinted by permission of the author and the publisher.

Excerpts from *Public Policy and Income Distribution* by Winifred Bell, Robert Lekachman, and Alvin Schorr Copyright © 1974 by New York University School of Social Work. Reprinted by permission of the author and the publisher.

Excerpts from "Recent Increases in Poverty," by Sheldon Danziger reprinted by permission from *Focus*, Vol. 7, No. 1 (Winter 1984). Copyright © 1984 by the Board of Regents of the University of Wisconsin System.

Excerpts from *The Politics of Neglect* by Bernard Frieden. Copyright © 1975 by MIT Press. Reprinted by permission.

Excerpts from *The Politics of Medicare* by Theodore R. Marmor (Hawthorne, NY: Aldine Publishing Company) copyright © 1970, 1973 by Theodore R. Marmor. Reprinted by permission.

Excerpts from "The New Despotism," by Robert Nisbet reprinted from *Commentary*, June 1975, by permission; all rights reserved.

Excerpts from *Revenue Statistics of OECD Member Countries 1965–1980* reprinted by permission, copyright © 1981 by the OECD.

Excerpts from *Progress Against Poverty* by Robert Plotnick and Felicity Skidmore (Madison, WI: Institute for Research on Poverty) copyright © 1975 by Academic Press. Reprinted by permission.

Excerpts from "Social Policy," by Alvin L. Schorr and Edward C. Baumheier from *Encyclopedia of Social Work, 16th Edition*, Robert Morris, editor, p. 1362 copyright © 1971 by the National Association of Social Workers, Inc. Reprinted by permission.

Excerpts from *EMIC: A Study of Administrative Experience* (Ann Arbor, MI: Bureau of Public Health Economics, School of Public Health, University of Michigan) copyright © 1948 by the University of Michigan. Reprinted by permission.

Excerpts from "The Model Cities Program, An Assessment," by Roland Warren from *The Social Welfare Forum* copyright © 1971 by Columbia University Press. Reprinted by permission.

The Scope of Public and Social Policy

A Confusion of Meanings

1

The term *social policy* is popularly used with varied and ambiguous meanings. *Policy* is generally interpreted as meaning an organizing principle to guide action. It has long been used in reference to the positions taken by sovereign governments on matters of state. With the growth of corporations, whether profit making or not, the term came to be applied as well to the principles determining daily management procedures and eventually to the primary or basic aims of corporate entities.

However, the growth of governmental and corporate structures since the late 1920s has made this limited definition of policy obsolete, for many of their actions now affect almost all aspects of the lives of most citizens. Those principles of action that affect citizens as individuals or group interrelationships most directly have come to be called *social* policies, to distinguish them from policies more directly related to the more traditional areas of power, political control, and economic production. The borderline between acts that might be defined as social, political, or economic is necessarily unclear, but in general, social policies are identified as those through which government seeks to correct inequities, to improve the condition of the disadvantaged, and to provide assistance to the less powerful. They have come to include actions directed toward equalization of the well-being of all citizens, adjustment of social relationships, and regulation of aspects of living not dealing with physical safety, economic and commercial activity, or foreign relations. T. H. Marshall, a founder of social policy theory, has defined this difficult new arena as "the policy of governments with regard to action having a direct impact on the welfare of the citizens by providing them with ser-

1

vices and income."[1] The need for a better understanding of the concept of
social policies—how they evolve and to what extent their development is influenced by professional or technical competence—has been forced upon
citizen and public official alike, for public action now affects the lives of all,
indirectly if not directly.

Before World War II, social policy was often defined to mean those actions intended to benefit the poorest or least advantaged in an industrial
society. After World War II, it became increasingly apparent that policies of
government dealt with the redistribution or flow of resources to all
economic levels of society. National accounting took note of the fact that
legislation to benefit citizens often benefited the middle class and the
economically comfortable as often as it benefited the poor. Tax benefits that
reduce tax payments for owners of real estate or of industry are just as
clearly "social policy" as are laws that govern the payment of tax income to
the needy. Both methods have the effect of altering or smoothing out the
relationships between income classes. At the highest level of social policy,
the struggle is for an equitable balance among the various decisions that
benefit various populations.

Early definitions need only one modification in 1984: Social policy now
works through government influence over the conditions in which citizens
pursue their private activities as often as it acts by giving income or services
to the dependent—the shape of taxation on income, the regulation of industry, investment in urban development, protection of civil rights, control
of environmental pollution or of military build up, and the innumerable
other ways that modern government affects the lives of all citizens, not just
the poor.

A striking example of this shift in perception is the recognition that the
organizations of health and welfare service employ large numbers of professional and clerical workers. It has been estimated that, at least 13% of all
private sector professional service workers in America are employed, indirectly, if not directly, through funds which flow into the welfare system.
These workers are as much beneficiaries of welfare as are the client consumers.[2]

Ernest Becker, a distinguished social scientist and philosopher, has tried
to understand how it can be that intelligent, reasoning human beings continue to create and to recreate worlds with so much violence, inequality, and
suffering. He states that governments are one, if only one, device for giving
meaning to group survival.[3] In recent decades we have turned to govern-

---

[1] T. H. Marshall, *Social Policy*, (London: Hutchinson, 1965), p. 1.

[2] Lester Turow, *The Zero Sum Society*, (New York: Penguin Books, 1981).

[3] From Ernest Becker, *The Denial of Death* and *Escape from Evil* (New York: Free Press,
1973 and 1975).

ment to make wise choices on our behalf, yet at the same time, we are often repelled by what governments do. Becker concludes that reasoning has failed thus far to influence man's fate, but that we now seem to realize we must choose between inaction or using reason to keep the world from destruction. In electoral campaigns we seek a compromise between our deepest emotional wishes for peace, plenty, and equity and our reluctance to trust too much to the reasonableness and thoughtfulness of others—that is, to judgments expressed through government.

At one level William D. Carey notes that the election of 1976 seemed to be mainly a struggle over the transfer of influence and power, and not at all over the substance of the choices that political leaders must make once power is achieved. He notes poignantly:

> It is the substance that defines the quality of choice. What are the terms on which an affluent and technologically powerful nation proposes to conduct its affairs in a troubled world? For that matter, are affluence and power ... to be continued goals of our public policies and the measures of effective leadership? If *not* affluence and power, then what? Candidates speak for or against the power of a national government or say "trust me"; but few discuss issues concretely.[4]

In many ways the election of 1976 tested certain broad premises underlying governmental policy. For example, one premise is the desirability of unrestrained growth—growth in the economy, in consumer goods and consumerism, in freedom, in size, in power, and, finally, in government. Against this view lies a deep, uneasy sense that unqualified and unlimited growth will not only exhaust physical resources but lead to new confusion and disorder and even to limitations in human tolerance. Such concerns are not expressed in the course of an electoral campaign in which the acquisition of power seems to be the major aim, but they lie uneasily beneath the surface, appearing as distrust of governmental growth and activity, coupled with a yearning for ever increased economic and physical well-being. What emerges is a fear, not only that we are reaching the limits of growth, but also that we are nearing the limits of confidence in political solutions to our continuing problems.[5] The 1980 election of a Republican administration in Washington reflected this concern about the limits of growth and the influence of a national government's power. For the first time since the depression of the 1930s, the United States had a national government clearly and strongly committed to a reduction in the size and role of government responsibility for transferring resources to the poor.

---

[4] William D. Carey, editorial in *Science*, 13 August 1976, p. 535.

[5] See, for example, R. E. Miles, Jr., *Awakening from the American Dream* (New York: Universe Books, 1976).

Diminishing Confidence in Government Policy

For much of human history, individuals, organizations, and governments were preoccupied with physical survival—prevention of starvation and protection against enemies. The Industrial Revolution and its accompanying promise of relief from some of the pressures of physical survival allowed for an increase in individual aspirations and in governmental capacity to satisfy them. Nineteenth-century optimism about science and technology expanded to include new, hopeful beliefs for society. It was no longer sufficient merely to avoid starvation. Hazards of the human condition that are centuries-old suddenly became proper objects of public attention. Disease could be controlled, the pain of death and dying postponed, the frustration of drudgery and labor diminished. The material comforts an industrial economy could provide came to be seen as the right of all citizens, not merely a favored few. Where these conditions did not result naturally, people began to look more to the government to accelerate the progress toward a better world.

The fully developed expectation on the part of the people that government should assume this responsibility and governmental acceptance of its new role reached a peak of expression in American politics of the 1930s with the promise of a New Deal. Succeeding generations and governments adopted variants on the theme: Square Deal, Fair Deal, and finally, the Great Society of the 1960s.

Governments at all levels became engaged in modifying the distribution of resources, in allocating jobs, in controlling working conditions, in providing health and social services, and in developing housing. In effect, all aspects of human and social existence became the proper concern of government. In communist societies these functions were totally preempted by the state, and planning for the delivery and distribution of all goods was closely controlled. In noncommunist societies the borderline between private activity and governmental intervention was subject to constant modification, experimentation, and change.

By the 1970s the number of federal governmental aid programs of all kinds totaled about 1000 (this figure includes only programs listed in the Federal Catalogue of Domestic Assistance Programs, so the number can be arbitrarily revised upward or downward). In 1975 half of the federal budget, half of local government budgets, and a fifth of the gross national product (GNP) were devoted to social programs intended to realize the expectations for the well-being of citizens.[6] But the results of this flood of programs became the focus of dissatisfaction. Consumers, professional experts, policy makers, and taxpayers all expressed their special complaints. Some

[6] Advisory Commission on Intergovernmental Relations, Fiscal Federalism, 1. Trends, 1976 ed. (Washington, D.C.: 1976), pp. 7, 11, 17.

argued that government was permanently incompetent; others, that policies were unwise or benefited the wrong persons.

This frustration over federal social problems was compounded by further disillusionment with governmental wisdom resulting from the expeditions in Southeast Asia that were maintained through both Republican and Democratic administrations, and from the distortions, manipulations, and dishonesty of the early 1970s and of the Nixon administration.

The swing of the pendulum from high hope to great disillusionment produced in 1976 a period of pause and hope. Could a new national administration regain some sense of the confidence that the past represented? Or would dismay and apathy deepen? There were polarized views as to the proper approach to action. A conservative, widely held view was expressed by Robert A. Nisbet, who concluded that the national government has so deeply penetrated the most minute aspect of the daily life of all citizens that a real tyranny has entered into our society, a tyranny more insidious and dangerous than the political tyrannies of fascism or communism.

> "The most absolute authority," wrote Rousseau, "is that which penetrates into a man's inmost being and concerns itself no less with his will than with his actions." The truth of that observation is in no way lessened by the fact that, for Rousseau, genuinely legitimate government, government based upon the general will, *should* so penetrate. In the name of education, welfare, taxation, safety, health, and environment, to mention but a few of the laudable ends involved, the new despotism confronts us at every turn. Its effectiveness lies, as I say, in part through liaison with humanitarian rather than nakedly exploitative objectives but also, and perhaps most significantly, in its capacity to deal with the human will rather than with mere human actions. By the very existence of one or another of the regulatory offices of the invisible government that now occupies foremost place, the wills of educators, researchers, artists, philanthropists, and enterprisers in all areas, as well as in business, are bound to be affected: to be shaped, bent, driven, even extinguished.[7]

Nisbet argues that present practices are pragmatic, beginning with the best intentions but ending by placing government at the center of all activity. The accumulation of petty rules and regulations conceals the real predicaments of human existence that trouble many citizens, making it impossible for the so-called practical programs to do much good in ameliorating the very difficulties with which they are intended to deal; they may, indeed, do great damage. At the opposite extreme, others argue that our national commitment to deal with serious human dilemmas has not been strong or firm enough, so that we end up with half measures neither adequately funded nor administered.[8]

[7] Robert Nisbet, "The New Despotism," *Commentary* 59, no. 6 (June 1975): 31–34.
[8] James L. Sundquist in *Centrally Planned Change: A Re-examination of Theories and Concepts*, eds. R. Mayer, R. Maroney, and R. Morris (Urbana: University of Illinois Press, 1974): 178–204.

Most people probably fall between the extremes, wanting the government to attend to certain kinds of difficulties, provided governmental action appears to be well focused, efficient, and not too preemptive of private life. This vague aspiration of the center probably explains why the national investment in human services, through a growing body of social programs, continues to expand. Even between 1980 and 1983, under a government committed to reducing the federal role, the total national expenditure continued to rise, although the purposes shifted relatively more for military and somewhat less for other social purposes. The most vigorous debates over alternative policies under quite different national administrations—Republican (Eisenhower, Nixon, Ford) and Democratic (Roosevelt, Truman, Kennedy, Johnson)—have produced a steady rise in federal budget expenditures, in the proportion of federal taxes going for social purposes, and in the variety and range of programs introduced. What has varied is the *rate* of increase. For this middle range of public opinion, the concern seems to be that the "system" is out of control and subject to no reasonable direction or management, not that it is too big or too small.

Federal action in the social area since the 1930s has generally taken the form of problem-specific legislation resulting in an ever-increasing number of new programs. But starting in 1968, both Republicans and Democrats began to question the effectiveness of this approach, and both parties proposed new policy guidelines. One proposed policy was to improve government operations while imposing a moratorium on new programs. Another was to create more programs and increase funding for existing ones in order to secure a more sizable mass of intervention. A third and very beguiling policy would seek to cut back sharply the role of government. An extreme and idealized version claims that:

> a shift of the center of government to the citizen, the person, [makes] a new paradigm possible for social policy. The government defines problems; people experience predicaments. . . . The government acts through implementation; people seek to understand their predicaments through theories about their predicaments. . . . a true social policy will come into being (according to the popular paradigm), a governing principle will come into being, as people perceive their social predicaments, form theories about these, and on the basis of such theories make commitments which, if the theory is at least practically sound, will start a development through constructive conflict and cooperation by which people will lead themselves out of their predicament.[9]

The first two policy lines shift the attention of technical inquiry to the means by which service programs can be made more effective or a bureaucracy can be better trained and better controlled to assure respon-

---

[9] Quoted from an unpublished paper by Robert McClintock, resident scholar in the U.S. Department of Health, Education, and Welfare, Office of the Secretary, 1976.

siveness to human needs. The third approach advocates the complete abandonment of existing approaches in order to start over again. It would build up new social mechanisms through the widest participation of citizens, relying on citizen self-help rather than on government.

Unfortunately, the last proposal leaves unanswered the question of how the popular paradigm will come into being. What is the mechanism through which 250 million citizens will begin to express constructive conflict and cooperation? Who will be involved in the confrontation—government agencies, or the policymaking units of the legislature, or citizens outside the government? The first two approaches also leave questions unanswered. How can the existing procedures and programs be reformed without destroying them?

Whatever the identifiable flaws in such shifts in policy, each could constitute a long-range general goal. However, in order to serve as an effective guide for action, more middle-range social policy guidelines would also have to be adopted. Examples of these are dealt with in succeeding chapters, but a brief reference to them can be made here.

The Middle Range: Social and Sectoral Policies

Middle-range policies are best understood in terms of tangible human dilemmas, not in terms of social abstractions alone. The following illustrate some persisting human dilemmas for which some governmental action at a middle range of policy is still sought, despite dissatisfaction with past efforts. These middle-range policies may be better identified as sectoral policies; they affect the entire society indirectly, but they focus on specific sectors of human affairs.

Income Security

The private economy has not been able to provide work and income for all persons at a level that meets their economic expectations. Public action is accepted for the retired, the physically disabled, the very young, and—reluctantly—for those unemployed through no fault of their own and for single-parent, female-headed families with small children. But the programs in effect keep some people out of work who the rest think ought to be working, even if at substandard wages. Other programs are at cross-purposes: Retirement programs are designed to get people out of the labor force, while work-incentive programs are designed to get others in, neither working very neatly in relation to the other. The cost of such programs rises, regardless of boom or depression cycles. Meanwhile, hope persists that more jobs can be generated, but only as a result of "proper" governmental action, following which government should resume its narrower role of helping a few unfortunates who cannot work at all.

The single most troublesome area of income policy is that of obligation for the able-bodied. There seems to be little objection to policy that benefits those who work. Tax benefits for home ownership or retirement payments to those who have worked are widely accepted. But there is reluctance to be equally generous for those able-bodied and without work. These may be middle-aged workers displaced by technological change or able-bodied elderly who want to work, but more likely they are young adults of minority groups or teenaged unmarried mothers. This able-bodied unemployed population seems to be slowly increasing as technology abolishes jobs as fast or faster than it creates new ones, but public and policy judgment often continue to function on premises of past generations that assumed that the able-bodied could and should be able to find some work, that public support is unjustified. The unemployed become the scapegoats of much policy debate.

Health

Guaranteed access to health services by government was first supported as a way to keep people off relief by keeping them healthy, but it became in time a right of citizenship in a humane society. Some improvement of access for the aged and poor minorities has occurred, but at the cost of depersonalizing health care and increasing expenditures. The inflated costs of medical care consumed 9% of the gross national product in 1976 and 10% in 1983. Growing investment in high-technology curative programs produces a growing, not diminishing, number of disabled persons.

Housing and the Urban Environment

Decent housing at a reasonable price for all has been a vaguely articulated goal for decades. But a succession of governmental programs, designed to improve the physical quality of housing and to bring it within the reach of the poorest, seems to have coincided with a steady decline in the quality of the urban environment, ending in an ugly urban sprawl, wasting energy, and eroding the amenities of normal living. All this has incurred a further inflation, so that low-cost housing for families with modest incomes demands a rising percentage of disposable income and becomes less and less attainable.

The Aged

The elderly have been the object of major public programs to assure economic and health security. But the costs have proven unexpectedly high so that more and more of each generation's earnings has been siphoned off in rising taxes to assure this security for a growing percentage of the population retiring from productive work. At the same time, the idea of forced retirement to draw benefits has been increasingly challenged by the aged themselves, and their new social, not economic, circumstances have attracted federal action—loneliness, isolation, deficient nutrition, housing, transportation. The boundaries of federal protection of the elderly have greatly widened.

Other Problems

A variety of other human difficulties continue to distress public and private citizens: mental illness, mental retardation, delinquent behavior (especially among youths), drug and alcohol abuse or addiction, and overinstitutionalization of the disabled. A group of programs that may, for lack of a better phrase, be called the personal social services are now underwritten by the federal government, and these involve federal control on a wholly new frontier. They raise the question of how far the federal government's obligations extend into the individual's daily life and the family domain. At the same time, the reasons for this development are compelling human concerns about real problems and a faith, perhaps vestigial, that government can make a difference in reducing these hazards.

In the 1976 presidential election campaign, one candidate announced a major task force on governmental actions as they affect the family. The statement was so loosely phrased that it could have meant either a wide-ranging assessment of many government programs or a narrow study of the Aid to Families and Dependent Children (AFDC) relief program as it operates to break up natural family ties. But whatever its meaning, the fact that the statement was made at all confirms the movement of government into the family domain. The basic decision must be made as to whether to withdraw a little or to improve the programs' impact on family life. But in either case, further decisions must be made—in what areas to withdraw, how can the programs be made more effective, and so forth.

Older views held that giving financial relief to poor widows or deserted mothers or giving health examinations to poor mothers was a sufficient expression of our national desire to help those in trouble. But we have discovered that, if we give relief under strict controls, we encourage troubled fathers on the edge of survival to desert so that their children can be fed. And if we remove controls, we risk encouraging whole family units to withdraw from the labor force altogether. If they do, can we conclude that family life is strengthened or weakened?

A desirable policy would be one that gives all individuals maximum choices about how they shall live, but such a policy becomes one of public financial support for private choice making. The cost of such a policy may prove higher than most citizens want to pay, and the results may increase inequity rather than reduce it. (Is it equitable to guarantee the same income to one family that works 40 hours a week and to another family that does no work?) But if we feel that this type of policy loses sight of social or collective needs, what course should we follow?

These are, of course, oversimplified formulations, but they still reflect emotional responses that are widely expressed. Single-action remedies are thus found wanting, and social policies become more complex as we move from the generalized aim of helping those in trouble to guiding principles to direct actions to realize that aim.

The sectors we have listed are representative areas for social policy action. They suggest that social policy seeks to realize the largest of human aims—to shape a more perfect world—but that it does not specify just how that perfection will be achieved or how it will alter our social and political forms. Policy seems to reflect peoples' efforts to improve life's conditions with the imperfect techniques now at hand and in the face of many contradictory wants and beliefs. But saying this much tells us little about what social policy is. Does an accumulation of programs or any one program of services constitute a policy? And whose policy do we mean—that of the Congress, the president, "the government," or "the people"?

Conflicting Definitions of Social Policy

Social policy slowly came to mean that area of organized human activity that somehow sought to impose reason and order on a mass of rapid and often untidy change. But the concept of social policy in the public mind developed as haphazardly as the social changes that led to its rise. Considering the explosion of diverse wants and aspirations, it is not surprising that the term has acquired many different meanings and has been used as a label to cover many different approaches. At least four common usages can be distinguished. Each has some validity and some defects.

Social Policy as the Sum of Society's Actions: Societal Policy

Social policy is sometimes considered to be the sum of all choices made in society governing the nature of relationships among individuals and social units. One especially ambitious effort to encompass all of human knowledge into one science is that of David G. Gil, who argues that social policies constitute a system which links all relationships between individuals, groups and nations and which regulates the distribution of statuses, constraints, rewards and entitlements.[10]

It is clear that in the aggregate a set of behaviors and decisions reflects the current balance in any society's views about a social problem. This is perhaps self-evident, since this broad use of the term means that the social policies of society follow from the behavior of individuals, laws, acts of groups, etc. Such usage might be better termed *societal policy* or *social norms*. For example, until 1860 American societal policy permitted the coexistence of slavery in the South and absence of slavery in the North. After the abolition of slavery in 1865, society still permitted racial discrimination. Since 1950, however, the nation's sum of actions has shifted in the direction of abolishing, or at least reducing, racial discrimination. If one adds together the combination of legislative enactments, court decisions, and attitudinal changes, it would appear that, while discriminatory attitudes and behavior still exist, the national society overall has embarked on an antiracist policy. Such societal policy may be too slow moving, but it does represent some measurable line of norm development.

Such a broad concept of social policy thus becomes more a matter of historical reconstruction—that is, the recognition, after the fact, of changes that have taken place. It is doubtful whether it lends itself to the development of a discipline in social policy development since, at least in the United States, we do not have a monolithic society in which all aspects of social relationships are controlled and planned from any center. At best, such a usage of the term helps those engaged primarily in political activism, a career for which formal study has been unnecessary.

Social Policy as an Appeal to Do Something Comprehensive

In another usage, social policy is defined as the aim of a group of citizens for action on a particular problem. Thus, it is frequently argued that the nation requires a family policy, a national health policy, an income policy. In its more elementary sense, this usage simply identifies an area of human relationships in which advocates of action want society, through its mechanisms of government, to respond to a need, although the direction and details of action are not specified. In this usage, a comprehensive approach is usually preferred to a piecemeal one. A comprehensive approach is one in which all aspects are logically connected and neatly packaged, at least on paper, with no loose ends.

There is a tendency for advocates to conclude that, if programs of ac-

---

[10] David G. Gil, "A Systematic Approach to Social Policy Analysis," *Social Service Review* 44, no. 4 (December 1970): 411–426.

tion or behavior do not conform to what they desire or believe to be "right," then a policy on the subject is lacking. For example, in the human resource or social welfare area, it is commonly argued that there is no policy about the family or about health or about children, but such a conclusion ignores certain underlying realities. While there is certainly not "a health policy," adopted as such by the Congress and implemented by the federal government, certain sets of decisions and acts can be said to define American society's attitude to the health of its people. The present cumulative actions, viewed in their broadest context, can be said to contain the following elements: a belief in the ability of science and technology to effect cures and the consequent emphasis on cures as opposed to prevention of disease; a belief in the usefulness of distributing and sharing the cost of such curative services through insurance, so that individuals are not personally confronted with the costs of the services they receive; a strong preference for supporting individual access to private physicians rather than to collective health services, such as polyclinics; the appropriation of tax funds and governmental services, added perhaps reluctantly, to the health system to fill in gaps that the private system refuses to fill; and, finally, the appropriation of public funds to assure widespread access by all, regardless of income, to the kind of system that the foregoing components produce. Such a set of acts is a far cry from a comprehensive scheme, but it can be said to represent a national policy, being the best compromise that conflicting and contradictory forces can achieve. At best the effective policy stance has been one of improving access to an existing medical system organized by innumerable private providers. It is not a policy to change the system in any significant way; to give more or less emphasis to the long-term disabled, to the aged or to prevention; or to reverse the trend toward defining health care as *medical* care, usually organized around a large costly hospital complex.

Social Policy as Acts of Government

In a third sense, social policy seems to refer to a set or group of programs, developed either by government or by private organizations, to deliver particular health or welfare services or a combination of health and welfare services to achieve some loosely defined general aim. Thus, it can be said that there is a policy concerning child health when programs have been enacted for well-baby clinics, maternal and child health services, immunization, and nutrition. In this usage, it is not clear where the term *policy* differs from the details of program organization; it is sufficient to believe that the fact of "doing something"—that is, the existence of a set of programs—is an expression of society's having some policy about a particular problem.

  If we consider a narrower usage—for example, social policies as representing the specific enactments of government—we immediately en- counter two levels of complexity. If "enactments of government" is inter- preted as meaning legislation passed by Congress, how do we deal with the often contradictory intentions of many acts? If "enactments of government" is interpreted as meaning the sum of actions taken by the three branches of government, how do we reconcile the often contradictory effects of such ac- tions?

We must recognize that we can refer to an act of Congress only at a par- ticular point in time. Legislative history is replete with instances in which the Congress enacts legislation in one session and enacts quite contradictory legislation on the same subject in a following session, without troubling to repeal the former. Federal income maintenance policies originally were designed to provide emergency cash or in-kind income to people who had no work and who would, lacking such income, starve to death. But succeeding income programs, attempting to deal with the complexities of income distribution in America, produced an elaborate superstructure. There are income programs to fend off starvation, but there are also income programs to discourage people from working (social security retirement) and, simultaneously, income programs designed to force people to work (the work-incentive program of public assistance). To make the situation even more complicated, the income programs originally designed for emergency relief were based on the assumption that only the unemployed would lack the minimum means of subsistence. But if means of subsistence was taken as the standard for need for relief, then the borderline between the unemployed and those who had low-paying jobs became more difficult to maintain and such programs as the food stamps program were developed to give additional income to people who, although working full time, were con- sidered poor. The boundaries between relief and income redistribution became progressively blurred.

Rather than concluding from such an accumulation of contradictions that our nation lacks a policy, it can equally well be argued that our policy as regards income maintenance is one of rectifying the major distortions in in- come security without at the same time completely destroying our basic economic system. One may argue that our basic economic system should be replaced by a system in which all the means of production are managed by the national government and all citizens in effect are employees of one vast corporation: the state (as in the Soviet Union or China). Equally, one can believe that human needs are best met by an infinitely complex economic system, with many relatively independent producers offering employment opportunities, with the state moving progressively and pragmatically to cor- rect inequities and to bring about continuous equalization of opportunity and condition.

There are social policies embedded in both the above approaches, and in either it can be said that there is a clear guide to action by the national government. Unfortunately, at least in the United States, the national government is not simply the legislature. The executive branch has as much influence over the nature of policy as does Congress, exercised in the executive's capacity to formulate operating regulations that govern the development of any program enacted by Congress. This power of the executive is further enlarged by a tendency of Congress to enact programs with general purposes and with guidelines, but to leave the organization of administrative details to the executive branch. For example, Congress may enact a mental health program to return care for the mentally ill from hospitals to the community, but executive regulations can, and have, assured that mental health services are primarily controlled by a medical profession oriented to hospital care as the treatment of choice.

The situation in the United States is further complicated by the existence of a third, coequal branch of the national government, the courts, which in recent decades have become a major force in shaping social policies. When a court decides that a patient in a mental hospital must either be given active treatment or be discharged and that a patient cannot be constrained against his or her will, it can no longer be argued that the formulation of policy about the mentally ill is solely within the hands of either Congress or the executive branch. When the courts order busing of school-children to reduce school segregation, educational policy is no longer solely a legislative or executive matter.

This three-tiered government forces one to consider the distinction between policies advanced for consideration and the ones actually adopted by all three elements through the checks and balances of constitutional government.

Policy as Daily Administrative Guidance

The term *policy* may also be used to refer to the rules and regulations that govern the day-by-day delivery of specific services. In other words, policy is defined as the operating guidelines for formal organizations that deliver human services. Thus, an income maintenance program can be governed by a policy that requires that able-bodied recipients register for work or take any work that is offered. Mental health services may have a policy of not accepting chronic alcoholics and drug addicts or, on the contrary, of especially trying to reach alcoholics and drug addicts.

Like the other common usages, this narrowest concept of policy also presents difficulties. In terms of the delivery of services, it may be said that an agency has a policy to close at 5:00 P.M. or to offer emergency services at night and on weekends or to require a client's consent form to secure information from other agencies. Such minor administrative policies may also reflect wider social norms, as when an agency in the 1940s could require segregated entrances for minorities or could refuse applications from black applicants. An agency may or may not apply a rigid work test before giving relief, or a psychiatric service may or may not admit alcoholics. But such policies are of a wholly different order from the societal norms or the national directions we have just discussed. They certainly do not address directly the larger questions of income distribution and mental illness that originally gave rise to the demand that organized society deal with these problems.

It may be evident from this brief listing that some groups use the term *policy* to identify specific achievements they want to aim for, whereas others use it to identify a general desire to deal with some loosely defined social difficulty without distinguishing among the diverse and often irreconcilable wants of constituencies, which may impede any course of action.

In effect, the broadest definitions of social policy are so general that they defy any attempt to construct a professional discipline or a governmental structure that can simultaneously handle all the dimensions of life. The broader use is, therefore, most valuable in trying to identify a state of affairs in society at a given time without doing more than suggesting tension points requiring action. Similarly, the narrowest definition does no more than deal with minor organizational symptoms of the basic social problems with which we are concerned. What remains is a substantial middle range of subject matter touching on reasonably identifiable social difficulties that are sufficiently troublesome as to warrant organized intervention by some social entity. These troublesome issues are likely to be ones that provoke substantial controversy, at least as to means, if not ends. Opponents can agree that there should be equity and stability in income for the entire population but disagree vigorously on what constitutes equity and how any agreed-upon definition might be achieved. The matter next to be considered is whether a more utilitarian concept of social policy can be formulated.

Additional Readings

Anderson, Wayne; Frieden, Bernard; and Murphy, Michael, eds. *Managing Human Services.* Washington, D.C.: International City Management Association, 1977.
Gilbert, Neil, and Specht, Harry. *Dimensions of Social Welfare Policy.* Englewood Cliffs, N.J.: Prentice-Hall, 1974.
Marshall, T. H. *Social Policy.* London: Hutchman, 1965.
Rein, Martin. *Social Policy.* New York: Random House, 1970.
Schorr, Alvin. *Explorations in Social Policy.* New York: Basic Books, 1968.
Titmuss, Richard M. *Essays on the Welfare State.* New Haven: Yale University Press, 1959.
Walzer, Michael. *Spheres of Justice.* New York: Basic Books, 1983.

A Framework for Understanding Social Policy

Societal Norms, Public Policy, and Social Policies

2

The term *social policy* may be more usefully developed from the sense in which it is defined in the *Oxford English Dictionary:* "a course of action adopted and pursued by a government, party, ruler, statesman, etc.; any course of action adopted as advantageous or expedient."[1] Schorr and Baumheier expand this definition by identifying social policy as

> the principles and procedures guiding any measure or course of action dealing with individual and aggregate relationships in society. It is conceived as intervention in and regulation of an otherwise random social system. Established social policy represents a subtle course of action with respect to selected social phenomena governing social relationships in the distribution of resources within a society.[2]

Elaborating on these definitions, we can identify social policy as a guide to action in future unanticipated situations. Policy identifies the general principles that an individual party or a government uses to make choices and decisions in unfamiliar circumstances that may arise in the future. Policy is, therefore, a guiding principle. It is a guide to action to be taken by individuals or groups capable of influencing the course of events.

For purposes of this volume, this usage of the term is to be distinguished from an ethical concept or a set of values; value may be fervently held and

---

[1] Oxford English Dictionary, compact (New York: Oxford University Press, 1971), p. 171.
[2] Encyclopedia of Social Work, 16th ed. (New York: National Association of Social Workers, 1971), p. 1362.

yet not lead to action. Policy is to be distinguished by the fact that it involves a choice to be made by an individual or a group, resulting in actions that affect the lives of others.

This usage also needs to be distinguished from ideology, primarily by the flexibility inherent in a view that is treated as a guide rather than an immutable law. Ideologies are significant in shaping the course of human events, but they are frequently rigid in operation, and deviation from the ideology is considered to be treasonable. Rigid adherence to ideological purity may result in a form of self-destruction or failure in action.

Thus, we will here interpret policy as a set of guiding principles employed with flexibility by public officials able to make choices affecting large numbers of other people to assure decisive action when unanticipated conditions are met.

A Typology for Social Policy Analysis

The foregoing definition, to be useful, needs to be considered against a framework of those other dimensions that affect both the evolution and implementation of guiding principles. If one examines the various uses of the term *policy* more closely, a new pattern begins to emerge. The idea of social policy can be seen to consist of several elements, each of which needs separate attention and each of which has an effect on the rest.

Society's Aspirations

The aspirations of a society are in the nature of *preamble goals* for a society, much like the statement in the American Declaration of Independence that "all men are entitled to life, liberty, and the pursuit of happiness."

Social Norms or Societal Policy

Societal policy represents the accumulation of values and normative standards that a society builds up over time. These norms determine what a society will allow its organized structure of governance to do on behalf of its members. They are an unwritten blend of what a people think their society ought to be, what they wish to do collectively for the good of all, and how they prefer to act to achieve such ends.

Collective acts take place at two levels: that of government and that of nongovernmental informal or primary associations. Social norms control activities at both levels, but government is likely to be more rigidly limited because its acts can affect everyone. Informal associations are less rigidly constrained because their acts may affect only those who are members of the associations. Informal associations can test out variations in normative behavior and can, over time, alter the norms of the whole society, sometimes by trying out ideas that everyone is later willing to adopt and sometimes by forceful imposition, as in the case of dictatorial societies.

Thus policy as social norms means the premises, values, and general mind set of the country. Such values shape our political choices and our scientific and technological pathways for exploration.

Public Policy

Public policy provides a guide to the priority aims of governing and to the means that are acceptable to or preferred by a particular government. These guides are general in that they indicate which problems a government will choose to deal with and which way a government will choose to move when it is confronted with the necessity to take action. They are useful over time to assure some continuity in governmental behavior; they assure a sense of direction and provide a base from which to confront new or unexpected situations. In this sense policies are guiding principles for a government.

A government may choose a general policy of stressing its citizens' domestic well-being over acquisition of power in foreign affairs. When the well-being depends upon control over external resources, the policy choice is whether or not to concentrate on domestic resources alone. Within such a general policy, a government must also decide to what exent it will regulate the acts of its citizens in order to pursue the goal of general well-being, to what extent it will direct its citizens to act in their private capacities to satisfy their own needs, or to what extent it will provide for its citizens' needs directly through government agencies.

Sectoral Public Policy

In the guidance sense, not only is policy general, applying to all of government, but it can be *sectoral*, in that policy affects only a segment of a society, as in the case of health or child welfare policy.

Administrative Policy

Policy also includes the rules and regulations that are adopted by private or governmental agencies or units to govern their day-to-day activities.

We will concentrate in this book on the third and fourth elements, but will consider also how the first and second impinge upon the third, for the interaction of these four determines, over time, how social policies evolve.

Much of the recent discussion of social policy has assumed that development takes place as a result of political controversy, and this is essentially correct if, by politics, one means the maneuver for position and influence among political groups that have different objectives. Unfortunately, the ambiguity in language that we outlined in Chapter 1 introduces a rather sterile element into the political process. Political antagonists may argue that the "other" party is opposed to a preamble goal when, in fact, the argument is over the means to be used. Equally, the arguments may overlook the fact that general social norms can obstruct the adoption of particular public policies just as much as the views of extremist groups. These forms of political controversy lead to two indictments of American social policies: either that we lack a social policy altogether (e.g., we have no health policy) or that our social policies are destructive. This latter view is held by critics of the existing situation who are identified by their political opponents as conservative (or reactionary) or as progressive (or radical).

The later chapters will seek to establish that neither of these indictments is quite accurate. At the level of national government, consistent policies (in the sense of general guiding principles) can be identified for income maintenance, health, housing, personal social services, and children and the aged.

It will further be argued that the policies we have, however well or ill conceived and administered, have been constricted by societal policy, which represents the limits within which the general body of the electorate will allow its agents to function. This is not to deny that the norms of the citizenry are influenced by their political leaders. It is only to say that these social norms, however they have been shaped, do limit what governments are allowed to do.

This will lead us to a further consideration of the leadership role of government. Is government wholly passive, or can it alter the constraints imposed by social norms without being disowned by its people? An examination of several social policy areas will produce some evidence that national government has sought to widen the boundaries of governmental action on social policy matters, often trying to go beyond the limits of approved norms.

Finally, our exploration into the development of social policy will lead us to distinguish between social policies that are advocated and those that are adopted. Usually this is discussed as advocacy by political parties and groups of citizens acting in unofficial capacities. For our purposes, we will look at the advocacy roles played by the executive and legislative branches of national government.[3] We will indicate how in several social policy areas the executive or the legislative branch has taken initiative to advocate policies that went beyond the societal norms of a given period in history. While these efforts may have reflected pressures from constituency groups, we

---

[3] In recent years, the courts have also played an active role in advocating the adoption of social policies, but these judicial efforts lie outside the bounds of this volume.

will focus primarily on the official acts of governmental units to translate advocated into adopted policies, regardless of the origins of the advocacy.

Our analysis of American social policies will thus use these elements for a paradigm:

1. Underlying social norms that shape and constrict as much as they direct governmental action
2. Public policies reflecting the guiding principles with which governments meet new situations
3. Sectoral public social policies
4. The leadership role of governmental units in moving beyond or in modifying social norms

The interplay among these elements produces one dynamic in the evolution of the American society and in the role of its government vis-à-vis the wants of its citizens.

The Creative Tension: Social Norms versus Public Policy

The succeeding chapters trace a few index social policy areas in American life. But before we examine them in detail, it will be useful to assess what has been happening since the late 1920s in the United States regarding social policies. The basis for assessment is derived from evaluation of the exemplars of national policy discussed in succeeding chapters.

The central character of American social policies has a direction and a continuity. It is shaped by a few basic attitudes or social norms shared by most citizens as well as by their public officials. This societal policy—the sum total of laws, habits, mores, and practices—appears to consist of the following.

Preference for private or marketplace decision making. There is a preference for allowing marketplace forces the widest and fullest expression—that is, to find the solution to problems through the interaction of many decisions made privately, if at all possible. The term *marketplace* as used here refers to private-party decision making, sometimes mediated through some economic exchange between parties. Such marketplace exchanges exist among nonprofit and governmental units, but the conventional usage does not extend to those exchanges, since government has a power to enforce decisions commonly considered to be absent in private activities. As used here, the term reflects a vague confidence that individual decision making is preferred above all other forms of action.

As social and economic structures have become more elaborate, especially since the Industrial Revolution, more and more decisions that govern the distribution and access to goods and services have been made by corporate entities and collectivities. Simple, one-person choices have become virtually impossible, since these entities decide on the basis of corporate interests what goods and services can be produced or provided. Of course, such corporate-serving choices respond to a degree to the aggregated wants of many individuals, but the choice of action is determined primarily by the need of corporate units to satisfy their members—to show profit. Thus, the belief that the market will respond to individual wants or needs is diminished by the recognition that we as individuals get what others are willing to do or to produce for us.

This disjunction between individual and collective wants and responses leads to the discovery that the market does not keep up with expectations as fully or as rapidly as we would like, and, more serious for our purposes, it does not adequately meet all wants with equal efficiency. Thus, some groups remain relatively neglected, giving rise to the second facet of our normative social framework.

Belief in government aid to the weak and helpless. With the recognition that the market does not serve all individuals' needs equally comes the belief that government should act on behalf of vulnerable individuals and groups. The accepted definition of vulnerable individuals is limited mainly to certain groups who are perceived to be relatively weak and helpless—the aged, widows, orphans, the crippled, and, by recent extension, anyone in serious trouble not of his or her own making, as, for example, unemployment following an acceptable work history.

Continued belief in the saving virtues of work. If we assume that hard work by the individual will bring about the satisfaction of each individual's needs, then private decision making is to be preferred. The vulnerable are then defined as those who are deprived of work by forces beyond their control—the widowed, the aged, the ill, the uneducated, and so on. The other poor are poor because they are lazy.

Continued optimistic view of progress through science. The nineteenth-century belief in progress toward a better world through science and technology leads to a belief that actions can be seen as short term on the assumption that science will abolish current difficulties. As a result, there is little interest in adopting long-range policies that will be adhered to over many years in order to achieve a fixed result. There is a continuing belief that too many changes will be produced by science, or that too many unpredictable political events may erupt, or that constant social change will make today's actions useless in the future.

Preference for shared responsibility. The sharing or division of responsibility among the several layers of government is basic to our system. As an extension of this, there has always been a preference for shifting or distributing costs of any government action as far away from the individual as possible. If possible, let small insurance premiums anticipate large costs. Or levy small taxes to protect a few against grave trouble, and levy those taxes through "painless" payroll deductions for the federal government rather than levy local taxes that are more visible and "painful." If responsibility for any problem is assigned to the farthest removed level of government, the happier everyone is, for a time. But if the "pain" of costs builds up too heavily and quickly at any one level, a blocking reaction sets in.

For several decades the electorate has supported federal programs because federal taxation was more extensive and less visible. As the total tax burden rose to 30% of the gross national product, a reaction set in, captured by the Republican elections of 1980. But when that administration sought to divest the federal government of certain social obligations and to return them to state governments, those governments resisted on the grounds that they lacked the means to reassume burdens.

This sharing preference extends to the relationship between government and private enterprise. In the welfare field, private nonprofit and proprietary agencies alike have flourished. Citizens and public officials both are more comfortable when a variety of private organizations share with the government the responsibility for social programs. Local or state agencies for the mentally ill, the retarded, the aged, and children are seldom highly regarded, but private agencies for the same purposes are, even if they are financed by tax funds. In recent years, proprietary and profit-making agencies have entered the welfare field at a rapid rate. Profit-making agencies are now encouraged and accepted by both federal and state laws to provide nursing home and home health care, youth training, and housing. So the national preference for shared responsibility now involves several levels of government, nonprofit and profit-making private organizations.

The five preferences discussed here are the parameters of public policies. They establish the direction in which policies are, by and large, permitted and expected to develop. The public, national policies on such issues as income, health, old age, and housing have grown in volume and specificity, but they remain guided by the sense of direction and continuity of our basic norms. The fact that the norms are implicit, rather than stated explicitly as the basis of government policy, does not make them in any sense less powerful in determining decision making in public policy.

Although public policy is thus always limited by the basic norms, it would be a mistake to assume that it is unchanging. The norms themselves undergo change, and policy sometimes pushes beyond the implicit limits. The guiding norm of responsibility for vulnerable groups has led to the many social welfare programs that account for a large proportion of the federal budget and governmental activity. These programs have by now become so extensive in relation to other actions in the social fields that they represent an unexpected change in policy direction that goes well beyond the intent of the original concept of responsibility. The scope and dynamism of public programs produced by these policies have given such programs a vigorous life of their own. Their existence has expanded the limits set by another social norm, as the reliance upon private actions and decision making has in many areas been overshadowed by public decision making and the range of subjects considered suitable for public intervention into private lives has widened.

It may be concluded that a new stage in policy evolution has been reached. Governmental actions have now moved beyond these sanctioning preferences or societal policies. A tension or strain has been introduced: Either the government programs will be pulled back within the old confines, or the social norms will alter as a result of leadership changes introduced by governmental action. Present evidence suggests that it is the constrictions of social norms of the past that will give way and that the new, wider platform for public policies in social needs will be used for the next generation of governmental actions.

Gone is the need to defend governmental action and policy as a basic violation of old norms. Instead, controversy now rests on such questions as: How much further shall the national government go? What is it possible and desirable to expect out of government action? How will the boundaries between government and private actions be redrawn? How much private disposable income will citizens permit to be used for public provisions? How will private action be used?

If this analysis is correct, certain assumptions about the debate over specific public policies will have to be altered. It has long been assumed by liberal-minded activists who seek to enlarge government actions that obstacles inhere in the nature of the governmental system and in the blocking capacity of some powerful groups, but the very societal guides upon which these advocates rely and upon which they call for justification may prove to be the difficulty. All desire a better world, but the guiding principles by which this better world is to be approached are circumscribed. It is the cumulative effect of public policies and actions which constitute the vanguard pushing beyond the old guidelines and creating new ones, albeit slowly.

Others who argue for a cutback in governmental action, whether for conservative reasons or because of a radical mistrust in government, will find that some of the normative impulses serve to push toward more government rather than toward less.

An illustration of this tension is found in the dilemma about what to do with the long unemployed able-bodied adults. As alluded to earlier, this population has seldom been regarded with generosity or favor in any nation or at any time. Societal norms favor work for this group and disfavor helping them very much. At the same time, social norms hardly favor a starving population, but the effects of modern technology produce a significant minority of able-bodied citizens who cannot find work with the best efforts they make. The policy choice in the near future will be to keep this minority, between 10 and 15% of the labor force, as a positive part of the society or, alternatively, to let it fall into an underclass of neglected impoverished persons for whom society makes no decent place, a kind of untouchable class (not caste).

The distinction between norms and policy can be drawn thus: Guiding social norms are the result of an accumulation of preferences produced by a people as they shape their specific society. This accumulation represents the most widely held, deeply felt beliefs, although smaller groups with divergent views or preferences coexist within any society. The dominant beliefs and norms are embedded in innumerable laws and organizational modes of behavior, as well as in personal and informal group mores. These norms are not amenable to specific alteration by acts of government, although they do change slowly over time as social forces work their way through inherited belief systems and norms.

Public policies, meaning the explicit sectoral actions of government, are less grandiose, although they are also cumulative. They do not cover all of life. Such policies are discerned through the actions of public officials and the legislating elements of government and cover relatively specific aspects of a society's life. These policies can be expressed by individuals or by political parties. They can routinely conform to social norms, or they can express leadership action taken by public bodies to respond to new conditions that require new steps outside of or beyond the prevailing norms. Such leadership action makes public policy the cutting edge of social change and helps a people to exploit the opportunity for change that a new social situation demands. In some instances, public officials may seek to introduce public policies for relatively specific aspects of social life quite at variance with the underlying social norms, with the result either that a variant approach must be imposed by some force upon a people not yet ready or that the proposed policy becomes a subject for perhaps decades of debate and discussion during which public acceptance emerges. As we will discuss later, the over 50-year effort to secure some form of national health insurance may illustrate such a lengthy process. In this sense, public policy contains another level of guiding principles that are introduced by individuals or by parties to guide public actions of public officials. Such policies may lead or follow social norms, but they do influence government actions over time.

Thus, the evolution of social policy occurs through the tension between pressures exerted on governments to act beyond the confines of social norms and the restraining influence of the norms to precipitate movement. Except in periods of great upheaval and catastrophe, the result is to ensure that new assumptions of authority by government over the lives of citizens are tested and that, if too little action is taken or the testing is too prolonged, the pressure for movement builds up.

Evidence for this type of creative tension between norms and policy is first found in the accompanying tables. Tables 2.1, 2.2, 2.3 and 2.4 show how governmental allocations in social welfare, income maintenance, and

TABLE 2.1
Social Welfare Expenditures Under Public Programs, Selected Fiscal Years, 1950–80[1]

(In millions)

Program	1950	1955	1960	1965	1970	1975	1977	1978	1979	1980[2]
					Total expenditures					
Total	$23,508.4	$32,640.0	$52,293.3	$77,175.3	$145,855.7	$290,080.4	$360,602.0	$394,631.7	$430,684.5	$493,354.5
Social insurance	4,946.6	9,834.9	19,306.7	28,122.8	54,691.2	123,013.1	160,883.3	174,950.9	194,176.4	229,552.3
Old-Age, Survivors, Disability, and Health Insurance (OASDHI)[3]	784.1	4,436.3	11,032.3	16,997.5	36,835.4	78,429.9	105,410.1	117,431.9	131,719.4	152,110.4
Health Insurance (Medicare)[4]					7,149.2	14,781.4	21,548.8	25,189.2	29,123.6	34,991.5
Railroad Retirement[3]	306.4	556.0	934.7	1,128.1	1,609.9	3,085.1	3,818.6	4,019.8	4,310.6	4,768.7
Public employee retirement[5]	817.9	1,388.5	2,569.9	4,528.5	8,658.7	20,118.6	26,495.9	29,935.8	33,929.8	39,490.2
Unemployment insurance and employment services[6]	2,190.1	2,080.6	2,829.6	3,002.6	3,819.5	13,835.9	15,448.8	12,598.4	11,313.1	18,326.4
Railroad unemployment insurance	119.6	158.7	215.2	76.7	38.5	41.6	107.3	134.0	86.9	155.4
Railroad temporary disability insurance	31.1	54.2	68.5	46.5	61.1	32.9	81.8	73.4	65.6	68.7
State temporary disability insurance[7]	72.1	217.5	347.9	483.5	717.7	990.0	1,042.2	1,124.6	1,232.2	1,379.1
Hospital and medical benefits[8]	2.2	20.0	40.2	50.9	62.6	72.9	75.7	77.6	75.9	49.6
Workers' compensation[9]	625.1	943.0	1,308.5	1,859.4	2,950.4	6,479.1	8,478.6	9,633.0	11,518.8	13,253.4
Hospital and medical benefits[8]	193.0	315.0	420.0	580.0	985.0	2,470.0	2,530.0	2,820.0	3,215.0	3,665.0
Public aid	2,496.2	3,003.0	4,101.1	6,283.4	16,487.8	41,308.3	53,266.5	59,394.3	63,945.1	72,385.1
Public assistance[10]	2,490.2	2,941.1	4,041.7	5,874.9	14,433.5	27,360.4	35,086.0	37,208.3	40,008.6	45,474.0
Vendor medical payments[11]	51.3	211.9	492.7	1,367.1	5,212.8	13,501.6	18,206.6	20,395.9	23,431.0	27,394.2
Social services[11]					712.6	2,622.4	3,216.8	2,840.1	2,725.9	2,342.8
Supplemental Security Income[12]						6,091.6	6,818.9	7,193.7	7,532.3	8,226.5
Food stamps				35.6	577.0	4,693.9	5,472.0	5,139.5	6,478.1	9,083.3
Other[13]	6.0	61.9	59.4	373.0	1,477.3	3,162.4	5,889.6	9,852.8	9,936.1	9,601.3

Health and medical programs [14]	2,063.5	3,103.1	4,463.8	6,246.4	9,906.8	17,787.6	20,129.1	23,237.1	25,387.9	28,118.8
Hospital and medical care	1,222.3	2,042.4	2,853.3	3,452.3	5,313.4	9,219.6	9,049.1	10,542.1	11,314.9	12,202.8
Civilian programs	886.1	1,297.6	1,973.2	2,515.5	3,553.8	6,405.6	6,022.1	7,209.1	7,622.9	8,142.8
Defense Department [15]	336.2	744.8	880.1	936.8	1,759.6	2,814.0	3,027.0	3,333.0	3,692.0	4,060.0
Maternal and child health programs [16]	29.8	92.9	141.3	227.3	431.4	567.0	674.0	713.0	760.0	798.0
Medical research	69.2	132.8	448.9	1,165.2	1,635.4	2,928.0	3,728.0	4,368.0	4,647.0	5,218.0
School health (education agencies)	30.6	65.9	101.0	142.2	246.6	350.0	414.0	485.0	520.0	569.0
Other public health activities	350.8	383.7	401.2	671.0	1,348.0	2,919.0	4,165.0	5,067.0	6,025.0	6,848.0
Medical facilities construction	360.8	385.4	518.1	588.3	932.1	1,804.0	2,099.0	2,062.0	2,121.0	2,483.0
Defense Department	1.1	33.0	40.0	31.1	52.5	94.0	300.9	226.7	215.2	31.0
Veterans' programs	6,865.7	4,833.5	5,479.2	6,031.0	9,078.0	17,018.9	19,015.3	19,744.0	20,601.6	21,465.5
Pensions and compensation [17]	2,092.1	2,869.7	3,402.7	4,141.4	5,393.8	7,578.5	9,081.9	9,676.5	10,578.2	11,306.0
Health and medical programs	748.0	761.1	954.0	1,228.7	1,784.0	3,516.8	4,670.6	5,237.5	5,700.9	6,203.9
Hospital and medical care	582.8	721.5	879.4	1,114.8	1,651.4	3,287.1	4,321.2	4,855.6	5,307.9	5,749.9
Hospital construction	161.5	34.1	59.6	77.0	70.9	136.7	245.4	269.9	276.0	323.0
Medical and prosthetic research	3.7	5.6	15.1	36.9	61.8	93.0	104.0	112.0	117.0	131.0
Education	2,691.6	706.1	409.6	40.9	1,018.5	4,433.8	3,925.5	3,405.6	2,794.1	2,400.7
Life insurance [18]	475.7	490.2	494.1	434.3	502.3	556.1	607.2	614.3	638.2	664.5
Welfare and other	858.3	186.5	218.8	185.8	379.4	933.7	730.1	810.1	890.2	890.4
Education [19]	6,674.1	11,157.2	17,626.2	28,107.9	50,845.5	80,834.2	93,878.3	101,517.8	109,261.5	120,587.6
Elementary and secondary	5,596.2	9,734.3	15,109.0	22,357.7	38,632.3	59,745.6	68,218.5	73,133.1	77,714.6	86,773.0
Construction [8, 20]	1,019.4	2,231.9	2,661.8	3,267.0	4,659.1	5,746.0	6,235.1	5,245.2	5,449.3	6,524.0
Higher	914.7	1,214.4	2,190.7	4,826.4	9,907.1	16,384.1	20,034.4	21,893.3	24,129.8	26,090.7
Construction [8]	310.0	198.6	357.9	1,081.4	1,566.9	1,512.7	1,505.7	1,458.5	1,417.4	1,528.1
Vocational and adult [20]	160.8	204.9	298.0	853.9	2,144.4	4,441.3	5,312.0	6,133.3	7,029.4	7,375.2
Housing	14.6	89.3	176.8	318.1	701.2	3,171.7	4,358.1	5,224.7	6,225.8	7,209.1
Public housing	14.5	74.7	143.5	234.5	459.9	1,456.4	2,763.5	3,626.0	4,504.0	5,246.1
Other social welfare	447.7	619.0	1,139.4	2,065.7	4,145.2	6,946.6	9,071.4	10,562.9	11,076.2	14,036.1
Vocational rehabilitation [21]	30.0	42.4	96.3	210.5	703.8	1,036.4	1,251.9	1,297.6	1,309.2	1,251.1
Medical services [22]	7.4	9.1	17.7	34.2	133.8	217.7	242.6	255.6	264.6	261.8
Medical research [22]	.3	6.6	22.4	29.6		13.8	22.5	13.1		13.5
Institutional care [23]	145.5	195.3	420.5	789.5	201.7	296.1	359.7	410.1	444.0	482.4
Child nutrition [24]	160.2	239.6	398.7	617.4	896.0	2,517.6	3,268.3	3,585.0	4,374.6	5,289.3
Child welfare [25]	104.9	135.1	211.5	354.3	585.3	597.0	810.0	800.0	800.0	800.0
Special OEO and ACTION programs [26]				51.7	752.8	638.3	748.7	881.4	896.9	2,302.7
Social welfare, not elsewhere classified [27]	7.1	6.5	12.4	42.3	1,005.6	1,861.2	2,632.8	3,588.8	3,251.5	3,910.6

(continued)

See footnotes beginning on next page.

TABLE 2.1 continued

(In millions)

Program	1950	1955	1960	1965	1970	1975	1977	1978	1979	1980[2]
					Federal expenditures					
Total	$10,541.1	$14,622.9	$24,956.7	$37,711.7	$77,337.2	$167,426.0	$218,370.6	$240,033.7	$263,789.8	$303,344.9
Social insurance	2,103.0	6,385.0	14,307.2	21,806.6	45,245.6	99,715.0	134,744.7	147,252.0	163,872.2	191,106.9
Old-Age, Survivors, Disability and Health Insurance (OASDHI)[3]	784.1	4,436.3	11,032.2	16,997.5	36,835.4	78,429.9	105,410.1	117,431.9	131,719.4	152,110.4
Health Insurance (Medicare)[4]					7,149.2	14,781.4	21,548.8	25,189.2	29,123.6	34,991.5
Railroad Retirement[3]	306.4	556.0	934.7	1,128.1	1,609.9	3,085.1	3,818.6	4,019.8	4,310.6	4,768.7
Public employee retirement[5]	507.9	808.5	1,519.9	2,780.5	5,516.7	13,338.9	17,833.3	20,144.7	22,892.8	26,982.9
Unemployment insurance and employment services[6]	328.6	320.8	473.5	699.8	1,036.1	3,429.2	5,939.1	3,767.6	2,460.3	4,407.6
Railroad unemployment insurance	119.6	158.7	215.2	76.7	38.5	41.6	107.3	134.0	86.9	155.4
Railroad temporary disability insurance	31.1	54.2	68.5	46.5	61.1	32.9	81.8	73.4	65.6	68.7
Workers' compensation[9]	25.1	50.5	63.1	77.6	147.9	1,367.4	1,554.5	1,680.6	2,336.6	2,613.2
Hospital and medical benefits[8]	5.2	6.9	9.0	11.3	20.7	50.2	71.9	88.2	103.8	129.5
Public aid	1,103.2	1,504.2	2,116.9	3,593.9	9,648.6	27,186.5	35,399.3	40,013.0	43,015.3	49,252.2
Public assistance[10]	1,097.2	1,442.3	2,057.5	3,185.4	7,594.3	14,528.6	18,764.8	19,447.3	20,710.6	24,127.8
Vendor medical payments[11]		23.3	199.8	555.0	2,607.1	7,056.4	9,713.3	10,578.6	12,147.9	14,550.3
Social services[11]					522.0	1,962.6	2,461.2	2,130.1	2,044.4	1,757.1
Supplemental Security Income[12]						4,801.6	5,272.9	5,573.4	5,890.5	6,439.8
Food stamps				35.6	577.0	4,693.9	5,472.0	5,139.5	6,478.1	9,083.3
Other[13]	6.0	61.9	59.4	373.0	1,477.3	3,162.4	5,889.6	9,852.8	9,936.1	9,601.3
Health and medical programs[14]	603.5	1,150.3	1,737.1	2,780.6	4,775.2	8,521.0	10,150.0	11,461.0	12,132.0	13,348.0
Hospital and medical care	382.6	811.5	983.5	1,074.7	2,045.0	4,045.0	4,637.0	5,292.0	5,760.0	6,451.0
Civilian programs	46.4	66.7	103.4	137.9	285.8	1,231.0	1,610.0	1,959.0	2,068.0	2,391.0
Defense Department[15]	336.2	744.8	880.1	936.8	1,759.6	2,814.0	3,027.0	3,333.0	3,692.0	4,060.0

Maternal and child health programs [16]	20.1	23.7	35.3	73.4	196.0	271.0	317.0	338.0	351.0	351.0
Medical research	69.2	132.8	425.9	1,110.2	1,485.4	2,642.0	3,378.0	3,975.0	4,220.0	4,756.0
Other public health activities	63.8	65.0	57.3	222.9	590.3	1,150.0	1,211.0	1,211.0	1,239.0	1,250.0
Medical facilities construction	67.8	117.4	235.1	299.3	458.1	413.0	562.0	645.0	560.0	540.0
Defense Department	1.1	33.0	40.0	31.1	52.5	94.0	300.9	226.7	215.2	31.0
Veterans' programs	6,386.2	4,771.9	5,367.3	6,010.6	8,951.5	16,569.8	18,860.6	19,570.3	20,411.9	21,253.6
Pensions and compensation [17]	2,092.1	2,689.7	3,402.7	4,141.4	5,393.8	7,578.5	9,081.9	9,676.5	10,578.2	11,306.0
Health and medical programs	748.0	761.1	954.0	1,228.7	1,784.0	3,516.8	4,670.6	5,237.5	5,700.9	6,203.9
Hospital and medical care	582.8	721.5	879.4	1,114.8	1,651.4	3,287.1	4,321.2	4,855.6	5,307.9	5,749.9
Hospital construction	161.5	34.1	59.6	77.0	70.9	136.7	245.4	269.9	276.0	323.0
Medical and prosthetic research	3.7	5.6	15.1	36.9	61.8	93.0	104.0	112.0	117.0	131.0
Education [19]	2,691.6	706.1	409.6	40.9	1,018.5	4,433.8	3,925.5	3,405.6	2,794.1	2,400.7
Life insurance [18]	475.7	490.2	494.1	434.3	502.3	556.1	607.2	614.3	638.2	664.5
Welfare and other	378.8	124.9	106.9	165.4	252.9	484.6	575.4	636.4	700.5	678.5
Education [19]	156.7	485.1	867.9	2,469.8	5,875.8	8,629.4	9,741.0	10,900.8	12,107.9	12,990.2
Elementary and secondary	47.1	309.2	441.9	776.8	2,956.6	4,562.5	4,676.8	5,507.4	6,165.1	7,052.7
Construction [8, 20]	5.2	139.9	70.6	77.0	35.9	20.9	14.6	19.3	24.3	40.9
Higher	48.5	101.8	293.1	1,217.0	2,154.6	2,863.5	3,867.7	4,077.0	4,524.9	4,382.3
Construction [8]	5.7	5.1	1.2	324.0	466.3	273.9	251.6	132.6	74.7	42.1
Vocational and adult [20]	58.7	70.5	104.5	406.2	602.6	940.2	883.1	958.3	1,030.3	1,206.5
Housing	14.6	74.7	143.5	238.2	581.6	2,540.7	4,005.5	4,887.3	5,801.9	6,608.1
Public housing	14.5	74.7	143.5	234.5	459.9	1,456.4	2,763.5	3,626.0	4,504.0	5,246.9
Other social welfare	174.0	251.7	416.7	812.0	2,258.9	4,263.6	5,469.5	5,949.3	6,448.6	8,785.9
Vocational rehabilitation [21]	21.0	64.3	143.3	567.5	814.0	973.2	1,006.6	1,039.6	1,006.1	
Medical services [22]	5.1	5.7	11.2	21.2	107.0	174.2	194.1	204.5	211.7	212.8
Medical research [22]		.3	6.6	22.4	29.6	22.5	13.8	18.0	13.1	13.5
Institutional care [23]	20.5	40.3	20.5	34.5	22.5	20.3	18.0	20.0	55.5	74.2
Child nutrition [24]	121.2	170.7	306.1	503.7	710.9	2,064.0	2,758.3	3,040.0	3,374.6	4,209.3
Child welfare [25]	4.2	7.1	13.4	36.5	44.7	49.8	56.5	56.5	56.5	57.0
Special OEO and ACTION programs [26]	...	...	...	51.7	752.8	638.3	748.7	881.4	896.9	2,302.7
Social welfare, not elsewhere classified [27]	7.1	6.5	12.4	42.3	160.6	677.2	914.8	944.8	1,025.5	1,136.6

1 Expenditures from Federal, State, and local revenues under public law; includes capital outlay and administrative expenditures unless otherwise noted. Includes some payments abroad. Until 1977, fiscal years for the Federal Government, most States, and some localities ended June 30. Federal fiscal years subsequently ended September 30.
2 Preliminary estimates.
3 Excludes financial interchange between OASDHI and Railroad Retirement.
4 Included in OASDHI total.

5 Excludes refunds of employee contributions; includes payments to retired military personnel and survivors. Administrative expenses for Federal noncontributory retirement not available.
6 Includes unemployment compensation under State programs; programs for Federal employees and ex-servicemen; trade adjustment and cash training allowances; and payments under extended, emergency, disaster, and special unemployment insurance programs.
Footnotes continued on next page.

(continued)

TABLE 2.1 continued

(In millions)

Program	1950	1955	1960	1965	1970	1975	1977	1978	1979	1980[2]
					State and local expenditures					
Total	$12,967.3	$18,017.1	$27,336.6	$39,463.5	$68,518.5	$122,654.4	$142,231.4	$154,598.0	$166,894.7	$190,009.6
Social insurance										
Public employee retirement [5]	2,843.6	3,449.9	4,999.4	6,316.2	9,445.6	23,298.1	26,138.6	27,698.9	30,304.2	38,445.4
Unemployment insurance and employment services [6]	310.0	580.0	1,050.0	1,748.0	3,142.0	6,779.7	8,662.6	9,791.1	11,037.0	12,507.3
	1,861.5	1,759.9	2,356.1	2,302.8	2,783.4	10,406.7	9,509.7	8,830.8	8,852.8	13,918.8
State temporary disability insurance [7]	72.1	217.5	347.9	483.5	717.7	990.0	1,042.2	1,124.6	1,232.2	1,379.1
Hospital and medical benefits [8]	2.2	20.0	40.2	50.9	62.6	72.9	75.7	77.6	75.9	49.6
Workers' compensation [9]	600.0	892.5	1,245.4	1,781.8	2,802.5	5,121.7	6,924.1	7,952.4	9,182.2	10,640.2
Hospital and medical benefits [8]	187.8	308.1	411.0	568.7	964.3	2,419.8	2,458.1	2,731.8	3,111.2	3,535.5
Public aid	1,393.0	1,498.8	1,984.2	2,689.5	6,839.2	14,121.8	17,867.2	19,381.3	20,939.8	23,132.9
Public assistance [10]	1,393.0	1,498.8	1,984.2	2,689.5	6,839.2	12,831.8	16,321.2	17,761.0	19,298.0	21,346.2
Vendor medical payments [11]	51.3	188.6	292.9	812.1	2,605.6	6,445.2	8,493.3	9,817.3	11,283.1	12,843.9
Social services [11]	…	…	…	…	190.6	659.8	755.6	710.0	681.5	585.7
Supplemental Security Income [12]	…	…	…	…	…	1,290.0	1,546.0	1,620.3	1,641.8	1,786.7
Health and medical programs [14]	1,460.0	1,952.8	2,726.8	3,465.8	5,131.6	9,266.6	9,979.1	11,776.1	13,255.9	14,770.8
Hospital and medical care	839.7	1,230.9	1,869.8	2,377.6	3,268.0	5,174.6	4,412.1	5,250.1	5,554.9	5,751.8
Maternal and child health programs [16]	9.7	69.2	106.1	153.9	235.3	296.0	357.0	375.0	409.0	447.0
Medical research	…	…	23.0	55.0	150.0	286.0	350.0	393.0	425.0	462.0
School health (education agencies)	30.6	65.9	101.0	142.2	246.6	350.0	414.0	485.0	520.0	569.0
Other public health activities	287.0	318.8	343.9	448.1	757.7	1,769.0	2,909.0	3,856.0	4,786.0	5,598.0
Medical facilities construction	293.0	268.0	283.0	289.0	474.0	1,391.0	1,537.0	1,417.0	1,561.0	1,943.0
Veterans' programs	479.5	61.6	111.9	20.4	126.5	449.1	154.7	173.7	189.7	211.9

...	5,549.1	9,425.1	14,667.1	21,580.0	35,675.5	55,183.1	63,541.7	67,655.7	71,549.5	79,720.3
Elementary and secondary	1,041.2	2,091.9	2,591.2	3,190.0	4,623.2	5,725.1	6,220.5	5,225.9	5,425.0	6,483.1
Construction 8, 20	866.3	1,112.6	1,897.7	3,609.4	7,752.4	13,520.6	16,166.7	17,816.3	19,604.9	21,708.4
Higher	304.6	356.7	757.4		1,100.6	1,238.8	1,254.1	1,325.9	1,342.7	1,486.0
Construction 8	102.1	134.4	193.5	447.7	1,541.8	3,501.1	4,428.9	5,175.0	5,999.1	6,168.7
Vocational and adult 20	14.6	33.2	80.0		119.6	631.0	352.6	337.4	423.9	601.0
Housing										
Other social welfare	273.7	367.3	722.8	1,253.6	1,886.3	2,683.0	3,601.9	4,613.6	4,627.6	5,250.2
Vocational rehabilitation 21	9.0	15.3	32.1	67.1	136.3	222.4	278.7	291.0	269.6	245.0
Medical services 22	2.3	3.5	6.6	13.0	26.8	43.5	48.5	51.1	52.9	49.0
Institutional care 23	125.0	155.0	400.0	755.0	179.3	275.8	341.7	390.1	388.5	408.2
Child nutrition 24	39.0	69.0	92.6	113.7	185.1	453.6	510.0	545.0	1,000.0	1,080.0
Child welfare 25	100.7	128.0	198.1	317.8	540.7	547.2	753.5	743.5	743.5	743.0
Social welfare, not elsewhere classified 27	...	...	...	...	845.0	1,184.0	1,718.0	2,644.0	2,226.0	2,774.0

7 Cash and medical benefits in five geographical areas. Includes private plans where applicable and State costs of administering State plans and supervising private plans. Administrative expenses of all private plans and all data for Hawaii not available.

8 Included in total directly above; excludes administrative expenses not available separately but included for entire program in preceding line.

9 Cash and medical benefits paid under Federal and State laws by private insurance carriers, State funds, and self-insurers. Includes Alaska and Hawaii beginning 1960. Administrative cost of private carriers and self-insurers not available. Starting 1970, Federal expenditures include black lung benefit programs.

10 Represents categorical cash and medical payment programs under the Social Security Act and General Assistance. Starting 1969, includes work incentive activities.

11 Included in public assistance total above; includes administrative expenses of Medicaid program.

12 Benefits began January 1974; fiscal year 1973 data represent administrative expenses only.

13 Work relief, other emergency aid, surplus food for the needy, repatriate and refugee assistance, temporary and emergency employment assistance, and work-experience training programs under the Economic Opportunity Act and the Comprehensive Employment and Training Act. See footnote 27.

14 Excludes State and local expenditures for domiciliary care in institutions other than mental or tuberculosis. Services in connection with OASDHI, State temporary disability insurance, workers' compensation, public assistance, vocational rehabilitation, and veterans' and antipoverty programs are included in total expenditures for these programs.

15 Includes medical care for military dependent families.

16 Includes services for crippled children.

17 Includes burial awards. Starting 1965, includes special allowances for survivors of veterans who did not qualify under OASDHI. Starting 1974, subsistence payments to disabled veterans undergoing training shifted from veterans' pensions and compensation to veterans' education subgroup. Starting 1973, includes clothing allowance.

18 Excludes the Servicemen's Group Life Insurance program.

19 Federal expenditures for administrative costs (Department of Education) and research included in total only.

20 Construction for vocational and adult education included with elementary-secondary school construction.

21 Starting 1974, excludes administrative expenses.

22 Medical services and research included in vocational rehabilitation total.

23 Federal expenditures represent primarily surplus food for institutions.

24 Surplus food for schools and programs under National School Lunch and Child Nutrition Acts. State and local funds represent direct appropriations through 1979; all such expenditures starting in 1980.

25 Represents primarily child welfare services under the Social Security Act. Starting 1969, excludes administrative expenses.

26 Includes domestic programs consolidated in fiscal year 1972 under ACTION and special OEO programs consolidated in fiscal year 1974 under Community Services Administration. Other OEO programs listed in appropriate subsections under public aid and education.

27 Federal expenditures include administrative and related expenses of the Secretary of Health and Human Services, Indian welfare and guidance, aging and juvenile delinquency activities, and certain manpower and human development activities. State and local expenditures include amounts for antipoverty and manpower programs, day care, child placement and adoption services, foster care, legal assistance, care of transients, and other unspecified welfare services; before 1970, these amounts included with institutional care.

SOURCE: Social Security Bulletin, 46, no. 8: (August 1983) 10–12.

TABLE 2.2
Total and per Capita Social Welfare Expenditures under Public Programs; in Actual and 1979 Prices, Selected Fiscal Years, 1950–79

Fiscal year	Total social welfare expenditures		Per capita social welfare expenditures							
	Amount in millions [1]	Per capita [2]	Social insurance	Public aid	Health and medical programs	Veterans' programs	Education	Other social welfare	All health and medical care [3]
Current dollars:									
1950	$23,420.8	$152.56	$32.19	$16.26	$13.44	$44.18	$43.47	$2.92	$19.97
1955	32,511.8	194.66	58.71	17.98	18.58	28.46	66.68	3.71	26.47
1960	52,106.3	285.42	105.35	22.46	24.45	29.52	96.43	6.24	35.03
1965	76,928.6	391.15	142.29	31.95	31.76	30.30	142.73	10.50	48.48
1970	145,483.9	701.27	262.47	79.48	47.75	43.27	244.94	19.98	121.65
1975	289,336.0	1,335.89	565.51	190.81	81.76	77.89	373.20	32.07	238.58
1976	331,611.0	1,520.95	665.60	223.33	88.94	86.44	402.31	38.85	275.10
1977	360,077.0	1,639.66	729.63	242.56	92.94	85.86	427.52	41.31	308.30
1978	393,456.4	1,775.73	786.26	268.06	103.49	88.36	458.31	47.67	347.19
1979	427,326.9	1,911.92	862.63	289.25	109.60	90.74	484.24	47.61	389.33
Percentage increase from—									
1950	1,725	1,153	2,580	1,679	716	106	1,014	1,530	1,850
1955	1,215	882	1,383	1,509	490	220	626	1,183	1,371
1960	720	570	719	1,188	348	208	402	563	1,011
1965	456	389	506	805	245	200	239	353	703
1970	194	173	229	264	130	110	98	138	220
1975	48	43	52	52	34	17	30	48	63
1976	29	27	30	30	23	5	20	23	42
1977	19	17	18	19	18	6	13	15	27
1978	9	8	10	8	6	3	6	0	12

Constant (1979) dollars:									
1950	$66,725.9	$434.64	$91.71	$46.32	$38.29	$125.87	$123.85	$8.32	$56.90
1955	81,893.7	490.33	147.88	45.29	46.80	71.69	167.96	9.34	66.68
1960	117,621.4	644.29	237.81	50.70	55.19	66.64	217.68	14.09	79.07
1965	161,614.7	821.74	298.93	67.12	66.72	63.66	299.85	22.06	101.85
1970	255,234.9	1,230.30	460.47	139.44	83.77	75.91	429.72	35.05	213.42
1975	375,273.7	1,732.67	733.48	247.48	106.04	101.02	484.05	41.60	309.44
1977	408,891.5	1,875.40	820.72	275.38	109.67	106.58	496.07	47.90	339.21
1978	418,694.2	1,906.58	848.41	282.05	108.07	99.84	497.12	48.04	358.49
1977	428,135.4	1,932.24	855.56	291.69	112.61	96.15	498.71	51.87	377.79
1979	427,326.9	1,911.92	862.63	289.25	109.60	90.74	484.24	47.61	389.33
Percentage increase from—									
1950	540	340	841	524	186	-28	291	472	584
1955	422	290	483	539	134	27	188	410	484
1960	263	197	263	471	99	37	122	238	392
1965	164	133	189	331	64	43	61	116	282
1970	68	55	87	107	31	20	13	36	82
1975	14	10	18	17	3	-10	0	14	26
1976	4	2	5	5	0	-15	-2	-.6	15
1977	2	.3	2	3	1	-9	-2	-.9	9
1978	-.2	-1	1	-1	-3	-6	-3	-8	2

[1] Excludes expenditures within foreign countries for education, veterans' payments, and OASDHI and civil service retirement benefits; see table 1 for data including these expenditures.

[2] Includes housing, not shown separately.

[3] Combines "health and medical programs" with medical services provided in connection with social insurance, public aid, veterans', vocational rehabilitation, and antipoverty programs.

Source: Based on Jan. 1 Bureau of the Census data for total U.S. population, including Armed Forces and Federal civilian employees and their dependents overseas, and the civilian population of territories and possessions. Prices based on implicit price deflators for personal consumption expenditures prepared for the national income accounts by the Bureau of Economic Analysis, Department of Commerce (1979 = 100): 1950, 35.1; 1955, 39.7; 1960, 44.3; 1965, 47.6; 1970, 57.0; 1975, 77.1; 1976, 81.1; 1977, 86.0; 1978, 91.9.

SOURCE: Social Security Bulletin, 44, no. 11: (November 1981) 8.

TABLE 2.3
Social Welfare Expenditures under Public Programs as a Percentage of Gross National Product, Selected Fiscal Years, 1950–1980[a]

Fiscal year	Gross national product (in billions of dollars)	Total[b]			Social welfare expenditures as percentage of gross national product						
		Total	Federal	State–local	Social insurance	Public aid	Health and medical programs	Veterans' programs	Education	Other social welfare	All health and medical care[c]
1950	264.8	8.9	4.0	4.9	1.9	0.9	0.8	2.6	2.5	0.2	1.2
1955	379.7	8.6	3.9	4.7	2.6	.8	.8	1.3	2.9	.2	1.2
1960	498.3	10.5	5.0	5.5	3.9	.8	.9	1.1	3.5	.2	1.3
1965	658.0	11.7	5.7	6.0	4.3	1.0	.9	.9	4.3	.3	1.4
1970	960.2	15.2	8.1	7.1	5.7	1.7	1.0	.9	5.3	.4	2.6
1975	1,452.3	20.0	11.5	8.4	8.5	2.8	1.2	1.2	5.6	.5	3.6
1976	1,625.4	20.4	12.1	8.3	9.0	3.0	1.2	1.2	5.4	.5	3.7
1977	1,836.5	19.6	11.9	7.8	8.8	2.9	1.1	1.0	5.1	.5	3.7
1978	2,043.4	19.3	11.8	7.6	8.6	2.9	1.1	1.0	5.0	.5	3.8
1979[d]	2,313.4	18.5	11.4	7.1	8.4	2.8	1.1	.9	4.7	.4	3.7
1980[e]		18.7	11.5	7.2							

[a] SOURCE: Ann Kallman Bixby, "Social Welfare Expenditures, Fiscal Year 1979," *Social Security Bulletin* 44, no. 11: (November 1981) 9.
[b] Includes housing, not shown separately.
[c] Combines "health and medical programs" with medical service provided in connection with social insurance, public aid, veterans', vocational rehabilitation and antipoverty programs.
[d] Preliminary estimates.
[e] Ann Bixby, "Public Social Welfare Expenditures, Fiscal Year 1980," Research and Statistics Note, Report #1, April 27, 1983, pp. 1–2.

health grew between 1950 and 1975, but especially since 1965, regardless of changes in political party control of government. Table 2.5 documents the incidence of costs on income classes. What has distinguished the policies of different parties is a difference in emphasis on what increasing government actions will concentrate on and how government should use its growing influence. The continuities and the cutting edges of change will be explored in succeeding chapters.

The Social Components of Policy

In all these views of social policy, there is further confusion resulting from ambiguity over the meaning of the term *social*. Is social policy distinct from public policy? If they were coequal, one could make an arbitrary choice as to which term to use, but it is reasonably clear that social policy means something different from public policy. There can be public policy, meaning the policy of the national government as reflected by Congress, the executive, the courts, or all three together regarding the economy. Economic policy can be mandated nationally by a control of money supply, by a decision to fund public service employment as the last resort, by encouraging inflation, or by accepting a high level of unemployment.

Economic policy is not quite the same as social policy. By and large, economic policy deals with macro levels of society—with aggregates of consumers and producers—and is based on economic concepts about the behavior of that artificial construct known as the economic man. But it is now widely recognized that economic policy is affected by a set of circumstances not contained in economic theory. The state of a culture, psychological motivation, the character of family ties all alter and affect the individual's actual behavior so that it is different from that predicted for the abstract economic model. Acceptance of the idea that women with small children ought to compete in the labor force changes the nature of that labor force. The belief that people should have a minimum income changes the functioning of economic rewards. What is not altogether clear, however, is the way in which these less firm social considerations are to be treated at the level of national policy. Are they to be incorporated as a part of economic policy? Is there a distinct social component of economic policy or a completely separate policy that affects economic behavior?

One common treatment of this subject avoids any attempt to distinguish among policies—all are equally social, be they economic or not. Anything governmental or public is social. A situation can be labeled a social condition when that condition becomes a problem to or is important to a particular society. This requires that the condition be one that the existing institutions

TABLE 2.4
Social Welfare Expenditures under Public Programs, Selected Fiscal Years, 1950–1979 (in millions of dollars, except percentages)[a]

Fiscal year	Total social welfare[b]	Social insurance	Public aid	Health and medical programs	Veterans' programs	Education	Housing	Other social welfare[c]	All health and medical care[d]	Total social welfare as percentage of: Gross national product	Total social welfare as percentage of: Government expenditures for all purposes[e]
Total											
1950	23,508	4,947	2,496	2,064	6,866	6,674	15	448	3,065	8.9	37.4
1955	32,640	9,835	3,003	3,103	4,834	11,157	89	619	4,421	8.6	32.7
1960	52,293	19,307	4,101	4,464	5,479	17,626	177	1,139	6,359	10.5	38.4
1965	77,175	28,123	6,283	6,246	6,031	28,108	318	2,066	9,535	11.7	42.2
1970	145,856	54,691	16,488	9,907	9,078	50,845	701	4,145	25,391	15.2	48.2
1975	290,047	123,013	41,326	17,708	17,019	80,863	3,172	6,947	51,673	20.0	57.4
1976	332,385	145,703	48,693	19,392	19,005	87,749	3,371	8,472	59,979	20.4	60.3
1977	360,925	160,883	53,266	20,409	19,015	93,921	4,358	9,071	67,704	19.6	59.4
1978	394,382	174,935	59,394	22,930	19,744	101,592	5,225	10,563	76,928	19.3	57.8
1979[f]	428,401	193,588	64,649	24,496	20,523	108,279	6,226	10,640	86,240	18.5	56.8
Federal											
1950	10,541	2,103	1,103	604	6,386	157	15	174	1,362	4.0	26.2
1955	14,623	6,385	1,504	1,150	4,772	485	75	252	1,948	3.9	22.3
1960	24,957	14,307	2,117	1,737	5,367	868	144	417	2,918	5.0	28.1
1965	37,712	21,807	3,594	2,781	6,011	2,470	238	812	4,625	5.7	32.6
1970	77,337	45,246	9,649	4,775	8,952	5,876	582	2,259	16,600	8.1	40.1
1975	167,436	99,715	27,205	8,513	16,570	8,629	2,541	4,264	34,125	11.5	53.8
1976	197,407	119,600	32,527	9,909	18,843	9,023	2,906	4,598	41,010	12.1	57.0
1977	218,407	134,745	35,399	10,182	18,861	9,745	4,006	5,470	46,476	11.9	56.3
1978	240,121	147,252	40,013	11,566	19,570	10,884	4,887	5,949	52,960	11.8	55.3
1979[f]	264,186	163,744	43,612	12,150	20,333	12,097	5,802	6,449	59,437	11.4	55.0

State and local

Year											
1950	12,967	2,844	1,393	1,460	480	6,517	—	274	1,704	4.9	59.2
1955	18,017	3,450	1,499	1,953	62	10,672	15	367	2,473	4.7	55.3
1960	27,337	4,999	1,984	2,727	112	16,758	33	723	3,478	5.5	60.1
1965	39,464	6,316	2,690	3,466	20	25,638	80	1,254	4,911	6.0	60.4
1970	68,519	9,446	6,839	5,132	126	44,970	120	1,886	8,791	7.1	64.0
1975	122,612	23,298	14,122	9,195	449	72,234	631	2,683	17,581	8.4	63.7
1976	134,978	26,103	16,165	9,483	162	78,726	465	3,874	19,047	8.3	66.2
1977	142,519	26,139	17,867	10,227	155	84,176	353	3,602	21,303	7.8	65.6
1978	154,261	27,683	19,381	11,364	174	90,708	337	4,614	24,042	7.6	62.7
1979[f]	164,215	29,844	21,037	12,346	190	96,182	424	4,192	26,868	7.1	60.4

State and local as a percentage of total

Year										
1950	55.2	57.5	55.8	70.7	7.0	97.6	0	61.2	55.6	55.1
1955	55.2	35.1	49.9	62.9	1.3	95.7	16.9	59.3	55.9	54.7
1960	52.3	17.8	48.4	61.1	2.0	95.1	18.6	63.5	54.4	52.4
1965	51.1	22.5	42.8	55.5	0.3	91.2	25.2	60.7	51.5	51.3
1970	47.0	17.3	41.5	51.8	1.4	88.4	17.1	45.5	34.6	46.7
1975	42.3	18.9	33.2	52.0	2.6	89.3	19.9	43.4	32.9	42.2
1976	40.6	17.9	32.2	48.8	0.9	89.7	13.8	49.2	31.2	40.7
1977	39.6	16.2	33.1	50.7	0.8	89.4	8.1	42.8	31.5	39.6
1978	39.0	15.9	31.3	50.2	0.9	89.9	6.4	44.5	31.1	38.9
1979[f]	38.3	15.4	32.5	50.4	0.9	90.7	6.8	39.4	31.2	38.4

SOURCE: Based on U.S. Department of Health, Education and Welfare, Social Security Administration, Office of Policy, Research and Statistics Note No. 4, June 4, 1981, *Public Social Welfare Expenditures, Fiscal Year 1979*, by Ann Kallman Bixby, Division of Retirement and Survivor Studies.

a SOURCE: Advisory Commission on Intergovernmental Relations.
b Represents expenditure under public law and from trust accounts, including administration, capital outlay, and some payments outside the United States.
c Includes outlays for vocational rehabilitation, institutional care, child nutrition and welfare, and social welfare expenditures not elsewhere classified.
d Combines "health and medical programs" with medical services provided in connection with social insurance, public aid, veterans', and "other social welfare" programs.
e Expenditures for that part of workers' compensation and temporary disability insurance payments made through private carriers and self-insurers omitted in computing percentages.
f Preliminary data.

TABLE 2.5

A Comparison of Direct Tax Burdens Borne by Average and Upper-Income Families, 1953, 1966, 1977, and 1980[a]

| | Selected direct taxes as a percentage of family income | | | | | | Family income (percent) | | | Percentage decrease in after tax income | | | |
| | Federal personal income tax | Social Security Tax[b] (OASDHI) | State–local taxes | | | | Total | Decrease due to direct taxes | After tax income | 1953 to 1966 | 1966 to 1977 | 1977 to 1980 | 1953 to 1980 |
Year			Local res. prop. Tax	State–local personal Income Tax	State–local general sales tax	Total selected taxes							
Average family[c] ($21,500 in 1980)													
1953	7.6	1.1	2.2	0.3	0.6	11.8	100.0	11.8	88.2	—	—	—	—
1966	9.5	3.2	3.1	1.0	1.0	17.8	100.0	17.8	82.2	6.8	—	—	—
1977	9.6	5.9	3.9	1.8	1.3	22.5	100.0	22.5	77.5	—	5.7	—	—
1980	10.1	6.1	3.2	2.2	1.1	22.7	100.0	22.7	77.3	—	—	0.3	12.4
Twice the average family[d] ($43,000 in 1980)													
1953	12.8	0.5	1.8	0.9	0.5	16.5	100.0	16.5	83.5	—	—	—	—
1966	12.7	1.6	2.6	1.6	0.8	19.3	100.0	19.3	80.7	3.4	—	—	—
1977	14.8	3.0	3.2	2.9	0.9	24.8	100.0	24.8	75.2	—	6.8	—	—
1980	16.6	3.7	2.4	3.2	0.9	26.8	100.0	26.8	73.2	—	—	2.7	12.3
Four times the average family[e] ($86,000 in 1980)													
1953	16.6	0.3	1.7	1.2	0.4	20.2	100.0	20.2	79.8	—	—	—	—
1966	17.3	0.8	2.4	2.4	0.5	23.4	100.0	23.4	76.6	4.0	—	—	—
1977	22.6	1.5	2.6	4.0	0.7	31.4	100.0	31.4	68.6	—	10.4	—	—
1980	24.3	1.8	1.9	4.1	0.6	32.7	100.0	32.7	67.3	—	—	1.9	15.7

[a] In computing federal personal income tax liabilities, deductions were estimated to be 14% of family income for the $5,000 and $8,750 families and 12% of income for the $10,000 family. Estimated itemized deductions were assumed for the remaining families. Interest on state and local debt, dividends, and nontaxable capital gains (estimated, based on IRS *Statistics of Income*) were excluded from family income for these computations.

Residential property tax estimates assume average housing values of approximately 1.8 times family income for the average family in both 1953 ($5,000) and 1966 ($8,750); 2.2 times in 1977 ($16,000), and 2.4 times in 1980 ($21,500). The ratios for the remaining family income classes are 1.5 for $10,000 income (1953) and $17,500 income (1966); 1.8 for $32,000 income (1977); 1.9 for $43,000 income (1980); 1.4 for $20,000 income (1953) and $35,000 (1966); 1.5 for $64,000 income (1977) and $86,000 income (1980), with average effective property tax rates of 1.35% in 1980, 1.75% in 1977, 1.70% in 1966, 1.20% in 1953. Based on U.S. Bureau of the Census, Governments Division, various reports, and *U.S. Census of Housing;* Commerce Clearing House, *State Tax Reporter;* Internal Revenue Service, *Statistics of Income, Individual Income Tax Returns;* and Advisory Commission on Intergovernmental Relations staff estimates.

In computing state income tax liabilities, the optional standard deduction was used for $5,000, $8,750, and $10,000 income families, and estimated itemized deductions for the remaining families.

Estimated state–local general sales tax liabilities are based on the amounts allowed by the Internal Revenue Service as deductions in computing federal personal income taxes. The percentages shown for state–local personal income and general sales taxes are weighted averages (population) for all states, including those without a sales or income tax.

SOURCE: Advisory Commission on Intergovernmental Relations staff computations. "Significant Features of Fiscal Federalism, 1980–81 Edition" p. 49. Washington, D.C. Dec. 1981.

[b] Personal contributions.

[c] Estimates for average family (married couple with two dependents) earning $5,000 in 1953, $8,750 in 1966, $16,000 in 1977, and $21,500 in 1980, assuming all income from wages and salaries and earned by one spouse.

[d] Estimates for twice the average family. Family earning $10,000 in 1953, $17,500 in 1966, $32,000 in 1977, and $43,000 in 1980 and assumes that earnings include $165 (interest on state and local debt, and excludable dividends) in 1980, $125 in 1977, $50 in 1966, and $25 in 1953; also assumes the inclusion of net long-term capital gains of $1,600 in 1980, $1,200 in 1977, $625 in 1966, and $350 in 1953.

[e] Estimates for four times the average family. Family earning $20,000 in 1953, $35,000 in 1966, $64,000 in 1977, and $86,000 in 1980 and assumes that earnings include $1,515 (interest on state and local debt, and excludable dividends) in 1980, $1,100 in 1977, $525 in 1966, and $265 in 1953; also assumes the inclusion of net long-term capital gains of $9,200 in 1980, $7,300 in 1977, $3,360 in 1966, and $1,730 in 1953.

cannot handle to the satisfaction of enough members of that society. Thus, a condition or situation with which established institutions and agencies can cope to the satisfaction of most members is not yet a social problem, although it may be a problem to individuals or groups within the society. Only when a problem becomes sufficiently important to enough members of society, meaning that enough are dissatisfied with the ways their institutions are handling it, does it become social. Once defined as a social problem, it requires collective action. Thus limited, the only collective action that matches this concept of a social problem is one that involves the institutions of government, for they represent the desires of citizens and their means for acting collectively on those desires.

Seen in this light, illness becomes a social problem only when the ways in which medical institutions cope with it are seen as inadequate by a large segment of the population. Caring for sickness has been a problem for many people, but Americans for many reasons have not seen fit to adopt one strongly advocated policy, that of health insurance. The pain of the difficulty has not been severe enough, or it has not yet affected enough people to force collective action, or a few political forces have been strong enough in relation to advocates of change to block action. All these reasons have probably contributed to the fact that national health policy is still in turmoil. Unemployment is another example of a difficulty that has not yet become enough of a social problem to produce a major change in policy. Long-term unemployment for some parts of the population has thus far affected certain minorities whose condition has not yet aroused to action the sensibilities of the majority of more secure voters. As a result, this social problem, while a topic of much debate, has not yet pushed further the boundaries of public responsibility. The same can be said about crime, income, and so on. When a critical state is reached, any action taken through the formal mechanisms of society becomes social action, and its guiding principles become social policies. When medical, police, or income institutions take care of illness or poverty in ways that satisfy enough citizens, then it is not a social problem. If institutional methods are altered to the satisfaction of most citizens, one can say that social problem has been taken care of. It is then possible to identify the guiding policies that govern the acceptable solution, or it is possible to discuss alternative policies if the solution is not acceptable.

However, a large variety of public, governmental institutions and programs have evolved in recent decades to deal with conditions that fall within the foregoing definition of social but yet are viewed as different from economic, cultural, or foreign policy conditions. An attempt should be made to see if an additional meaning can be given the term *social policy* when it is applied to this new cluster of governmental actions.

For the purposes of this volume the word *social* is used to characterize those aspects of government policy that can be directly traced to individuals in society rather than to the society as an impersonal abstraction. For example, public policy about income can be called social policy if redistribution among broad classes is intended or if needs of specific subgroups of persons are targeted (the aged or the American Indian family). A tax policy that limits taxation for home owners is a broad public and also a social policy, since it directly improves the well-being of individuals, poor and well-to-do alike. Aid to Families with Dependent Children also represents a clear policy, for it redistributes tax revenue directly to a smaller class whose condition is also improved by redistribution. In this instance, government acts directly on the lives of its beneficiaries.

Increasing or decreasing the rate of economic growth or increasing or decreasing national economic self-sufficiency are less likely to be considered here as social policy matters. Employment, income, or health programs affect and reach minorities, women, and the aged differently and the attention to these differentiations is more clearly part of the social meaning. We can speak also of the social component of otherwise general policies when we take into account how policies intended to achieve wider employment are affected by the ways in which individuals and groups are differentially motivated. There also exists a social dimension when we find unintended personal consequences of general policies, as when a policy to get working mothers off relief produces a generation of disturbed children because mothering care has been diminished by forced work policies.

The term *social* also covers that cluster of public programs that are intended to meet the needs of vulnerable subpopulations. These can be rather narrow, such as the protection of abused children or the feeding of infants in low-income families, or they can be very broad, such as consideration of whether day-care facilities should be provided for all families who wish them, to permit mothers to pursue careers or simply to relieve women from household drudgery. In this area, the term refers to subjects usually identified with social (i.e., collectively provided) services or to welfare, as in the concept of the welfare state. In such cases, the social *policy* is distinguished from the *program* by the ends intended to be achieved. Day care for children, as a policy, is not valued by its details but by whether it is intended to encourage mothers to seek work outside the home, or to reduce the costs of combined work and child care for mothers, or to make life more comfortable for mothers who stay home and thus help them to be more loving rather than more harassed mothers.

The term *social*, therefore refers to the human impact of government, to alternatives in patterns of relationships and to arbitrarily selected types of action addressed to the needs of vulnerable groups. In both the broad and narrow uses, we will be speaking of relationships across categorical lines. General policies affecting the economy can no longer be wholly isolated from effects on individuals and from the effects that individual and psychological phenomena have on economic policy. Health policy cannot be isolated from the reactions and the behavior of consumers. But equally, the setting up of organizational mechanisms to carry out any policy, social or otherwise, must consider the interface between the bureaucratic structure, its behavior, the behavior of persons who staff those bureaucracies, and the behavior of the persons who use them. These interfaces are here considered social because they also affect the ways in which any policy of government reaches individual citizens, whether those citizens are many or few, privileged or vulnerable.

None of these uses of our term stops at the level of criticism. It is necessary but not sufficient to note that work policies discriminate against minorities or that urban policies produce alienation and depersonalized environments. Such critiques are not social policies. When these critiques are linked specifically to explicit acts of government or to explicit lines of action proposed to produce a more desirable state of affairs for individuals, then it can be said that the social dimension has a *policy utility*, as these terms will be used.

To recapitulate, *policy* is used in this text to denote a continuing guide for action by individuals or groups in a position to make choices over time affecting the lives of others in a flexible fashion. It is a nonidealized guidance mechanism. By contrast, *societal policy* or *social norms* (a variant on the common usage of the term *social policy*) may be said to represent the sum of actions, attitudes, and choices made in a society, often with contradictions but with rough identity, but a sum of choices so broad as not to be amenable to decision making by responsible individuals or groups. *Public policy* may be seen as the sum of what governments use as guides for their actions. And *social policies* represent those aspects of policy that directly address individuals and groups in a society and social relationships as distinguished from technical or economic relationships.

Criterion Measures for Social Policy Analyses

Our discussion thus far lacks measures by which citizen, scientist, or policymaker can assess the direction of the evolution of public policies. Much attention has been given to the political process: how various subgroups exert power or influence to effect or prevent change and how society's political structure facilitates or obstructs change.

Less attention has been given to a more technical side of the problem. The term *technipol* has been coined to identify the twin functions that must be performed by anyone in the policy arena. At the level of organizational detail, many technical facets have, of course, been elaborated. We have a plethora of devices to measure different ways of providing medical care, to control budget expenditures, or to prevent fraud. We have been less inventive when it comes to broader issues of policy that touch on the basic attitudes and permitted behavior in a given society. A start has been made by Lowi and by others to translate the old questions about "who gets what from whom" into more technical categories.

Lowi has suggested that such age-old questions can be traced out through a study of major policy types, classified according to their content. Public policies can be classified as: (1) *distributive* (the parceling out of public benefits among parties to the division, as in the case of "pork barrel" actions by Congress); (2)*regulative* (the control of the relations among parties, thus altering the rules by which they secure shares of the public benefits); or (3) *redistributive* (the reallocation of benefits and burdens among broad socioeconomic sectors of the population, rather than among organized narrow-interest groups).[4] In this formulation, it appears that distributive and regulative policies lend themselves to the creation of coalitions among relatively well-organized political entities, in or outside of government. Redistributive policies strike more deeply at the roots of society's values and structure and are likely to produce polarization rather than coalitions among basic political forces.

The social policies we will be discussing began as distributive or regulative ones, but over time they have taken on a redistributive character. Thus, they challenge deep-seated historical patterns of group behavior and involve both the legitimacy of new governmental functions and certain unexpected limitations to private initiative. Patterns of the scope of government and the role of private initiative have strong roots in the past, but such marked changes have taken place since the late 1930s and a new level of decision making has been reached. Old norms about the proper scope for government no longer match the realities of government actions that touch the lives of all citizens directly and pervasively. Shall we try to return to old standards or construct new guidelines appropriate to the present reality?

For our purposes, the new distributive–redistributive character of policy requires a choice between two possible paths of program development in the future. Both paths raise questions about the much widened scope of government intrusion into what has until recently been considered a private domain. Marmor, citing Friedman, has classified social welfare policies by the path they follow—that is, whether they are based upon a charity- or middle-class perspective:[5]

[4] Theodore Lowi, "American Business Public Policy and Political Theory," *World Politics* 16 (1964): pp. 677–715. See also David Gil, *Unravelling Social Policy* (Cambridge, Mass.: Schenkman, 1973) and Theodore Marmor, *The Politics of Medicare* (Chicago: Aldine, 1973).

[5] Lawrence Friedman, "Social Welfare Legislation," *Stanford Law Review* 21 (January 1969): 247, cited in Marmor, *Politics of Medicare*, p. 120.

Criterion	Middle-class program	Charity program
Benefits	Broad demographic unit, not selected by means test	Needy persons selected by means test
Benefits	Earned, noncomprehensive, for a given problem	Given, not earned, more comprehensive
Financing	Regressive, as with social security taxes, earmarked	General revenues, more progressive
Administrative	Centralized, nondiscretionary, clerklike, with developed rules of entitlement	Discretionary, decentralized

Another way of dichotomizing social policies is to distinguish between rights and philanthropy. Philanthropy, in conventional usage, means an exchange between individuals or, more often, a charitable giving by one person to another. Such gifts can be based on a feeling of obligation owed another, on grounds of religious belief, or on fear, to protect oneself from the hostility of another. The recipient can make no enforceable legal claim on the donor; the giving is voluntary. In public policy terms, the charitable rationale is still present, since it assumes that public programs represent the use by citizens of government to do what they would voluntarily do. But in the past century, the belief has spread that all people have certain *social rights* that complement the political rights of the eighteenth century. The rationale is advanced that the poor or the unemployed, for example, have a legal right to relief, and even a right to a level of relief comparable to that of all other citizens, that is enforceable on others even when they are not willing to make the gift. The rights approach, epitomized most concretely in the welfare rights organization of the 1960s, introduces a basis for evaluating social policy in ways quite different from that of the philanthropic approach. Rights involve some concept of just desert, or deserving, and also require that the rights of recipients be balanced against the rights of givers (or of taxpayers). This is quite different from trying to establish social policy for the poor on the basis of need or humane concern for a fellow citizen. While the discussion that follows will not choose among these alternative bases for social policy, the force of difference needs to be kept in mind, since public thinking is more attuned to principles of charity in helping the poor than it is to the enforceable rights of the poor that turn the disadvantaged into claimants, not beneficiaries.[6]

[6] Olive Stevenson, *Claimant or Client?* (London: George Allen and Unin, 1973).

Another view of social policy is to treat it as consisting of giving things, or benefits, to people in need. It is therefore associated with the dependency of some people on others. In modern society these dependents are often complete strangers to those who help them through the mechanisms of a welfare state. In recent years, another approach has evolved: social welfare as the creator of conditions that improve the living conditions of all citizens, not only of the poor. This is dealt with further in Chapter 8 when alternative policies are reviewed. Such broad approaches mean that the horizons of social policy can no longer be limited as a self-contained area for study with its own rules and dynamics. Instead, it is studied as part of a national economy. This perspective does not yet characterize social policy or analysis, but it will define it in the future. For the present, this volume limits itself to somewhat more narrow definitions as outlined above.

The final framework for analyzing the evolution of American social policies consists of examining:

1. Social norms
2. Public policies
3. Sectoral public social policy
4. Leadership role in government
5. Advocated versus adopted policy
6. Criteria for assessing policy guidelines: rights versus charity

Ideology beyond a Policy Framework

These elementary efforts to introduce a technical aspect to policy analysis, as distinguished from administrative detail, complement rather than replace certain value or ideological considerations that underlie all policy actions. In social work as in many professions, the term *values* is used instead of *ideology* to express a faith in certain enduring beliefs upon which all professional, political, and technical behavior *should* be based. Some of these values are general, such as respect for individuality. Others represent more specific ideas, such as basing choices on a capitalist, marketplace system of organization, on government ownership and management, or on small-scale neighborhood forms of group association.

Such basic ideological preferences can constitute the core of policy as guidance, but they require some operational framework for translation into action. Political structure or form of organization satisfies part of this requirement. The political processes of policy formation have been discussed in numerous case examples and will not be repeated here since our concern is with other less publicized aspects of policy evaluation.[7]

---

[7] Readings listed at the end of Chapters 3–6 include references that outline the ideological facets of debate in each sector.

It is evident that some structure, organization, or mechanism must be in place, or must be created, through which policies are shaped and moved. These structures are the formal mechanisms of any society, even if policy is perceived to have its original dynamic in the actions of individuals or of unofficial informal organizations, such as associations or parties. Abstract concepts about policy require complementary attention to these mechanisms and also to technical tools, which will be briefly considered in Chapter 9.

Ideology is, nonetheless, an important force in the politics of policy formation, for it evokes deep emotions in human beings and thus energizes political activity. Confronted with the seemingly intractable problems and often bizarre or persistent consequences of complex human society, citizens seek direct and simple solutions. Ideology becomes a rallying point and can also inform the practical choices made by advocates when they reach public office and power. The beliefs in political freedom and pluralism guide concensus choice taking; belief in a free market guides policies that seek to limit the authority of government; confidence in the wisdom and responsiveness of state planning encourages growth in government authority. But advocates of each of these ideologies, when in office, find that the inherited structure of programs and laws, plus the complexity of competing interests that make up the foundation of social organization, require time, patience, and infinite care in constructing any change in the direction that a society had previously adopted. This process of fitting ideological conviction to pragmatic reality in an open society is made especially difficult in the United States, where carefully thought out ideological positions and platforms that are not characteristic of practical and often contradictory beliefs motivate the average voter, who in turn governs the position taken by major political parties.

Why Social Policies Warrant Expert Technical Attention Now

In a period of great flux, we may ask why it is not sufficient to hold strong ideological positions as a framework for evolution or ask whether revolution rather than evolution in human affairs may not be more consistent with satisfying human needs. There are numerous illustrations, at least in the United States, that indicate the urgency of evolving steady policies in a situation of uncertainty. Policies are desired that do not straightjacket action and that avoid randomness in response. At almost every level of society, citizens seek a society in which there is an opportunity for constructive employment for all. In the United States, most prefer some looseness in an economic system where varieties of positions and opportunities for mobility and advancement are offered by a variety of nominally competing economic enterprises. A substantial proportion of the citizenry recognizes that this marketplace system works imperfectly and are prepared to accept some level of governmental intervention. This intervention is sometimes viewed as residual, meaning that it is intended to take care of areas in which the marketplace system fails (as, for example, when public assistance or public service employment is offered as the last resort). Others believe that progressive governmental intervention may slowly lead to sufficient improvement in the functioning of the economic system so that the economic wants of individuals are more adequately met. As recently as 1930, the idea of the national government's intervention in the economic system in even residual activities was fought out bitterly, but it is now widely accepted. What is not yet accepted (except by a minority) is the new boundary between private enterprise and government. This constitutes a mine field through which responsible groups and officials need to maneuver if they seek to develop consistent policies that will satisfy such conflicting desires.

If we turn to a less economic arena—that of medical care—it is by now reasonably clear that there is no overwhelming public demand for a national, exclusive, governmentally administered health service. While compulsory health insurance remains a live option, the readiness to shoulder its cost is less definite. What does exist, however, is the determination to guarantee access to medical care for all, to remove the pain of paying for medical care as far from the individual as possible, and to retain some aspect of choice through private physician and hospital delivery of medical care. The costs of such a system in economic and human terms are now seen as very great (as will be discussed in Chapter 4), so that a new crisis can be said to have arisen and some steady guiding policy is necessary to confront it.

In a less well-defined arena—family policy—similar crises, conflicting wants, and difficulties emerge. We do not have a national position that says families must take care of all their members or that families will be relieved of explicit responsibilities. There is no national policy that seeks to move all mothers into work or to keep them from work. On the other hand, it is clear that most individuals believe that the family does constitute a fundamental social institution that needs to be sustained and that it constitutes the most flexible "social service" of first resort. At the same time, there is widespread acceptance of the belief that the family is overburdened in specific areas and needs to be relieved, primarily by public intervention. The real difficulty lies in how far to go. We are not ready to force mothers with small children into employment, but neither are we prepared to make it too easy for them to avoid it altogether. We have fairly well settled that families with severely retarded children can be completely relieved of the burden of care, but we are less certain when it comes to other forms of disability. Families had been presumed to be the final arbiter in matters of education, but the crises of racial discrimination forced a major shift in emphasis so that now a large area of ambiguity exists. The state is now attempting to force changes in family control of educational systems in order to remove gradually the vestiges of discrimination. At the same time, it is seeking to avoid a complete abdication of family responsibility.

It may be clear from such illustrations that the formulation of guiding principles becomes more and more desirable and even necessary. Confidence in scientific skill is also found in the social arena, and the belief persists that difficulties can be resolved without too much encroachment on the private sector. Our expectations have grown enormously, fueled by a succession of New Deal and Great Society programs and carried into 1976 by presidential candidates who argued that our society is a great one, that it can be gotten moving again, and that we are capable of mastering our destiny.

Unfortunately, the stated desire to resolve difficulties is frequently obstructed by a search for privacy and freedom from constraint and a fear that equity may mean equalization (the have's will have less). There is still a suspicion of "too much government"; there is an idealization of individual decision making; the acquisition of material goods and the search for pleasure are the modern-day interpretations of the pursuit of happiness promised in the Constitution. The citizens who believe that there must and should be a solution to these problems may feel that they should not have to pay high taxes or be limited in their choice to solve someone else's problem.

Such contradictory passions underlie the urgency for developing a more clear-cut understanding about policy as a guide for progress. Income maintenance is perhaps the most sensitive area; it is here that Americans may be most sharply tested in their capacity to be both fair and reasonable. Scapegoating and attacks upon the welfare system abound, but it is no longer possible to consider the problem of the poor and of income maintenance in light of nineteenth-century charity. Unfortunately, much policy debate has been framed by both public and private individuals as charity. The free mobility of Americans, the imperfections of its economic balance between technological requirements in the work force and rewards for labor are quite severe, and while insecurity mostly affects the poorest, no income classes are immune from economic uncertainty.

The belief in private choice for medical treatment runs very deep, and yet the enormous inflation in the costs of medical care and the enormous gap of resources in urban ghettos and rural areas begin to erode faith in our ability to deal with such difficulties. When we turn to the problem of aging, there is a deep-seated desire to assure the minimum security for the elderly who are retired from the work force. Long extension of life and freedom of family members to move about conflict with the realities of trying to support an increasing proportion of retired persons while ignoring the realities of long-term disability. At the same time, the fact that so many "younger" aged, between 60 and 75 years old, are still healthy and vigorous and desirous of an active life may force a reconsideration of our 1930s adopted policy that the aged are worn out and best removed from the work force by pensioning.

If we are to make any headway in relieving such social distress, there are quite practical reasons for developing guidelines for action and for training people to facilitate such action. Deep-seated conflicts of interest mean that any action taken is likely to be a compromise, at least among the major conflicting forces. Compromises seldom produce perfect solutions for any troublesome social condition. Therefore, although a succession of less-than-perfect solutions may modify its nature, the condition persists in the face of efforts to deal with it.

It may be discouraging to realize that some troublesome social issues are likely to be with us for a long time and are not amenable to clear-cut solutions. Differences among persons and groups, changing levels of aspiration, biological and physiological weaknesses, imperfections of any known economic system—all suggest that trouble will continue. In light of such reality, groups and individuals who make decisions affecting the lives of others need some guidelines. Such goals as the abolition of poverty or illness are essential but too broad to fit the realities of decision making. Hopefully, a path can be charted that moves steadily, though slowly, in the direction of such ideal goals, and it is policy that holds groups and individuals on course as they form a succession of less-than-perfect solutions.

A second, more realistic reason for a continuous guide to action lies in our imperfect social science and social technology. Many ideological views argue that the adoption of their proposed course of action is the only remedy for poverty, illness, or mental disease if adopted completely. No such remedies have been completely adopted by any society and, therefore, remain untested theories. Since our techniques for social intervention are imperfect, responsible individuals and parties require guiding principles with which to test imperfect intervention devices, making continual adjustments and improvements over time. Without steady middle-range policies based on goals and past experience, interventions become erratic, discontinuous, and random rather than building toward definable goals. Policy, therefore, draws a basic premise from its parent discipline, politics: Learn to distinguish the possible and the impossible, and then do what is possible. In the United States as elsewhere, it is natural to aim for the impossible. Policy, therefore, rides that uneasy course of balancing striving for the probably unattainable ideal, doing the possible, and avoiding the pitfalls of expediency, randomness, and impulsive experimentation without cumulative knowledge. It is in this uneasy no-man's-land between expediency and the ideal that government must act and that a new discipline must evolve to inform the processes by which policies are developed and acted upon.

We have touched on contradictions between aspirations and reality in American society that if not resolved, may erode confidence in government altogether. One consequence, of course, could be the creation of a wholly new governmental structure, but one cannot ignore the possibility of another consequence—namely, the growth of anomie and the breakdown in organized capacity to deal with problems, resulting ultimately in decay and nihilism.

In this text we, of course, cannot supply a solution to these dilemmas, but we can explicate an approach to analyzing social policy that through improved understanding of and discipline in policy development can provide a guide through the difficulties ahead. Policy promising neither too much nor too little can have a stabilizing effect on collective efforts in American society. Such efforts seek to improve progressively the way in which persisting social difficulties are managed without, at the same time, tearing the American fabric apart by violent internal conflict. Whether such a middle path can succeed remains to be seen.

Without proposing global solutions or specific programs, this volume will seek to perform a few limited tasks. It will seek to sharpen what the term *social policy* means. It will try to discover whether implicit, as well as explicit, social policies can be identified in certain areas commonly considered more social than economic: income, medical care, housing, personal social services, and care of the young and the aged. If such policies can be identified, an attempt will be made to review what disciplinary techniques and tools are currently available to improve the development of guiding principles for the future. Such tools may be used to alter the evolution of implicit policies or to improve those explicit policies that have established their utility. Such questions as the following will be examined:

1. Can the concepts of social policy be given meaning as a basis for equipping professionals and citizens to deal better with the subject matter or content of social policy?

2. Are there levels of policy that distinguish between the state of a society, the directions governments take, and the details of program administration?

3. Do we have anything that can be called national social policies, or do we at random act as a nation?

4. If we do have national policies, do they have any continuity or are they an accumulation of contradictory ad hoc reactions by government to problems?

5. Do tools, techniques, and concepts exist for a separate field of inquiry that also provide the basis for a separate career in policy development? Or is action, if any takes place, the result solely of political exchange among competing special interests?

Certain conclusions, based on the analysis of examples in Chapters 3–7, guide the treatment of such questions. First, the national government has, through many changes in national administration, adhered to a few basic principles as it acts on the social needs of its citizens. These principles constitute public policies and provide continuity in guiding national acts, contrary to the widely held view that the nation lacks consistent social policies. They conform to the best available definition of policy—a set of guiding principles by which accountable persons or groups make public decisions in reasonably consistent directions as they meet new and unanticipated situations.

Second, social norms generally circumscribe or set the boundaries for public policy action. These wider societal policies change slowly, and public policy (i.e., governmental choice) sometimes goes beyond these normal constraints and eventually alters the basic content of societal policies.

Third, the American system is at a new plateau in this evolution of social norms. As an unanticipated consequence of the incremental build up of governmental actions conforming to social norms, and guided by public policy, the weight and scope of national governmental actions is now so great and so widely accepted that the very norms that once circumscribed national policy have been altered. Government has become a leading force in modifying basic social norms, not only the follower of random political forces. We are ready to make new choices, unprecedented in the American system of government.

Fourth, we can now question commonly held assumptions about the sources of resistance to and pressure for change. These new insights into American policy processes provide a basis for elaborating the technical, analytic side of policy analysis, just as we have already probed the political dimension of a technipolitical process.

Additional Readings

Bell, Winifred. *Contemporary Social Welfare*. New York: Macmillan, 1983.

Cullingworth, J. B. *The Social Content of Planning*. Problems of an Urban Society, vol. 2. London: Allen and Unwin, 1973. Chaps. 5–6.

Gil, David. *Unravelling Social Policy*. Cambridge, Mass.: Schenkman, 1973.

Gilbert, Neil. *Capitalism and the Welfare State*. New Haven: Yale University Press, 1983.

Glennerster, H. *Social Service Budgets and Social Policy*. London: Allen and Unwin, 1975. Chaps. 2–5.

Graham, Otis. *Toward a Planned Society*. New York: Oxford University Press, 1976.

Titmuss, Richard. *Commitment to Welfare*. London: Allen and Unwin, 1968.

Income Maintenance Policies

Continuity and Change

3

Income, whatever its form, is the fundamental means by which citizens exchange or secure access to the goods produced by any society. It is not surprising, therefore, that the most important and sensitive area of social policy is that affecting income distribution. This holds true in economies organized on free enterprise capitalist lines or those organized on market-controlled socialist lines. Conditions of life are at stake. A too rapid change in the distribution pattern produces unsettling reactions ranging from passive resistance to strikes, riots, and revolts. These arise in all societies regardless of economic form. Some control of income by the state is omnipresent and sometimes omnipotent.

Social policy concerning income can be distinguished from economic policy in that social policy of a government focuses primarily on (1) assurance of minimum requirements for survival for all members of a society and (2) the distribution of income among various group and class strata (i.e., the proportion of the population with high, middle, and low income and the difference between the highest and lowest incomes. Economic policy may take these social dimensions into consideration, but they are not its primary concern.

Attention to these questions in the United States has been characterized by a continuing pressure for change following a consistent line of evolution from minimum assurance of survival to income redistribution. The evolution of American income policy resulting from the tension between pressure for and resistance to change can be divided into five major phases: the period before the 1930s, with minimum or no federal obligation; the New

Deal period of the 1930s, with the emergence of federal responsibility; the Great Society period of the 1960s, with an enlargement of the guiding principles; the 1970s, with an attempt to control government responsibility; and the 1980s, with an attempt to reduce federal responsibility.

Limitations of Social Norms and Their Expansion: Pre-1930–1980

Implicit social norms, as we have postulated, have both stimulated and limited American approaches to income policy. These underlying concepts have found differing expressions at different periods in history but have remained remarkably stable. In regard to income maintenance, they can be briefly summarized as follows.

1. Primary responsibility is expected to rest with the individual and the marketplace. Perhaps this is an inheritance from pioneer days, when it was assumed that any willing individual could acquire his own share of an apparently unlimited supply of land and resources and provide for his own subsistence. This attitude emerged from the conditions of the earliest American settlement by dissidents from older European nations or by wealth-seeking adventurers. In New England, at least, the earliest settlers were for the most part poor and lived in conditions of widespread poverty, but not of dependence on others. There was little surplus; all had to work and all helped close neighbors when they met some personal disaster. Ideas of community governed the Puritan settlement, with its emphasis on building the New Jerusalem in the New World. Religious beliefs about original sin and individual pathways to salvation through either faith or deeds were powerful shapers of public belief. As the nation became more secure, by the early nineteenth century, population grew, more immigrants came, and urbanization increased. Able-bodied adults without income or work were encountered more and more often but were considered lazy or sinful or both.

With the evolution of an industrial society, the uncertainties and inequities of corporate control of employment opportunities were gradually recognized and steps were taken, often after violent conflict, to correct the worst abuses. But until the 1930s, with a few exceptions, national action in the more industrialized states was primarily regulatory—control of working conditions, hours of work, and monetary policy. Income dilemmas were not considered a matter of governmental responsibility, and it was still expected that able-bodied persons could take care of their own needs if they would only work hard enough.

2. Government, whether local, state, or federal, has always played a role in income maintenance. Local communities, through their local govern-

ments, carried out responsibilities for the poor established in the English poor laws. For the most part, these poor were the sick, widowed, and aged. Estimates for the early 1700s suggest that less than 1% of local populations received any help other than from family. The able-bodied were often poor but not paupers.[1] However, even as government's role gradually expanded beginning in the eighteenth century, it was considered to be less desirable than, and only supplementary or complementary to, the free operation of the marketplace. However, the gradually increasing total amount of government income maintenance activities has increased the government role so that federal expenditures now represent over 20% of the GNP, or of all the goods and services produced in the economy.[2] Much of this expenditure is for direct income support for individuals or classes.

3. Government's supplementary role has been justified primarily for segments of the population considered to be vulnerable and helpless and therefore needing and deserving public attention—aged, sick, widows. In the eighteenth century, this was a modest obligation; but in the twentieth century, the governmental responsibility to satisfy this concept has an obligation representing nearly half the national budget. This expansion is accounted for by increasing the segments of the population believed to deserve help and by extending benefits to low- and middle-income citizens as much as by any increase in destitution.

4. Eligibility for most governmental programs is conditioned by present or former work.

5. Most national income maintenance policy has been predicated on a joint federal and state partnership.

6. Faith in science or technology to abolish poverty has persisted so that most income programs are assumed to have a short life (retirement for the aged excepted).

The national policy is guided not only by this set of stable principles, but also by another set of principles that are less stabilized and have been constantly expanding. In the earliest period, government, first local and only later national, was considered to have some responsibility for the helpless members of a pioneer society, primarily orphans and widows. In time, with the evolution of an industrialized nation in the late nineteenth and early twentieth centuries, the concept of governmental responsibility was expanded to include assuring minimum survival to other disadvantaged groups (unmarried mothers, the mentally ill, etc.), first as a matter of charity and then by the 1930s as a matter of right. But the concept of an essential minimum was also steadily enlarged until it came to mean not prevention of

[1] Gary Nash, "Urban Wealth and Poverty in Pre-Revolutionary America," *Journal of Interdisciplinary Studies* 6, No. 4 (Spring 1976): 556–560.

[2] Charles Schultz et al., *Setting National Priorities: 1973 Budget* (Washington, D.C.: Brookings Institution, 1972) Tables 1–3, p. 11.

starvation but a minimum of health and decency. The most recent stage of this development has been the use of income maintenance programs to achieve a higher degree of equity by a progressive raising of the income floor for all persons. Up to 1975 this development seemed on the verge of reducing the spread between minimum and maximum income in the United States. The supplementary role of government became more active and positive in reshaping economic relationships.

Before the 1930s: Limited Federal Obligation

The current dominance of the national government in social policy matters obscures the fact that local and sometimes state governments were actively involved in elementary forms of income support from the beginning of the Republic. At that time, policies were shaped primarily by charitable concepts: Neighbors discharged a charitable obligation to look after the widows and orphans. They were often recompensed by tax appropriations for the most elementary forms of relief payments. Such tax payments to citizens to perform charitable acts could be justified when most citizens were poor. However, a small beachhead of national obligation emerged when the national government reluctantly accepted some responsibility for large numbers of veterans of the Continental armies, many of whom were destitute.

The role of the federal government remained minimal during the nineteenth and early twentieth centuries, except for its continuing obligation to military personnel, who were considered to have earned special claims on the national government. However, the land-grant and homestead legislation of the nineteenth century represents national policies conforming to the principles outlined above. In the early days of industrializing, the major tangible asset available to the national government was its authority over vast expanses of land acquired by purchase or expropriation. Through various mechanisms land was made available to citizens, sometimes with preference to veterans, sometimes in a kind of lottery open to all competitors. It is true that large tracts of land were turned over to the railroads as an incentive to "open up the country" and, indirectly, to provide jobs and economic development, but other large tracts of land were made available to individuals. In a sense, land in the middle nineteenth century was the equivalent of contemporary dollar allocations from the treasury. The land distribution programs conformed to a basic policy of relying upon the individual and the marketplace, and yet also involved federal supplementation of the essentially private processes. They also involved a form of federal and state partnership, since jurisdiction devolved to the states once land was acquired by individuals or by corporations.

By the early twentieth century, the major industrialized states—New

York, Massachusetts, New Jersey, Ohio, Illinois—had elaborated other state-level programs based upon older English poor laws of local residence and poor relief. A few states enacted statewide, modest pensions for widows with minor children and for the aged. By 1929 these expenditures were estimated to total some $500 million, almost entirely state or municipality administered.[3]

The 1930s and the New Deal:
The Emergence of Federal Responsibility

The depression years and the enactment of the Social Security Act in 1935 are rightly considered watersheds in the evolution of American policy for welfare and especially for income maintenance. However, the significant breakthrough in this period was the assumption of an active role by the national government for income maintenance.

While this can be considered a major development in the history of the nation, it does not represent a new direction in policy if, by policy, we mean those guiding principles for action in unexpected and future circumstances. Social security legislation of the 1930s appears to conform in all major respects to the principles governing income maintenance outlined at the beginning of this chapter. Most programs were based upon past employment; income support was to be temporary (except for the aged), assuming that private work would be revived; continued income support was assured only to the widowed, disabled, and aged; and programs required cooperation and cost sharing by three levels of government.

If this was not quite a revolution in policy or a major change in direction, at least two significant advances in the nature of these policies were made:

1. The belief was introduced that income provided should be closer to a level of minimum health and decency than to a bare subsistence.
2. A first step was taken to use federal policy to equalize income as well as to provide access to minimum income.

The Federal Emergency Relief Administration (FERA) represented the national government's use of its fiscal resources to provide cash assistance not only to the widowed and orphaned but also to able-bodied workers. This was clearly an emergency program based on the assumption that the economy would, in time, provide the major sources of income and that the marketplace would resume its normal function. However, through its use of cash payments, the FERA represented an assurance of access to minimum income, a responsibility previously assumed by state and local governments.

[3] *Encyclopedia of Social Work*, 16th ed. (New York: National Association of Social Workers, 1971), vol. 2, Table 20, p. 1584.

The Public Works Administration (PWA) and the Works Progress Administration (WPA) of the same period represented another facet of the same guiding principle—namely, that, at least for the able-bodied, income and work went hand in hand. Over the life of the WPA, nearly 8 million persons, formerly unemployed, were given jobs building highways, bridges, roads, public buildings, hospitals, nursing stations, libraries, schools, and museums. Swampland was drained; water mains and sewer lines were rebuilt; parks and playgrounds were restored or constructed; the first National Guide Series to the United States was produced; and theater, music, and plastic arts were subsidized. In a peak year of 1938, 3,161,000 unemployed individuals were employed on such projects.[4] By the time of America's entry into World War II, both the FERA and the WPA were terminated, testifying to the emergency nature of these national administrations and to the continuity of basic policy that saw government as a complement or supplement to the marketplace economy.

The enactment of the Social Security Act in 1935 symbolized further the continuity of American social policy as now expressed in the public policy of the national government. First, the Social Security Act assured access of minimum income for certain vulnerable populations—namely, the elderly, widows, and orphans. This policy, however, was no longer left to impulses of local government or to the uncertainties of annual appropriations. Instead, a form of compulsory annuity was introduced—compulsory for almost all the working population (certain excluded groups, such as farm laborers, domestics, and employees of religious organizations and physicians, were later covered)—and contributed to by the beneficiary as well as by the employers. The assurance of security, meaning income access and nothing more, was riveted into our society by these devices. In the future, it would be very difficult indeed to remove this access, at least for the working population.

A crucial issue was the compulsory nature of the policy. There was strong conservative opposition to the idea of any compulsory program, and a competitive preference was strongly argued for some voluntary arrangements by which individuals would themselves choose whether or not to be protected under the new program. In the legislative controversy preceding the passage of the act, those who favored a completely voluntary system, which would have returned the entire security program for the elderly to the marketplace, were counterbalanced by advocates of the Townsend Movement, which called for a straight and simple pension of a fixed sum to be paid to all older persons regardless of their work status. The

[4] See Donald Howard, *W.P.A. and Federal Relief Policy* (New York: Russell Sage, 1943); A.E. Burns, *Federal Work, Security and Relief Programs*, Research Monograph No. 24 (Washington, D.C.: U.S. Government Printing Office, 1941), p. 54.

proponents of the Social Security Act compromised by inserting the require-ment that the annuity would become available only on retirement. This issue was left in doubt until final determination was made in the Senate Finance Committee in 1935. In the debate the president and his appointed Committee on Economic Security strongly supported compulsory annuities. The Congress represented the older policy, while the presidency repre-sented the cutting edge of the new. The policy and position of the executive branch was finally adopted by the Congress.[5]

Regardless of the economic aspects of this decision, it represented logical consistency in a social policy that assured minimum income access only for persons who were considered by the society at any given time to be outside of the effective labor force. In the eighteenth century, women fre-quently and orphans often were considered wholly outside of the labor force. In the 1930s, in the midst of a deep depression, the elderly—especially those over 65—were also considered (whether realistically or idealistically) as effectively out of the labor force and, therefore, qualified for minimum income assurance.

The firmness of federal policy was further tested by the debate over where to place the administration of the Social Security Act. There was strong support among presidential advisors to place all administration within the Department of Labor, the federal department most clearly iden-tified with employment and especially employment developments in the private economy. A compromise was reached whereby unemployment com-pensation would be administered by the Department of Labor and an in-dependent Social Security Board would be established to administer the old age pension program. This independent, permanent, new agency fell within the old norms for the federal government in that it attended to the needs of a part of the population considered most likely to be kept out of the work force and also considered vulnerable. At the same time, the fact that its crea-tion substantially widened the scope of the federal government's sup-plementary role would have consequences for the future shaping of public policies. The new programs were located in permanent instrumentalities of the national government and thus marked a turning point in the range of the national government's supplementary responsibility. This evolution modified the underlying policy boundaries of the past in one final respect: The administration of the old age retirement program was vested entirely in the national government, without the state and local government partner-ship existing in most other activities.

Income security for widows and orphans was translated by the Social

---

[5] For a discussion of this debate see Edwin E. Witte, *The Development of the Social Security Program* (Madison: University of Wisconsin Press, 1963).

Security Act into a program for mothers and dependent children. The legislation was not as generous with children as it was with the aged, at least with respect to federal sharing in the costs of security. But a federal program provided federal contributions to state programs for mothers with dependent children who qualified by lack of other income sources. The national government did not assume a commitment to provide assured income to this specially vulnerable group of citizens, but it acted within conventional boundaries by sharing costs and administration with state and local governments and by limiting its share to the poorest, most helpless.

The federal role of complementing the marketplace was, in 1935, further enlarged by the introduction of a national system of unemployment insurance. This was intended to assure steady access to some income for persons in the labor force but temporarily unemployed. Issues as to whether to limit or to widen federal policy were argued. To ensure enactment, the proponents of the program finally adopted compromises to maintain a central policy position. The insurance was limited to workers forced out of employment through no fault of their own, and the income security provided was kept to a minimum. Some proponents argued for a federally administered system with standard, federally determined premiums to be paid employers and with standard federally determined benefits. Others argued for a single fund, but one to be administered by each state. Still others argued for maximum openness, with states free to choose between a single unemployment insurance fund or several insurance funds set up for each major employer group. While the details of tax level and of insurance fund form are complex and significant, what proved most important in the enactment of this legislation was the enlargement of a well-established principle of governmental responsibility for income assurance. Between 1941 and 1970, the annual number of workers, applying for payments due to unemployment rose from 3,439,000 to 6,402,000. Average weekly benefits rose from $11.06 to $50.34, representing about 35% of average weekly earnings throughout the three decades, as benefits sought to keep up with inflation.

The steadfast work focus of federal policy was further demonstrated by the introduction of a program for vocational rehabilitation of the disabled. The Committee on Economic Security, which spearheaded the original executive branch planning for this legislation, considered invalidism or disability insurance and recognized it as an acceptable form of protection. However, the complexities of developing and administering an insurance program for invalids were considered to be so great that the committee felt it should be the last item introduced to round out a full program of security. Those who argued for a comprehensive program for the handicapped and those who were opposed to any further extension of protection were satisfied by a compromise that provided for the rehabilitation of the injured so that they could return to employment. Balancing the executive determination to enlarge and the congressional determination to contain, the compromise measure joined the concern of government for a vulnerable group unable to work with the commitment to the marketplace and self-employment by establishing a program for education and retraining supported by the federal government.

The principle of shared responsibility between the federal and the state governments and with private industry was also strengthened and extended in this period. Except for the annuity program for the retired elderly, all other programs of the Social Security Act involved some form of joint federal and state collaboration and sharing in both administration and costs. The nature of the collaboration varied by program. Old age assistance, as distinguished from the retirement program, was administered by state governments, with the federal government matching approved expenditures by one-half. Programs for mothers and dependent children were also state administered, with the federal government sharing in approved expenditures by one-third. Vocational rehabilitation proved to be a combination of state-administered programs and federal regulation and funding. Workmen's compensation was entirely state administered, with the federal government collecting and remitting taxes. Whatever the details of the form, the principle of federal–state sharing of both responsibility and financing was reaffirmed.

In another significant move, the 1935 legislation sought to raise the floor for income support from a bare subsistence level to one of minimum decency. The original Social Security Legislation stipulated that the states must furnish assistance sufficient to provide "when added to the income of the aged recipient, a *reasonable* subsistence compatible with decency and health."[6] This provision was derived from legislation in pioneer states, such as New York and Massachusetts. However, representatives of southern states were vigorously opposed to this introduction of a federal standard into a state's freedom of choice, primarily because it was viewed as a threat to the states' freedom to treat their minorities differently from the way in which others were treated. To secure enactment, this provision was dropped, but its proposal is another example of how executive branch activities sought to enlarge public policy beyond existing norms. In this case, the proposal went too far beyond what the American society was then prepared to accept. If the language proposed had been retained, the balance in partnership between federal and state government would have been altered: A tool to press for greater income equalization would have been placed in the hands of a federal agency, and federal intervention into the lives of its citizens would have deepened and widened. However, federal efforts persisted into later years. A proposed policy was delayed but finally

[6] Ibid.

adopted by 1965 when the Department of Health, Education, and Welfare began its systematic use of a formula to fix a "poverty line" for counting the poor. This became the target for most social programs.

The 1935 legislation also represents a major advance in redistributive policy, which uses income maintenance as a means not only to assure minimum income but also to reduce the disparity between income classes. The retirement program introduced a principle new to the American society: It payed relatively larger benefits to workers receiving low wages throughout their working life and thus discriminated slightly in favor of low-income workers at the expense of higher-earning employees, who contributed more substantially to the income fund. This did not mean that benefits were strictly graded according to past income, but rather that there was a slight increase in benefits to the lowest paid, while the higher-paid workers received slightly less than if the program paid an annuity based upon private pension plans.

In periods of overwhelming national emergency, the norms we have identified as governing income programs in the United States have been abandoned. During the depths of the depression, public assistance income was federally administered throughout most of the United States. The fact that this was considered an emergency measure comparable to the kind of national mobilization that takes place in wartime is revealed throughout all the debate of this period, in the very name of the Federal Emergency Relief Administration, and in its dismantling as soon as war and improvement in employment altered the economic profile.

Wartime introduced one interesting experiment in federal control of income maintenance indirectly through the health field. A large part of the work force was in the army; their wives were at the prime childbearing age. The low army pay left them unable to meet the costs of childbearing and rearing. A wartime emergency program, the Emergency Maternal and Infant Care Program, was introduced to assure that the medical costs of childbearing and rearing for military personnel would be properly covered. Although not vast by comparison with other income maintenance programs, this program was the first that, while nominally handled through the marketplace of private medicine, did so under strict regulations introduced by the United States Children's Bureau and administered as a national program.[7]

The Social Security Act succeeded in sustaining the implicit social policies of the past: reliance upon the marketplace, government supplementation, with acceptance of limited federal sharing with the states, and a commitment to help assure certain disadvantaged groups of access to steady income. The legislation's major contribution brought the national government

---

[7] See Nathan Sinai and Odin W. Anderson, *EMIC: A Study of Administrative Experience*, Research Series No. 3 (Ann Arbor: Bureau of Health Economics, School of Public Health, University of Michigan, 1948).

for the first time fully into the income arena as a matter of social policy, but without introducing any radically new thrust in policy.

Certain new and even revolutionary changes in policy were tested and by and large failed. The attempt to assure income, at least for the elderly, on a compulsory basis without requiring retirement from the work force was defeated, as was the attempt to introduce a level of income for assuring health and decency rather than minimum subsistence. However, an approach to radical change was adopted. The retirement program was the first step in the long process of narrowing disparities in income in American society, and full federal administration and control was tested, even if on a depression or wartime emergency basis.

The 1960s: An Enlargement of the Guiding Principles

Between 1935 and 1960, most of the emergency relief proposals induced by the depression were dismantled, leaving only the basic income maintenance programs initiated in the 1930s. This period was characterized by inflation and economic boom with recession, but a combination of war and postwar economic expansion and growth in the national economic product produced a general belief that the basic economy was proceeding soundly and that substantial governmental interventions were no longer necessary. However, expenditures for income maintenance programs by federal and state governments did not decline; in fact, they increased slightly. In 1935, at the depths of the depression, $22.4 billion were spent for these purposes; by 1960, the amount had increased to $24.4 billion.[8] Approximately half of these expenditures were in the form of federal payments to the states, representing continuity in the concept of federal–state partnership.

The persistence of government programs at these levels in a period of presumed economic health caused substantial anxiety, an anxiety increased by evidence that poverty continued at a high level even though the principle of access to minimum income still seemed to be at work. In 1959, for example, it was estimated that about 22% of the American population lived below an arbitrarily defined level of poverty.[9]

The existence of such levels of poverty produced not only political crises but also a serious, if poorly articulated, doubt about the whole economic system. Poverty was an issue in the political arena as the need to increase expenditures to maintain income was argued. However, this phenomenon also served to introduce a substantial challenge to another guiding principle for government policy in the income field—namely, that government existed primarily to supplement or complement the functioning of the marketplace.

[8] *Encyclopedia of Social Work*, Table 20, p. 1584.
[9] President's Commission on Income Maintenance. *Poverty Amid Plenty—The American Paradox* (Washington, D.C.: U.S. Government Printing Office, 1969).

The fact that nearly a quarter of the American population was not satisfactorily served in terms of income by the marketplace raised grave doubts about the American economy itself.

These doubts led to a continuing search for better technical means for identifying what is meant by the term *poverty*. In fact, the development of measures of poverty can be taken to represent one of the difficulties in policy planning—namely, the absence of widely accepted technical tools with which to carry planning forward. The instrument most widely used to measure poverty was a measure of absolute poverty developed by the Social Security Administration (SSA).[10] In its simplest form, this measure is based on the estimated cost of an economy food budget for families of various sizes, representing the proportion of income expended by family types for the purchase of food. Thus, if a family of a given size and location spends one-third of its income on food at an economy level, it is assumed that income required to keep the family just at or above the poverty line would be three times this figure; families with incomes below this fixed figure are considered to be below the poverty threshold.

Although this measure is widely used and does represent a significant advance over previous measures in the United States, it has nonetheless been criticized on several scores. It is considered to ignore accepted levels of decency as distinguished from a stringent or even bare subsistence budget. It also does not take into account price level variations in different regions or climatic and other factors that affect the costs of budgetary items, such as food, shelter, and transportation. More serious, it is often ignored in calculating relief payments. With all its limitations, the measure does, however, serve as a tool for national policy in that it does establish a generally accepted fixed minimum below which families should not fall.

Numerous proposals have been made to modify the Social Security measure, but most of them have been concerned only with raising the level of the poverty threshold. *Relative* measures of poverty are an important supplement to the social security index. The difference between the income that most Americans consider to be average or real for themselves and the income actually attained that falls below this real average is a useful measure of relative poverty in a dynamic society.

Plotnick and Skidmore have combined the official Social Security measure with a second relative measure of the poverty population.[11] Their modification divides a family's current cash income by the Social Security poverty line. This yields a welfare ratio that indicates the fraction by which

[10] Molly Orshansky, "Counting the Poor—Another Look at the Poverty Profile," *Social Security Bulletin* 28, no. 1 (January 1965): 3–29.

[11] Robert Plotnick and Felicity Skidmore, *Progress Against Poverty*, Institute for Research on Poverty series (New York: Academic Press, 1975), Chap. 2.

the family's income exceeds or falls below the SSA level of minimum decency defined in absolute terms.

These measures do not adequately account for the effect of taxes or of in-kind transfers, such as food in kind, subsidized housing, or free medical care, although some attempts are being made by the Institute for Research on Poverty of the University of Wisconsin to introduce these variables.[12]

Bearing in mind these technical problems of measurement and the more general concerns about poverty and the economy, it is instructive to re- view the decade of the 1960s. The 1960s can be called the period of the Great Society. The boundaries of governmental supplementation of the marketplace were substantially widened, and the guiding principle once limited to assuring a subsistence minimum was broadened by the op- timistically proclaimed War on Poverty. Underneath the rhetoric promis- ing a campaign to abolish poverty lay an important shift in national policy—namely, the move from subsistence to prevention. The dimensions of this shift can be seen by a review of trends between 1965 and 1974 in social welfare expenditures considered to be related to income programs. Tables 3.1, 3.2, and 3.3 dramatically outline the increases in federal, state, local, and total expenditures on social programs addressed primarily to low- income populations. The relationship of such federal actions to the number of households considered below poverty during this period is clear, as is the effect of such actions on the poverty gap between the periods preceding and following the transfer of public funds.

The tables show clearly the great escalation of total amounts expended in the 7-year period. The programs all conform to the basic principles developed during the 1930s: They rest on the assumptions that a combina- tion of job creation, education, and other incentives can reduce the number of families in poverty; that providing these incentives is a governmental responsibility; and that such governmental actions are essential to supple- ment the basic marketplace economy.

But job stimulation and cash relief were no longer seen as sufficient to reduce poverty and allow the market its old dominance. Deficits in educa- tion and in opportunity also had to be overcome by such short-term pro- grams. Therefore, government financing was extended to include adult education, special employment programs, remedial medical and nutritional services, family planning, various child-care programs designed to relieve parents and to start children early on constructive careers, migrant ser- vices, youth corps for out-of-school youths to condition them to employ- ment, counseling services, work experience opportunities, and the like. To provide resources to the poor so that they could take an active part in reme- dying their situation, special programs of the Office of Economic Opportu-

---

[12] Ibid., Chap. 14.

TABLE 3.1
Social Welfare Expenditures, 1965, 1968, 1972[a]

Year and Program	Federal		State–Local		Total	
	Expenditure (in millions of dollars)	Percent	Expenditure (in millions of dollars)	Percent	Expenditure (in millions of dollars)	Percent
1965						
OEO and related programs	359	17	0		359	(12)
Other low-income programs	5,995		2,503	(7)	8,498	
Other social welfare expenditures	31,420	83	34,205	(93)	65,625	(88)
Total	37,774	100	36,708	(100)	74,482	(100)
1968						
OEO and related programs	3,311	21	0		3,311	(15)
Other low-income programs	8,698		4,379	(9)	13,077	
Other social welfare expenditures	45,563	79	46,273	(91)	92,836	(85)
Total	58,572	100	50,652	(100)	109,224	(100)
1972						
OEO and related programs	4,695	24	0		4,695	(18)
Other low-income programs	19,959		9,149	(11)	29,108	
Other social welfare expenditures	80,362	76	70,707	(89)	151,069	(82)
Total	105,016	100	79,856	(100)	184,872	(100)

[a] SOURCE: Robert Plotnick and Felicity Skidmore, *Progress against Poverty*, Institute for Research on Poverty Series (New York: Academic Press, 1975), Table 1.3.

ABLE 3.2
asic Statistics of Pretransfer Poverty, 1965, 1968, 1972[a]

	Pretransfer poor households		Total pretransfer poverty gap (in billions of dollars)	Average per household poverty gap (in dollars)	Total pretransfer income of the poor (in billions of dollars)	Average pretransfer income (in dollars)
	Number (in thousands)	Incidence (in percentages)				
965	15,609	25.7	22.13	1,418	14.14	906
968	14,933	23.2	23.79	1,593	12.95	867
972	17,640	24.8	32.49	1,944	16.37	928

SOURCE: Robert Plotnick and Felicity Skidmore, *Progress against Poverty*, Institute for Research on Poverty Series (New ork: Academic Press, 1975), Table 3.1.

nity (OEO) allocated large sums to local community action agencies that directed funds to local citizens' groups close to the thinking, culture, and needs of the poor.

Table 3.3 summarizes the nature of the expenditures in this massive program. Most of the funds were allocated to cash payments as a means of income support (43.3% in 1972) and to education (33.7% in 1972). Allocations to nutrition, OEO, and health services, less in volume but nonetheless significant, were primarily intended to overcome employment deficits, rather than represent a commitment to general public provision of health or welfare services.

TABLE 3.3
Composition of Total Social Welfare Expenditures to Pretransfer Poor, 1965, 1968, 1972, by Functional Categories[a]

	Total social welfare expenditures		
	1965	1968	1972
Total dollars (in billions)	74.5	109.2	184.9
Composition (in percentages)			
Cash transfers	48.5	41.7	43.3
Payments to farmers	3.0	2.8	1.7
Nutrition	1.2	0.9	2.0
Housing	0.4	0.4	1.0
Health	7.6	12.9	13.3
Welfare and OEO services	1.9	2.3	2.9
Employment-manpower	0.9	1.8	2.1
Education	36.4	37.1	33.7
Total	100.0	100.0	100.0

[a] SOURCE: Data from Robert Plotnick and Felicity Skidmore, *Progress against Poverty*, Institute for Research on Poverty Series (New York: Academic Press, 1975), Tables 2–4.

A close analysis of this period indicates that, despite the surface confusion resulting from the introduction of many new federally funded services, most of these services still conformed with remarkable fidelity to the basic principles that we have identified. This period still is characterized by a primary reliance upon the marketplace for employment, with governmental supplementation. It is based upon minimum income standards as an expression of decent treatment of citizens. There is little if any shift in the principle of federal and state sharing.[13] In 1965, for example, $37.8 billion were provided by federal funds and $36.7 billion by state and local funds (see Table 3.1). In 1972 the federal share had increased to $105 billion and the state and local share to $79.8 billion. While the federal share had steadily increased from 50 to 56%, the principle of sharing had not been abandoned.

One of the guiding principles has been especially powerful—namely, the federal readiness to assure more generous security for those clearly unable to take part in the work force—the aged and the disabled. Much of the social welfare expenditure to abolish poverty, 60% by one estimate, has concentrated on payments to the elderly and the disabled who, before transfer of public funds, were considered in poverty. Such groups in 1972 received a share of the total expenditures, mainly through Social Security retirement benefits and Medicare, that some considered disproportionate. For example, programs that do not depend on poverty-line conditions of eligibility (Medicare and retirement) grew from $28 billion to $59 billion between 1965 and 1972; programs especially limited to those in the poorest economic circumstances (which do rely upon poverty-line determination of eligibility) increased from $19.6 billion to $41 billion. While the elderly and permanently disabled constitute the total beneficiary population of the first set of programs, they also constitute a large proportion of those in the second.

This principle may have been breached—or extended—by the fact that retirement benefits are paid regardless of income status of the recipients; only two conditions, old age and disability, are necessary to trigger federal action, not three as in the past, the third being low income.

A variety of economic analyses now permit some assessment of the results of this incremental shift in public policy regarding income. These econometric analyses are still in an elementary stage of development and, while limited by the nature of the data available, are still useful first-stage assessment tools. Between 1965 and 1972, the average real income of families, without public income transfer programs, rose from $9,822 to $11,596.[14] The national unemployment rate fluctuated within a narrow range of 4.5–5.6% and the rate of inflation increased perceptibly from 1.7 to 5.9% and then dropped to 3.3%.

[13] Ibid.
[14] Ibid., p. 118, Table 5.4.

Approximately one-third of all pretransfer poor households were lifted above the poverty line, as measured in absolute terms, by cash transfers (see Table 3.4).

In absolute and percentage terms, households with aged heads benefited overwhelmingly in this removal from poverty, although a respectable one-fourth of households with nonaged male or female heads also were removed from poverty. Unfortunately, this movement has been quite unevenly distributed among population subgroups. For example, black households with nonaged female heads, a group that benefits less generously than others do from these programs, have grown proportionately, compared to other parts of the population. This unsatisfactory state is clearly connected with the prospects of various population subgroups entering the marketplace economy through regular employment. The aged and disabled are not expected, in the normative view, to be at work, but adult women are expected to work, even if opportunities are scarce. The latter are still afforded a lower level of economic security (see Table 3.5).

This picture of the effect of the programs of the 1960s should not be overstressed; it is suggestive only. This was a period in which by American standards unemployment remained relatively low and inflation reasonably controlled. Still, the number of persons requiring public income transfer programs remained high, and the movement out of poverty was mainly due not to a return to private employment but to income maintenance programs. This finding has seriously disturbed those adhering to the basic principle that federal involvement in income maintenance can be transient and supplementary, decline over time, and be resumed only in episodic periods of depression. In fact, the number of persons dependent upon public funds and the sums of money involved both increased steadily during this period.

A number of explanations have been advanced to account for this rather disappointing result. The most pessimistic view is that the dynamics of a marketplace economy are such that relative poverty as distinguished from absolute poverty can never be reduced. The economic system requires incentives to keep people in the work force, and these incentives must bring them income substantially above the income secured by those who are not employed. However, the wants and functioning of the bulk of the population are such that employment cannot be offered to all persons, especially not to those with limited skills. Also, as people need more income to satisfy their expectations, the number of persons seeking work increases, because families with several wage earners have a greater total family disposable income. In a society where employment for mothers, wives, husbands, and teen-aged children is considered desirable, the volume of positions that can be produced is not sufficient to meet the demand.

It is also argued that the programs designed cumulatively during the 1960s did not concentrate on the poorest, but on a combination of the poor,

TABLE 3.4
Number and Percentage of Pretransfer Poor Households Taken Out of Absolute Poverty by Government Transfers, by Demographic Groups, 1965 and 1972[a]

Demographic group	Pretransfer poor households	Pretransfer poor households made nonpoor by Social Security		Additional pretransfer poor made nonpoor by other nonpublic assistance transfers[b]		Additional pretransfer poor households made nonpoor by public assistance transfers[c]		Total pretransfer poor households made nonpoor by all cash transfers	
		Number (in thousands)	Percent	Number (in thousands)	Percent	Number (in thousands)	Percent	Number (in thousands)	Percent
1965									
All households	15,611	3,258	21	1,454	9	449	3	5,161	33
Households with aged heads[d]	7,512	2,699	36	880	12	222	3	3,801	51
Households with nonaged male heads, with children	2,761	75	3	182	7	45	2	302	11
Households with nonaged female heads, with children	1,395	171	12	54	4	77	6	302	22
Households with nonaged heads, no children[e]	3,943	313	8	338	9	105	3	756	19
1972									
All households	19,557	4,685	24	1,370	7	603	3	6,659	34
Households with aged heads[d]	9,158	3,875	42	611	7	243	3	4,729	52
Households with nonaged male heads, with children	2,682	129	5	231	9	100	4	460	17
Households with nonaged female heads, with children	2,395	178	7	45	2	148	6	371	15
Households with nonaged heads, no children[e]	5,322	503	9	483	9	112	2	1,098	21

[a] SOURCE: Robert Plotnick and Felicity Skidmore, *Progress against Poverty*, Institute for Research on Property Series (New York: Academic Press, 1975), Table 6.5.
Note: Percentages do not always sum to total because of rounding.
[b] Unemployment insurance, workmen's compensation, veterans' benefits, and government employee pensions.
[c] Old-Age Assistance, Aid to the Blind, Aid to the Permanently and Totally Disabled, and Aid to Families with Dependent Children.
[d] Includes unrelated individuals.
[e] Most are unrelated individuals, but childless couples are included.

TABLE 3.5
Poverty and Dependency on Cash Transfers, 1980 (in percent)[a]

Head of household[b]	Incidence of pretransfer poverty (1)	Receiving cash welfare[c] (2)	Taken out of poverty by cash welfare (3)	Receiving nonwelfare cash transfers[d] (4)	Taken out of poverty by cash nonwelfare transfers (5)	Official incidence of poverty (6)
					Percentage of pretransfer poor persons	
White nonaged						
Male	9.8	20.4	4.9	47.1	26.4	6.8
Female	35.9	46.0	6.5	33.4	15.8	27.9
White aged						
Male	49.3	9.1	1.8	97.7	81.6	8.2
Female	67.9	16.5	4.1	95.9	60.1	24.3
Nonwhite nonaged						
Male	21.0	38.2	7.2	42.1	14.3	16.5
Female	59.3	68.0	6.5	28.8	7.2	51.2
Nonwhite aged						
Male	67.2	31.7	8.3	93.3	50.6	27.6
Female	83.2	54.9	12.3	85.9	27.8	49.9
All persons	21.9	30.9	5.1	58.2	35.3	13.0

[a] SOURCE: Computations by Sheldon Danziger from March 1981 Current Population Surveys prepared for National Economic Association Session, December 29, 1982, "Exploring Black Welfare Dependency," unpublished manuscript (Madison, Wisc: Institute for Poverty Research, 1982).

[b] Heads of households 64 years of age or younger are nonaged; those 65 or older are aged.

[c] Cash welfare transfers include Aid to Families with Dependent Children, Supplemental Security Income, and General Assistance.

[d] Nonwelfare cash transfers include Social Security, Railroad Retirement, Supplemental Security Income, unemployment compensation, workers' compensation, government employee pensions, and veterans' pensions and compensation.

the marginally poor, and those above the poverty line. The elderly who receive increases in Social Security benefits or Medicare payments are not necessarily below the poverty line, and while some elderly are removed from poverty, through these increases, others below age 65 are not affected. In fact, one of the major incremental programs, food stamps, was designed to improve the position of the so-called working poor whose incomes hovered around the poverty line but might well be above it. The justification of this approach is not hard to see. It is argued that if the income of unemployed persons approximates the income of people who are fully employed at the lowest level of income but still above the poverty line, there is less incentive to remain in employment. Therefore, the condition of persons slightly above the poverty line needs to be improved relative to those below it. And for every improvement at the bottom of the income scale that results from a concentrated program focusing only on the poorest, there must be a consequent increase in income assured for those above the minimum. But since the functioning of the private marketplace economy does not smoothly assure these gradations, governmental intervention to provide supplements in the form of increasing income guarantees also increases government expenditures for a much wider segment of the population.

Finally, note must be taken of other unexpected consequences of a complex of income maintenance programs that have grown incrementally. First, there is the enormous variation in eligibility standards introduced in various categorical programs enacted by the Congress and in eligibility standards introduced by the states. Some people and families receive substantial cash transfers from these programs, and others in exactly the same objective condition receive no transfers at all. Some persons receive a combination of transfer benefits that raises them substantially above the average, whereas others fall far below it.

The chaos introduced by a series of incremental categorical programs all functioning within reasonable but broad national policies is well described by a series of reports by the Joint Economic Committee of the Congress of the United States.[15] It is possible for some households, depending upon location, size, and age, to receive as many as 10 or 11 different kinds of benefits that together have a high cash value. By 1970 there were 100 separate public welfare programs. In the committee reports, 1059 households in the sample studied (units that received benefits) received benefits in a minimum of 144 unique combinations. For example, in one community a female-headed family of four was found to have an average monthly combination of benefits totaling $714; in the same city a male-

---

[15] *Studies in Public Welfare* (Washington, D.C.: U.S. Government Printing Office, 1973), see especially Paper No. 6.

headed family of the same size received only $371. Some families receiving five or more benefits are likely to have total incomes above the federal poverty standard, but more families are entitled to fewer benefits and fall far below it.

The tangle of eligibility contradictions is also such that at least half of the persons who are likely to earn some income in private employment actually are worse off in employment than if they had not worked at all. Earning some income makes the families ineligible to receive certain welfare benefits, such as payment of medical expenses, access to food stamps, and housing supplements. This results in a "notch effect" or welfare trap; the keys to benefits are shaped by income earned. Categorical programs are intended to take care of segments of living: to assure access to health care, to improve housing, and so on. Each program is affected as much by the wants of the systems providing services as by the needs of poor people. There are many keys to eligibility, but no master key has yet been devised to eliminate the notch effect so that each program change does not adversely affect some group.

Whatever the explanation for the relatively disappointing results from this venture into prevention, a reassessment of public income maintenance programs was demanded by 1970. The fact that a relatively good economic situation did not reduce the role of government in its "interference" with or supplementation of the private marketplace sharpened the debate. Some argued that the venture into prevention was ill advised and that a more cautious return to basic guiding norms was essential. Others argued that the complexities of the modern economy require a further expansion of the government role, but with more complex and comprehensive planning to ensure a better expenditure of funds, not a reduction. For both, however, the belief persisted that the guiding principles remained acceptable and need not be substantially modified. Probing experiments to go beyond these principles were not yet persuasive in their effects, but no one argued the abandonment of income maintenance.

The 1970s: Controlled Responsibility and Management Reform

The Nixon era represented an attempt to withdraw from the preventive policy and return to the basic principles with a new focus—namely, the partial dismantling of the existing income maintenance programs and their reconstitution conforming to contemporary standards of business management. In this period, it was assumed that a cap could be placed upon the total federal investment in order to stem the increase in the federal share. The principle of government responsibility was not denied, but it was to be controlled. At the same time, the welfare system was to be simplified and its management rationalized. It is not altogether clear whether in this period the faltering first step taken in the Social Security Act to use income maintenance to equalize or reduce the disparity in income spread was to be continued or not. From some points of view, arguments for welfare reform, based on some variation of a negative income tax or family assistance plan, seemed to suggest the introduction of greater equalization of benefits paid but not necessarily of greater equity in the economic structure of society.

The search for a simplified and presumably equitable income maintenance program concentrated in this period almost entirely on public assistance and did not substantially alter the historic trend in workmen's compensation or retirement. For these programs, except for improvement in benefits, the basic principles as laid down in the 1930s were presumed to be sufficient. True, the demographic shift toward a larger proportion of older persons in the population, the tendency toward earlier retirement, and a significant increase in permanent and total disability among the adult population increased the cost of Social Security retirement programs beyond that originally anticipated. However, concern over the increased cost was expressed in debate over various financing forms rather than any major change in this basic component of the income system.

When one turns to public assistance, the situation is quite different. An attempt was made to rationalize more thoroughly the national responsibility. The Supplementary Security Income (SSI) program was adopted in 1972, whereby the federal government finally assumed full responsibility for a minimum national standard of security for parts of the dependent population outside of the labor force: the elderly other than those on Social Security, the blind, and the permanently and totally disabled. This was clearly consistent with the ongoing social norm for government.

Although the full responsibility was assumed by the federal government, the principle of state and federal sharing was retained in that state governments were enabled to maintain higher than minimum benefit standards for this population by contributing the additional costs. The net effect of the program was to raise significantly the level of income for this population in southern, western, and poorer states without an increase in burden to those states, while the older industrial states of the northeast and far west were placed in the unenviable position of maintaining their higher than average standard only through their own taxation. Nonetheless, the principle of sharing the responsibility seems to have been significantly modified, with the federal government finally taking total responsibility for an average minimum to prevail throughout the country.

In 1972, 15 million individuals received some payments from federally assisted or state relief programs. By December 1975, about 4 million aged, blind, and disabled were transferred to the new SSI program with a national uniform floor of income, leaving some 11 million under the AFDC and general assistance programs that depend on state-determined standards.[16]

Those who transferred to SSI in southern and southwestern states benefited most directly. In six states (Georgia, Mississippi, South Carolina, Indiana, Tennessee, and Texas), average payments for the aged had been below $60 a month, whereas the new SSI minimum became $140 for individuals and $210 for married couples. In three states (Alaska, California, and New Hampshire), the average payments had been above $110 so that their elderly benefited, but not as significantly as in the southern states: Actual SSI payments averaged $102 for aged couples, $142 for blind couples, and $139 for disabled couples. The difference from the national minimum reflects income received from other sources and differences in living arrangements.

Fifty-five percent of the aged, 51% of the disabled, and 61% of the blind received increases in income under SSI. In seven states (New Mexico, South Carolina, Tennessee, Louisiana, Mississippi, Ohio, and North Carolina), 90% or more of aged or disabled individuals or couples received SSI payments above former state levels. On the other hand, in eight states (California, Delaware, Massachusetts, Minnesota, Maine, Iowa, Arkansas, and Alaska), less than 10% of the aged or disabled units received an increase.

By 1975 average payments, including state supplements of federal minimums, ranged from $82.23 a month in Indiana to a high of $145.93 in Massachusetts. By contrast, AFDC payments to mothers ranged from a low of $14.39 per recipient in Mississippi to a high of $111.77 in New York.

For the rest of the dependent population, primarily families with dependent children and unemployed fathers, the early 1970s was a period of experimentation without clear direction. The AFDC program for unemployed parents continued with full state and federal sharing of cost and administration. These families were generally not considered suitable for permanent government intervention; aid was presumed to be assurance of a minimum access to income until employment could be secured. Various devices were tested to encourage them to seek employment in the private sector: Recipients had to register for job training and for work, and deserting fathers were pursued by legal means. However, such special training programs and harsh incentives were soon cut back. At the same time, a search was introduced for a more standardized program for underpinning the income of marginal families.

The most widely debated of these standardizing measures was the

[16] Lenora Kennedy, Dorothea Thomas, and Jack Schmulowitz, "Conversions to Supplementary Security Income from State Assistance," *Social Security Bulletin* 38, no. 6 (June 1975); and Annual Statistical Supplement 1975, *Social Security Bulletin*, Tables 157, 175.

variation of a family assistance plan or some form of the negative income tax introduced in the hope of devising some formula whereby standardized income levels related to family size could be adopted uniformly. Families would be entitled to income to bring them up to the standards. Assistance would be based on a sliding scale, so that the combination of public payments and earned income could increase as an incentive to seek employment up to some maximum figure, at which point public payments would disappear. However, as earned income declined, public payments would automatically increase so that in no instance would the family fall below a minimum floor, usually set around $2400 or $3000 per year. Such a major reorganization has not been adopted; it remains a proposed rather than an adopted policy. But it has been proposed in some form by at least three national administrations. Such "advanced" reforms retained the links between earned income and relief.

Small-scale tests of a negative income tax system were experimentally undertaken between 1966 and 1969.[17] The tests were mainly intended to ascertain whether workers would withdraw from the labor force in any significant numbers if some minimum income were assured, combining benefits and earned income at levels higher than it was possible to achieve without the program. While the payments were not large, they did measurably improve the income of low-income workers with some employment. Over the 3 years of experimentation, average payments made to continuous husband–wife families ranged from $91.03 per 4-week period in the first year to $96.84 in the third year. Black families received somewhat higher than average payments, $97.65 rising to $102.83 per week period, and Spanish-speaking workers received $86.96 rising to $100.32.

The research was complex and the results not altogether clear. In general, it appeared that there was some slight negative effect on the labor supply, meaning that a measurable percentage of families with earned income subsidized reduced their total work hours over time, as compared with a control population that had no such income supplement. But this effect was small; the percentage of withdrawal from employment accounted for about 5% of the estimated economic cost of the program. Black workers did not show the negative effect. Labor withdrawal seems concentrated among workers with especially low earnings and high family expenses. The fact that black workers did not withdraw may be accounted for by the fact that unemployment among black workers in control families was especially high in this period.

When one looks at the response of all family workers, not just the husband, it appears that the effect of such an income program on work is even less. Experimental and control families both reduced their work hours,

[17] See *Journal of Human Resources* 9, no. 2 (Spring 1974), whole issue.

although experimental families did so slightly more rapidly, and when work hours were increased, the experimental families increased their work total too, but less rapidly.

These studies also sought to ascertain whether there were any other social effects of such income guarantee. The findings suggest the following:

> Experimental families (receiving the guarantee) are *more* likely to buy a house, but this effect was more pronounced in families with higher incomes. Rent payments also increased suggesting movement into better housing, or at least out of public housing.
>
> Health and other aspects of life style were not significantly affected by a program of this brief duration. Attempts were made to test whether such programs would reduce family break-up and lead to more stable family life. The findings were inconclusive but suggest that when income assurances are more generous (i.e., a higher income achieved by a combination of earnings and guarantee) then some families do tend to stablize. But a significant number of families use the security to break up what seems to have been unhappy marriages.[18]

Other attempts to alter the income system concentrated on improvements in managerial efficiency. The federal government first encouraged states to reorganize state and local governments into larger units of administration with more comprehensive data systems to assure management control of expenditures. Under the guise of returning more responsibility to the states, federal administration of public assistance in fact increased the volume and detail of federal control. However, federal controls of a system based primarily on state determination of family incomes and eligibility for AFDC were founded on the use of statistical devices and management control procedures. Sampling methods were used to determine whether or not payments were made appropriately, and the federal share of payments to the states could be withheld on the basis of post hoc audits after the expenditures had in fact been made.

These efforts at management control occurred at a time when federal agencies for this purpose were demoralized by reductions and transfers, and state governments were increasingly harassed by large state budget deficits. The resulting confusion and dissatisfaction were increased by difficulties in launching the SSI program. It had been assumed that the program, using standardized payments once eligibility is determined, could be absorbed by the Social Security computer system and handled mechanically. However, the computer system, quite suitable for standard retirement programs, proved less than perfect when it came to handling a dependent population in fluctuating circumstances and with marginal total incomes. The system could not respond rapidly enough to changes in human needs

---

[18] Ibid., p. 253.

and to the built-in variations, which came from a combination of minimum federal standards with some above minimum payments in some states. This led to confusion, delays, and a great deal of human suffering.

Thus, efforts to improve public assistance programs only increased the demand for more basic reform of the welfare system, although the nature of that required reform is still not clear at this writing.

The 1980s: Attempts to Reverse National Policy

With the election of a Republican president and Senate in 1980, a new factor in national income policy was activated—an attempt to reassert the primacy of the marketplace and to reduce the force of federal intervention in the economy in general and in welfare in particular. This effort was partly a reflection of party principle, which offered a clear change from the two-party concensus approach to welfare of the preceding decades. But it was also a continuation of subtle shifts in national thinking that first emerged in the 1970s, brought about by a sluggish economy that continued to increase the burden of public responsibility without offsetting increases in income for a social increment that past economic growth provided.

The new administration proposed a clear change from the past: tax cuts, which especially favored the more affluent in order to increase investment in new economic activity; an increased military and defense expenditure program; and offsetting reductions in welfare expenditures. The result was an increase in unemployment, in corporate bankruptcies, and in reductions in existing income-support programs, such as unemployment insurance. At the same time, applications for AFDC and SSI continued to rise, as did expenditures and the number of aged, while income from taxes for Social Security declined along with the rate of employment. Inflation was reduced quickly, but the deficit in government budgets increased exponentially. The administration policies shifted from welfare to the marketplace as a solution. Prime reliance was placed on reactivating the economy in the belief that that would, in turn, produce new jobs that would provide more persons with necessary income so that government would be a less necessary resource. At the same time, there was a verbal commitment to caring for the "truly needy," meaning the disabled and others unable to work. The policy, despite protestations to the contrary, was not one of reducing the scale of government but of shifting it from welfare to economic and military incentives.

This attempted policy shift revealed most clearly how difficult it is to move the effective direction of a national political, economic, and social policy either quickly or radically. Dollar appropriations continue to grow for welfare, in part because entitlement programs (such as retirement, Medicare, and unemployment) could not be easily changed and because the Congress would not accept all the budgetary reductions proposed by pre-1980 administrations. This situation continued into the 1980s.

However, the 1980s introduced real shifts in policy, which slowly began to shift the direction of federal responsibility. This is further explored in Chapter 8, but as regards income programs, the following are significant.

1. The rate at which program support grows was cut, even if the programs themselves were not reduced legislatively. Still the effect of even modest inflation is to cut the reach of social welfare. Tables 2.1, 2.2, 2.3 show that, even before the new policy was introduced, the amount of federal support, in current or stable dollars, began to drop by 1979, and this has continued although firm current data are not available. For the first time in the modern era, the rate of increase in welfare moved from plus to minus in 1979. In per capita terms, the drop was most noticeable for veterans, for education, and for "other social welfare," which includes most of the social work personal services.

2. A variety of administrative management devices were tried out as a way to reduce costs and commitment without changing legal authorization. These steps are justified on the grounds of efficiency in management, or to reduce fraud and abuse. The final effects of such actions have not been evaluated, but certain consequences and problems can be noted. Administrative regulations shift eligibility for food stamps, making it more difficult for working adults with very low wages to qualify. Changing the procedures for establishing eligibility makes it more difficult for older clients and for those with small children to keep up with the requirements. Criteria for requalifying for Social Security benefits with disability were raised; individuals disqualified by new criteria were discontinued, and they receive no income while a lengthy appeals process is followed. Even if the applicant is successful on appeal, the program has been saved several months of payments. Similarly, requirements of eligibility for AFDC vary by state, and as state governments are burdened by a slow economy, high unemployment, and the backlash of some reduction in federal social programs, they raise the eligibility criteria for AFDC, increase requirements about work, delay cost of living increases, and make obstacles to clients who try to improve their position by studying to acquire new skills while on relief. State agencies that actually administer federal dollars are audited to see how many errors they make. If their daily actions result in too many mistakes—that is, eligibility approved in error or payments paid over or above an amount decided after the fact—then states are penalized by retroactive withholding of funds.

3. Most significant among these changes is a new approach to the so-called entitlement programs, such as Social Security, which benefit not only

the poor but even larger numbers of middle- and upper-income families. Such programs are not "welfare" or means tested in the traditional welfare sense. Rather, individuals become automatically entitled to benefits by objective conditions, not income, age, retirement, loss of work in an industry covered by unemployment insurance, etc. Until the 1980s Social Security retirement benefits were treated as true social benefits for all, not welfare—they were not taxed, regardless of individual income. This has been finally changed by action of the Congress, which in 1983 approved revisions in the act to begin taxing a part of retirement when an individual's total adjusted gross taxable income is above $25,000 ($32,000 for couples filing jointly). The formula requires inclusion of one-half of Social Security retirement income in taxable income if the inclusion will raise the adjusted gross taxable income above $25,000 (or above $32,000 for couples).

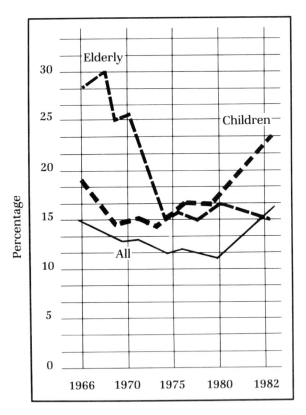

FIGURE 3.1.   The changing face of poverty: Poverty rates for children under age 18 and for persons aged 65 and over, 1966–1982. From the American Public Welfare Association, Washington Report 18, no. 7 (September 1983): 1, citing the National Journal © 1983.

TABLE 3.6
The Trend in the Incidence of Poverty among Persons, Selected Years 1965–82 [a]

Year	Pretransfer income (1)	Prewelfare income (2)	Posttransfer income (census income) (3)	Adjusted income [b] (4)
1965	21.3%	16.3%	15.6%	12.1%
1968	18.2	13.6	12.8	9.9
1972	19.2	13.1	11.9	6.2
1974	20.3	13.1	11.6	7.2
1976	21.0	13.1	11.8	6.7
1978	20.2	12.6	11.4	n.a.
1979	20.5	12.9	11.7	6.1
1980	21.9	14.2	13.0	n.a.
1981	23.1	15.1	14.0	n.a.
1982	24.0	15.9	15.0	8.8 [c]
% Change				
1965–1978 [d]	– 5.2	–22.7	–26.9	–49.6
1978–1982 [d]	+ 18.8	+ 26.2	+ 31.6	+44.3

[a] SOURCE: Sheldon Danziger in Danziger, Peter Gottschalk, Robert J. Rubin, and Timothy M. Smeeding, "Recent Increases in Poverty: Testimony before the House Ways and Means Committee," Focus, (Institute of Research on Poverty, Madison, Wisc.) 7, No. 1 (Winter 1984): 2.
[b] Adjusted income data are from Timothy Smeeding, "The Antipoverty Effect of In-Kind Transfers," Policy Studies Journal, 10 (1982), 499–521.
[c] This is an estimate from Peter Gottschalk and Danziger, "Changes in Poverty, 1967–1982; Methodological Issues and Evidence," IRP Discussion Paper no. 737–83.
[d] Percentage changes for adjusted income data are from 1965–79 and 1979–82.
n.a. = not available

This mechanism is known in England as a *clawback*. The term applies to benefits that are given to people on a non-means-tested basis. In effect, payments are made for a condition—retirement due to age, having minor children warranting children's allowances (not available in the U.S.), etc. Such conditions warrant social protection without stigma, but the result is that many beneficiaries are not poor, for there are more middle-income people than there are very poor in modern industrial society. The solution is to treat such benefits as true income, the same as if earned, and to tax them as part of general income taxes, especially if total personal income from all sources is above a minimum no-tax level.

The longer-term implications of this shift may be more significant than the short-term battle to prevent taxation of retirement benefits. The fairness of the taxation depends on the extent to which the basic income tax system protects the poorest, in relation to the rich. But for long-term welfare policy, the approach may make it easier in the future to develop other benefits, such as children's allowances, on an unstigmatized basis.

Such efforts by the 1980 administration to reverse policy has had an im-

TABLE 3.7
The Antipoverty Effectiveness of Major Income Transfers, Selected Years, 1965–82[a]

Years	Cash Social Insurance Transfers[b]	Cash Public Assistance Transfers[c]	In-Kind Transfers[d]	All Transfers
1965	23.5	3.3	16.4	43.2
1976	37.6	6.2	28.1	71.9
1978	37.6	5.9	n.a.	n.a.
1980	35.2	8.5	n.a.	n.a.
1982	33.8	3.8	25.8[e]	63.3[e]

[a] SOURCE: Sheldon Danziger in Danziger, Peter Gottschalk, Robert J. Rubin, and Timothy M. Smeeding, "Recent Increases in Poverty: Testimony before the House Ways and Means Committee," *Focus* (Institute for Research on Poverty, Madison, Wisc.) 7, No. 1 (Winter 1984): 8.
[b] Cash social insurance transfers include social security, railroad retirement, unemployment compensation, workers' compensation, government employee pensions, and vetarans' pensions and compensation.
[c] Cash public assistance transfers include AFDC, SSI (OAA, APTD, and AB in 1965), and general assistance.
[d] In-kind transfers include Medicare, Medicaid, Food Stamps, and, for 1976, school lunch and public housing; this figure also adjusts for direct taxes and the underreporting of cash transfers.
[e] Based on estimate for adjusted income poverty 1982.
n.a. = not available

mediate effect on the conditions of the poor although it has not yet reduced the scope of public commitment. As Table 3.5 indicates, social programs in 1980 still effectively lifted 35% of the pretransfer poor out of poverty. However, as the new policies took effect in 1982, the number and proportion of Americans living below the official poverty line began to increase. By one calculation (see Figure 3.1, Tables 3.6 and 3.7) those living in poverty increased from a low of about 11% in 1976 to 15% in 1982.[19] These calculations exclude in-kind benefits that some people may receive, such as food stamps or health care.

The effects of social programs continue to vary by population class. The elderly, of whom over 29% lived in poverty in 1966, were at the national average by 1982, although their proportion never dropped to the 1975 low of 11%. About 18% of children, on the other hand, lived in poverty in 1966, but this increased to 22% in 1982, due in large part to cuts in the AFDC program. In 1982, 35% of blacks and 30% of Hispanics lived in poverty, compared with an average of 12% for whites.

The policy issue raised by these trends goes well beyond a charitable concern over poverty. The national ethic as well as policy about minorities or subcategories are involved. In a nation where it can be claimed that only

[19] American Public Welfare Association, *Washington Report* 18, No. 7 (September 1983):1. Also U.S. Bureau of the Census, *Money Income and Poverty Status of Families and Persons in the U.S.*, Current Population Reports, Series P–60, No. 140 (Washington: U.S. Government Printing Office, 1983).

15% of the population are poor, there is cause for satisfaction. After all, this is the lowest rate in world history. In the 1930s in the United States, the rate was 30%. In England and Europe of the poor laws, the figure was as high as 60%. And in early Colonial America, most residents were poor, but not paupers or dependent. On the other hand, when the present 15% are made up so unevenly of racial minorities and of children, the focus of debate about future policy is shifting. The satisfaction about a reduction in poverty to 15% is now replaced by a deep concern over equity and fairness between a comfortable majority and a poor minority. As the nation approaches this debate in the 1980s, the scope of national commitment is not materially reduced in reality, but the longer-term potential for change still remains.

Income Redistribution or Control of the Poor

While most activity since the 1930s focused on raising the minimum income for the poorest in the nation, the issue remains whether the relative shares of national wealth or income are more equitably distributed now than in the years before 1935.

A common measure of distribution is the proportionate share of personal money income received in the aggregate by the lowest, the highest, and the middle quintiles in the population. By such measures, it would appear that some redistribution did in fact take place as a result of government income actions during the depression of the 1930s and also government regulation of income during World War II. Between the middle 1940s and the 1960s, there was a slight reversal, and since then, despite the Great Society programs of the 1960s, little change has occurred.[20] Income distribution among unrelated individuals did continue to rise, although slightly, in favor of those falling in the lowest quintile. Tables 3.6 and 3.7 trace this trend from 1929 to 1971.

But federal programs worked unevenly to carry out such redistributing tendences, slight though they were. Blacks tended to do less well, although they were not wholly excluded. For example, old age, survivors, disability, and health insurance (OASDHI), while treating all beneficiaries alike, has not completely closed the income gap that separates black and white workers who retire or become disabled. OASDHI benefits are based on earned income, and in the private economy blacks, on the average, earn less than

---

[20] See Winifred Bell, Robert Lekachman, and Alvin Schorr, *Public Policy and Income Distribution* (New York: Center for Studies in Income Maintenance Policy, New York University School of Social Work, 1974); Michael Barth, George Carcagno, and John Palmer, *Toward an Effective Income Support System: Problems, Prospects, Choices* (Madison: Institute for Poverty Research, University of Wisconsin, 1974).

TABLE 3.8
Percentage of Personal Income Received by Each Fifth of Families and Individuals and by Top 5%, 1929–1962[a]

Families and individuals ranked from lowest to highest	1929	1935	1944	1947	1957	1962
Total	100	100	100	100	100	100
Lowest fifth	12.5[a]	4.1	4.9	5.0	4.7	4.6
Second fifth	—	9.2	10.9	11.0	11.1	10.9
Middle fifth	13.8	14.1	16.2	16.0	16.3	16.3
Fourth fifth	19.3	20.9	22.2	22.0	22.4	22.7
Highest fifth	54.4	51.7	45.8	46.0	45.5	45.5
Top 5%	30.0	26.5	20.7	20.9	20.2	19.6

[a] Source: Winifred Bell, Robert Lekachman, and Alvin Schorr, *Public Policy and Income Distribution* (New York: Center for Studies in Income Maintenance Policy, New York University School of Social Work, 1974), p. 6.
[b] Lowest and second fifth combined.

white workers. As a result, retired black workers receive an average of 80% of the benefits received by white workers; disabled black workers receive an average of 85% of the benefits received by white disabled workers. (Between 1958 and 1973, black workers had mean taxable earnings of only 69–73% of the mean taxable earnings of white workers.)

A Note on the Social Component in Income Maintenance

The federal policy regarding income has usually been treated as an economic matter, although it may be clear from the foregoing discussion that several other considerations have become important in the determination of income policies. These are the values that are implicit in the guiding principles. Human motivation as reflected in the willingness to remain in the labor force or to struggle to leave a state of economic dependency is primarily a social and psychological phenomenon, and individuals do not always operate as the theoretical economic man is expected to function.

The development of modern, open economies, especially since the depression, indicates the extent to which social factors must be accounted for in income programs. The diversity of programs funded and modified as part of an attack on poverty illuminates the extent to which social programs are now a fixed part of any national approach to income maintenance: the provision of adequate education for the young to equip them for responsible lives in the working economy; the provision of day-care services in a society where women and mothers wish to work and often are expected to work; specialized training and retraining programs to reduce the segment of the population that lacks work skills suited to the modern economy; and sup-

TABLE 3.9
Percentage of Aggregate Money Income Received by Each Fifth of Families and
Individuals, 1962–1971, before Taxes[a]

Families ranked from lowest to highest	1962	1964	1966	1968	1970	1971
Total	100	100	100	100	100	100
Lowest fifth	5.1	5.2	5.5	5.7	5.5	5.5
Second fifth	12.0	12.0	12.4	12.4	12.0	11.9
Third fifth	17.5	17.7	17.7	17.7	17.4	17.4
Fourth fifth	23.7	24.0	23.7	23.7	23.5	23.7
Highest fifth	41.7	41.1	40.7	40.6	41.6	41.6
Top 5%	16.3	15.7	14.8	14.0	14.4	NA[b]

Unrelated individuals ranked from lowest to highest	1962	1964	1966	1968	1970	1971
Total	100	100	100	100	100	100
Lowest fifth	3.0	2.4	2.8	3.2	3.3	3.4
Second fifth	7.4	7.1	7.5	7.8	7.9	8.1
Third fifth	12.7	12.8	13.2	13.8	13.8	13.9
Fourth fifth	24.1	24.5	23.8	24.4	24.5	24.2
Highest fifth	52.8	53.1	52.7	50.8	50.5	50.4
Top 5%	21.1	22.6	22.5	20.4	20.5	20.6

[a] SOURCE: Winifred Bell, Robert Lekachman, and Alvin Schorr, *Public Policy and Income Distribution* (New York: Center for Studies in Income Maintenance Policy, New York University School of Social Work, 1974), p. 7.
[b] NA = not available

plementary employment opportunities to guarantee employment when it is not available in the private economy and to staff basic urban public services, such as hospitals and sanitation, police, and fire departments.

Although it is easy to identify many social aspects in an area once considered primarily economic, it is less easy to identify the form that the social component finally assumes in income programs. The social component was long considered to consist primarily of individualized personal services provided by income programs, services in the form of counseling, encouragement, guidance, and the like. While personalization of income services is still valuable in order to assure a minimally decent administration of income programs, it has now been established that counseling and psychological services are not significant variables in removing people from economic dependency.

The social component has taken on a nonclinical meaning. It involves the nonwork, noneconomic aspect of income procurement and management in modern society as reflected by the variety of programs noted above.

Policy Issues in the Mid-1980s

Certain conclusions can be drawn from this recital of events, which are the basis for events in the next decade. First, it is clear that the basic principles that guided the development of federal income policies were marginally, but not substantially, altered.

Second, it is clear that efforts to expand or add to these principles were accepted reluctantly and were not dramatically successful. There have been persistent episodic efforts by the executive branch to extend the scope of federal responsibility and to secure the adoption of public policies beyond old norms. These efforts have not received wide support, but some progress beyond the constricting norms of the past can be seen. Modest income redistribution has been effected, and minimum federal standards have finally been secured, at least for the elderly and disabled. The federal government has also become involved in managing a variety of social programs (such as training) that alter basic marketplace functioning, even though this intrusion is considered temporary.

Finally, the experiences of recent decades cast a doubt upon the viability of these guiding principles in their present form in the period ahead. The belief that primary reliance can be placed upon the marketplace for that part of the population not clearly considered inappropriate for work—mothers, young adults, male heads of households—is no longer justified. Despite fluctuations in the economy, there appears to be a straightline growth in public expenditures for dependent populations of working age.

Abuses of the Income Provision System

Dominant in the public view is the concern over so-called abuses of the system of income provision. From the inception of federal responsibility, the charge has been leveled that some proportion of persons benefitting from income programs are "undeserving"; that is, they have concealed other sources of income or they could secure income through work but avoid the search for work. The feeling has persisted that some persons benefit unfairly by contrast with others who either scrimp along on submarginal incomes or who work at any job no matter how difficult in preference to applying for some governmental benefit. When individual cases are cited, most citizens seem to agree that help should be given to the clearly "deserving" poor, such as the sick and the widowed. However, when programs are viewed as a whole and the tax cost identified, citizens are shocked and charge that there must be abuses, for it cannot be that so many need to be helped by others' contributions.

The facts are reasonably clear, but they do not seem to clarify the issue in the public mind. The confusion exists between fraud and income redistribution. Certainly, there have been cases of individuals who defraud income programs by concealing substantial earnings or assets. But agencies that have established strong antifraud departments have seldom found enough clear cases of abuse to cover the costs of looking for them. They have found that most charges of abuse can be accounted for by one of the following circumstances: (1) minor errors in which changes in income status are reported late, but only by a short time; (2) administrative errors of staff; (3) improvements in levels of income support so that a family of four may have an assured income of $9000 a year, the 1984 poverty base, but which is startling to taxpayers still accustomed to thinking that poverty can be relieved by an occasional basket of food; (4) claims that are entirely legal but made by persons not in dire distress; (5) provider, not consumer, fraud.[21]

How to Help the Able Bodied Adult

It is the fourth of these explanations that may prove most troublesome in the future. For example, workers who are unemployed may claim unemployment compensation benefits even though other family members are working or hold assets in property or bank accounts. Unemployment benefits are in no sense attached to other income, but only to the fact of being unemployed. Some argue that such persons should exhaust other assets, thus converting unemployment insurance into a means-tested relief program. Others argue that workers should be forced to take any job and not be allowed to try to remain in their occupational field; an engineer should take a ditchdigging job rather than apply for unemployment benefits. The force of this argument would be strongest in a situation of a labor shortage. There are areas where fishermen or construction workers, for example, can work only half the year. If there is a real shortage of workers to fill other empty jobs, an inequity is perceived in that some workers can draw benefits to fish, repair their homes, or go on vacation while useful economic tasks are unperformed for lack of workers. The fact is that such situations are relatively rare; for the most part, the empty jobs require high skills that unemployed workers lack or there is no significant number of empty jobs to start with.

---

[21] Several studies suggest that most families with low income have modest standards by which to judge what income is right and necessary for them to live by. See Sidney Bernard, *Economic and Social Adjustment of Low Income Female-Headed Families* (Ann Arbor: University of Michigan Microfilms, 1965). He found that employed low-income families and families on public relief held about the same view as to income necessary to survival. Relief families saw public assistance as only one of several ways—part-time work, borrowing, selling numbers, etc.—by which the needed total could be secured. The total proved to be only slightly above the level of relief then being paid but sufficient to explain the minor cases of delayed income reporting, etc. Charges of great rip-offs and fraud were not uncovered.

Where unskilled jobs are available, they are likely to be in household service or stoop farm labor, and the effect of income programs has been to raise the level of wages that must be paid to attract workers to perform unpleasant jobs. Overall, of course, there has been a persistent shortage of jobs in the nation, except possibly very menial ones.

Such situations illustrate the dilemma of the able-bodied adult in the American welfare system. Except for unemployment insurance for short periods of time, most of the income system is geared for people presumed unable to work because of illness, age, or mothering small children. The unemployed able-bodied are presumed to be lazy or cheating, but the facts of the modern economy are otherwise. Rapid technological change abolishes jobs as fast as or faster than it creates new ones, at least in the short run of any worker's life. A large part of the work force, about 10% in 1982, is unable to find work: These are the youths without skills, especially minority youths; middle-aged workers displaced by technical change and hard to retrain; and the able-bodied elders, 60 or 70 years of age, who are still vigorous and want to work but cannot find it. To these must be added the over 3.5 million female heads of single-parent families, who are usually young, able-bodied, and with limited skills. The latter are not the "deserving" widows of deceased worker husbands; they are unmarried or divorced mothers. This large part of the population poses difficult challenges to a society that is not prepared to accept that so many of its able-bodied adults may not be needed by the economy, at least not at wages that will assure decent subsistence. The concern is widespread that this population is not trying to find work or does not want to work at all.

Additional examples of difficulty are encountered in other quite legal uses of income programs. Adult children who go to college or who wish to set up households apart from their parents may be legally entitled to income support if they cannot find work, although some would argue that parents should continue to supply their children's incomes—even if that forces the children to delay establishing separate households.

These legal uses are further complicated when two families with similar incomes are not eligible for the same benefits. One family may be entitled to food stamps or medical assistance, and another may be ineligible, although their needs are similar, because of the vagaries of administrative regulations.

The significance of such arguments over who deserves what lies mainly in uncertainty over the future direction that income programs can take. The old debate continues over substandard relief given only to some persons on the basis of subjective judgments about "worthiness" versus income given as a matter of legal right because of objective conditions in which people find themselves. The latter course has led to a slow but steady raising of the income and living standard minimum for large numbers and has produced some modest redistribution of income. How much farther this process will go in the future may depend on our national ability to distinguish between identifiable fraud, which can be handled by improved administration, and the rising standards of living for all. The idea of income as a right requires acceptance of a redistributive income policy; increased benefits for all does not reduce relative poverty, while national resources limit the capacity to increase benefits without altering the shares of national income received by the more affluent.

Changes in Federal–State Shared Responsibility

The borderline between federal and state responsibility is currently under major review. Because of the economic distress to which the states have been subjected, there is current pressure to transfer the total cost of financing all public assistance to the federal government, a tendency that has been resisted in the past and that, if accepted, would represent a major change in national policy. One obstacle is the absence of social techniques by which a national administration of programs can suitably adjust to the most varied of human needs that change from day to day among vulnerable groups.

Various approaches have been proposed to redivide responsibility. Federal sharing of national revenues with the states has been one. Another is a redivision of function to match revenue sharing. In one version, the federal government would take over all costs of public financing for health care, while relief, such as AFDC or long-term care for the sick, would revert to the states. Negotiations between state and federal levels of government will be long and drawn out, as they seek to resolve at least two major difficulties:

1. Is the division, including a return to the states, accompanied by a fair division of financial resources?
2. Which functions are best handled at a state level and which nationally?

By some criteria, the 1980 proposals are awkward to justify, for they propose to return to the states income support for many of the poor, whose situation is inextricably tied up with the national, not state, economy, while health care, proposed for national support, would seem more suited to local variation.

National versus Regional Standards for Income

There seems to be a growing desire to reexamine the choice between national standards applicable to everyone in the country and regional and state variations in standards governing income. The SSI program represents a

significant departure from the past reliance upon state-determined variations in income support. The continuing debate over welfare reform that
could encompass some form of negative income tax indicates another potential for modifying the historic tendency to allocate government support on
an individualized basis. The trend toward reliance upon computerized
management systems would seem to promote a further standardization of
income procedures. If this direction is pursued, it is possible that a technical
aspect of income maintenance would be significantly modified. Present income programs are in part determined by the processing of eligibility by
personnel on an individualized basis. Entitlement by condition, such as that
built into the Social Security system, workmen's compensation, and
unemployment insurance, might produce a more standardized entitlement
for income maintenance programs.

Introduction of Children's Allowances and Disability Payments

Most income programs now in force apply to individuals in certain conditions of illness or unemployment or to families without income. Arguments
are advanced in support of expanding the mechanisms for income support
in two directions. One of these is based upon the special needs of children.
Proponents urge that families be paid children's allowances, a sum for each
child born and payments until the child reaches his or her majority. Such
payments would be based on the fact of a child's birth, not on the economic
status of the family. It has been argued that such an income program would
benefit most persons with limited incomes, would avoid the stigma that
comes from applying for relief, and would bridge the gap that separates the
poor from the working poor and the nonpoor families. Recently such programs have also been supported by those who believe that mothers and
housewives should have available income paid directly to them rather than
to the head of household, who may be a husband. Children's allowances are
paid in Canada and in many European countries.[22]

Another extension would attach payments to the condition of disability.
To a large extent, this is now a reality as far as minimum income subsistence
is concerned. However, the disabled have economic needs greater than
those of the able-bodied. The disabled are often immobile or require at least
some part-time care. It is argued that where there are no family members or
where relatives are all employed, the disabled person should be entitled to a
sum in addition to the minimum income relief payments now available to
cover the costs of personal care. Such additional sums would be paid upon
certification of the disabling condition and would not be dependent upon

---

[22] See, for example, Dorothy A. Projector, "Children's Allowances and Income Tested Supplements," *Social Security Bulletin* 33, no. 2 (February 1970): 3.

any means-test inquiry into other assets. Such payment programs are now provided to veterans with service-connected disabilities and are found in several European countries. Such new benefits could be introduced without means testing if they are taxed for recipients whose total income exceeds a fixed minimum.

Inequity versus Inequality

Finally, there remains the troublesome question of the relationship between persons entitled to income support, according to whatever basic principles are followed, and persons marginally above a level of entitlement. The argument is usually framed as: is it fair to pay a non-worker as much or more than is earned by those whose name is above relief eligibility levels? In other words, the debate over equity versus equality can be expected to continue without much resolution in the foreseeable future. There are no signs to date that the differential in income between those supported at the bottom of the income scale through public aid and those earning various levels of income by employment or investment is likely to be narrowed in the immediate future. What does seem to lie ahead is a steady raising of the floor so that persons entitled to public payments will have some absolute improvement in their situation, measured by dollar income at least, while the condition of those above that minimum can be expected to increase relative to the bottom as well. Paradoxically, the 1980 policies moved in an opposite direction: The working poor lost more benefits than others did because they, more often lost supplemental benefits, such as food stamps and medical care.

Trends in Policy Development

Although prediction is risky, it certainly appears unlikely that the basic principles that have governed income maintenance public policy to date will be quickly altered, but changes can be expected. The proportionate share of federal and state governments can be altered either by some increase in the federal proportion or by a clear division of federal responsibility for some categories and state responsibility for others.

Income programs once expected to move toward some redistribution of income by slowly extending the precedent established in the Social Security Act of 1935, have moved in the opposite direction despite strenuous political opposition. There is no sign that national public policy will soon introduce any radical steps to eradicate income disparities. Income inequities, however, can be expected to receive continuing political attention. Over time, the elderly, the disabled, and more recently, minorities and women have been the beneficiaries of public policy programs or administrative arrangements that have slightly improved their status, and such incremental changes are likely to continue.

Despite the constrictions of general policy guides, it is also clear that there has been a contradictory extension of the universality of some coverage, mainly in the improved access to minimum decent income for minority groups and the extension of some income supplement programs, such as food stamps to the so-called working poor. An increase in tax support, but within the guidelines of the past is likely to continue if economic conditions improve, but the tempo of income redistribution is unlikely to increase soon.

Within such predictions, administrative policy choices will affect the ways in which certain more technical questions will be handled.

1. How should the working poor, those with income at or just above the margin of poverty, be assisted? Liberalizing public welfare payments and eligibility might be an answer, but there is a reluctance to mandate this in every state for reasons already noted. Some form of an earning subsidy through tax reduction might be one solution.[23] In this approach, full-time workers with low earnings would be entitled to preferential tax treatment when filing income tax returns. The fact that over one-fourth of all poor families have wage earners working at least 50 weeks in the year indicates the scale of this measure.

2. Can the AFDC program be improved by mandating federal standards that would apply in all states?

3. How can the administration of assistance in the form of Medicaid and unemployment insurance be modified? These programs now represent a confusing and frequently unworkable melange of state variations with federal control exercised through postaudit devices.

[23] See Public Law 94–12, The Tax Reduction Act of 1975, The C.Q. Almanac, 1975 (Washington, D.C.: Congressional Quarterly Publishing Office, 1976), p. 95.

Additional Readings

Barth, Michael; Cavegno, George J.; and Palmer, John L. Toward an Effective Income Support System: Problems, Prospects and Choices. Madison, Wis.: Institute for Research on Policy, 1974.

Bell, Winifred. Contemporary Social Welfare. New York: Macmillan, 1983.

Burns, Eveline. Social Security and Public Policy. New York: McGraw-Hill, 1956.

Hochman, Harold, and Peterson, George. Redistribution through Public Choice. New York: Columbia University Press, 1974.

Institute for Research on Poverty. "Poverty in the United States," IRP Focus (University of

Wisconsin, Madison, Wisc: Institute for Research on Poverty 1984) 7, no. 1 (Winter 1984): 1–13.

Joint Economic Committee of the Congress of the United States, Studies in Public Welfare. No. 5. *Intergovernmental Relations;* No. 6. *How Public Welfare Benefits Are Distributed;* No. 7. *Issues in Coordination of Public Welfare Programs;* No. 12. *Factors Influencing Family Instability;* No. 15. *Welfare in the '70's.* Washington, D.C.: U.S. Government Printing Office, 1973–1974.

Lambert, Richard, and Weintraub, Sidney, eds. "Income Inequality," *Annals of the American Academy of Political & Social Science,* 1973.

Levitan, Sar, and Taggart, Robert. *The Promise of Greatness.* Cambridge, Mass.: Harvard University Press, 1976, especially Pt. 3 and Chap. 3.

Marmor, Theodore, ed. *Poverty Policy: A Compendium of Cash Transfer Proposals.* Chicago: Aldine, 1971.

Morgan, James. *Income and Welfare in the United States.* New York: McGraw-Hill, 1962.

Moynihan, Daniel P. *The Politics of a Guaranteed Income.* New York: Random House (Vintage Books), 1973.

Nathan, Richard and Doolittle, Fred. *Consequences of the Cuts: The Effects of the Reagan Domestic Programs in State and Local Governments.* Princeton: Princeton University Press, 1983.

Piven, Frances, and Cloward, Richard. *Regulating the Poor.* New York: Pantheon, 1971.

Steiner, Gilbert. *The State of Welfare.* Washington, D.C.: Brookings Institution, 1971.

Thurow, Lester. *Generating Inequality: Mechanisms of Distribution in the U.S. Economy.* New York: Basic Books, 1975.

Health Policies

Fifty Controversial Years

4

Next to jobs and the distribution of income, health policies have been the object of the most extended, continuous controversy in the history of American sectoral social policy. A continuous line of effort to shape public policy, first at the level of state government and then at the level of the nation, has been traced since at least 1900.[1] Societal policy has revealed remarkable strength and resistance to change. The guiding principles of the American society have been operative in the field of health as in the field of income distribution. In the twentieth century, the field of health policy has been characterized by a persistent and continuous effort to move beyond the socially sanctioned policies of distribution and regulation (as those terms are used by Lowi) and to effect a significant redistribution. However, the results have been meager and unevenly distributed.

The effort to move in a direction apparently outside of the constraining limits of societal norms has been noteworthy in that it has been made by both private groups and, at some intervals, the executive branch of the government. In this sense, health policy can be seen as an instructive example of the potential in and the limits to the executive when seeking by con-

[1] See especially Peter A. Corning, *The Evolution of Medicare*, Social Security Administration, Research Report No. 29 (Washington, D.C.: U.S. Department of Health, Education, and Welfare, 1969). See also Roy Lubove, *The Struggle for Social Security, 1900–1935* (Cambridge, Mass.: Harvard University Press, 1968); Daniel Hirschfield, *The Lost Reform* (Cambridge, Mass.: Harvard University Press, 1970); and Theodore Marmor, *The Politics of Medicare* (Chicago: Aldine, 1970).

scious means to introduce a change in direction at the level of government policy.

The fact that these efforts have not been notably successful has tended to concentrate historical attention upon the drama of the conflict between proponents and antagonists. It is the purpose of this chapter, instead, to identify, where possible, the nature of the proposed public policy and to separate such policy conception from the more global conventional ways of thinking and from the more limiting administrative uses.

Societal norms in health are in some ways similar to those prevailing in the income maintenance field. The belief in the operation of the private marketplace and the choices of individuals are principal guides to government action. Arrangements for the delivery of health services have consistently been left primarily in the hands of privately organized providers, and the tendency has been to enlarge this concept rather than to restrict it. As will be discussed shortly, for a brief period local and national governments did experiment with the direct governmental administration of health services for limited populations by means of city, Veterans Administration, and public health hospitals. However, in recent decades this activity has diminished; only the Veterans Administration remains as a strong force toward direct administration of services, and it too is under pressure to be absorbed within the private system through insurance.

The role of government is seen as complementary, regulatory, and limited, its primary function being to see that vulnerable groups are protected and that the burden of disadvantage does not become too heavy. Equality, while frequently a political slogan, has at no time been expressed as government action to assure it. Whenever government arrangements have been necessary, they have taken the form of a responsibility shared by the federal government with industry and private citizens, rather than with state governments.

Health policy at the levels of government and of the society, as in the economy, maintains a steadfast faith that science and technology will overcome all difficulties and that a greatly improved world for individuals and the group will result primarily because of the inventive, imaginative genius of scientists and technologists.

The points at which health policy has sought to deviate from social norms help explain the bitter and continuous controversy associated with it. First, executive health policy has sought to redistribute health benefits among various sectors of the population rather than to act as a balance wheel in the normal marketplace distribution of those benefits. Second, government force has become an equal if not dominant partner with the private sector, mainly because of the weight of the public investment. Government's role, following societal norms, has produced the kind of increment in government obligation (to fill gaps and to satisfy societal expectations) that exerted a cumulative impact so that the simplified policy guides we have been discussing proved to be no longer sufficient.

As the succeeding review will indicate, the private sector has been unable to satisfy socially acceptable expectations about access to health services. The omission of some groups in the population from access to medical care at some point became so extensive and, therefore, so noticeable that it was no longer acceptable. For reasons not fully explained as yet, access for the poor, the aged, and minorities through large, impersonal, and distant public clinics became unacceptable, and this led to acceptance of government financing of private-system medical care for them. It is quite possible that the belief in the private sector as capable of dealing with this unacceptable limitation on access reinforced societal viewpoints on the use of insurance mechanisms as a primary means by which inequities could be rectified.

Insurance involves a systematic scheme by which funds become available to beneficiaries for the purchase of specified services. For a long time, this was seen to be the simplest means by which Americans of all income classes could be assured access—namely, by assuring that the costs of medical care would be met without too much pain to the individual. This view has long been reinforced by all parties to the debate, including the medical profession, the insurance companies, and proponents of government action. What was unanticipated was that a dynamic would be set in motion by this continuous reliance upon insurance that would increase the share contributed by government until it became dominant in health financing.

A secondary, unexpected consequence was an introduction into the American belief system, of the idea that certain services, such as health, that are considered essential to all citizens and therefore become theirs as a matter of right, could be provided with minimal cost to the individual. If health bills could be met for many by insurance that cost no one too much, then there was no limit to the volume and type of services that could be paid for as a health charge; even those who could not pay the modest premium charges became entitled to the same coverage as all others, since health is so precious a commodity. Easy payment of medical bills seemed to be the route to fair access to health for all. As a result, the cost consequences of extending and enlarging access to the health system for more and more services produced more and more public allocations, until the public share reached a point where its distribution could no longer be considered as minor or supplementary.

The belief that spreading the costs through insurance in a private fee-for-service system could satisfy claims of equity and coverage at minimal cost to government or individual was undermined by several developments in the 1970s. Inflation was one, but fundamental changes in the nature of medical care played an even greater role. After World War II, acute care hospitals began to dominate the scene. Care in such hospitals depended on a large staff of nurses, aides, attendants, food service workers, etc. Their wages were so low that many worked full time and also qualified for public relief to secure a minimum subsistence income. Trade union and professional organization resulted in a significant improvement in wage levels for most employees. At the same time, a rash of new, constantly changing technology, made necessary a great increase in staff and in capital equipment budgets. The ratio of support staff to physicians in hospitals rose to 20 to 1. Medicine's capacity to keep many disabled and desperately ill persons alive for years required that medical facilities extend their services for long periods of time to long-term or chronically ill patients while also meeting the short-term acute needs of a still growing population. Specialist medical care also invoked the use of multiple high-cost physician services to deal with complex health problems. Popular and scientific expectations pushed research and education farther and faster. In the aggregate, such developments raised the total and the per capita cost of medical care to a level that became painful to consumers and third-party payers alike.

Between 1929 and 1950, health services (public and private) rose as a proportion of the GNP from 3.6 to 4.6%, or by less than 27% over the 21-year span. But between 1950 and 1970, the proportion rose by 67%, or from 4.6 to 7.7%. In dollar terms, total expenditures for health in 1929 were estimated to be about $3.5 billion. In 1974 this figure had grown to over $116 billion and by 1980 to $247 billion. Of this sum, public (primarily federal) expenditures rose from 13.6% of the total in 1929 to 42.2% in 1980.[2] This was 9.4% of the GNP.

The scope of these public expenditures is the battleground of current debate over health policy. They are roughly distributed in the following categories: health insurance coverage for the elderly, health payments for persons of very low economic status, health benefits for injured workers, preventive health programs for mothers and children, rehabilitation of the injured and disabled, special primary medical services for the poor in ghetto areas, construction of hospitals, programs for veterans, and support of biomedical research. About 92% of all expenditures is in the form of cash payments to individuals to enable them to pay all or part of their hospital bills or in the form of assured payments to vendors as, for example, the purchase of medical care for the poor. Only 8% thus far involves direct provision of health services for some or all citizens, via Veterans Administration, army,

[2] See *Encyclopedia of Social Work*, 16th ed. (New York: National Association of Social Workers, 1971), p. 1602, Table 39; and *Health U.S. 1975* (Washington, D.C.: Health Resources Administration, U.S. Department of Health, Education, and Welfare, 1975), Table A6. Also Ronald Gibson and Daniel Wald, "National Health Care Expenditures," *Health Care Financing Review* 3, no. 1 (September 1981).

OEO, school health, maternal and child health, and public health programming. The confidence in scientific solutions now offered by medicine is reflected in the purposes for which most of these sums are expended. About 91% of Medicare and 49% of Medicaid expenditures go for the payment of services in hospitals and by physicians. Medicare and Medicaid combined represent 60% of all public expenditures.[3] An additional $1.9 billion is allocated for the conduct of various forms of biomedical research, either by the National Institutes of Health or by contract and research grants to private research institutions.

Unfortunately, the results of this trend in policy have been less than satisfying both to citizens and to political and scientific personnel. Some disadvantaged groups in the population, primarily minorities, inner-city residents, the long-term sick, and rural groups, are still relatively untouched. Redistribution has taken place, in favor of the elderly and to a lesser extent in favor of black minorities, but the scale of redistribution working through the private marketplace has been limited.

At the same time, as we have seen, the total cost has escalated, rising to 9.4% of the GNP. The cost of delivery of service to the individual has also risen dramatically; for example, care in a hospital for a single day, exclusive of intensive care, surgical, medical, and diagnostic fees, is several hundred dollars. This escalation has suddenly confronted both policymakers and average citizens with the consequences of the policies they have thus far accepted. The long-held belief that certain social benefits could become available by means that remove the individual from any confrontation of costs has been shaken.

As a result of these unanticipated consequences of the societal policies that have been expressed through public policies, a new set of issues have arisen. These policy issues are clearly social rather than scientific or technical in nature and have been brought about by a recognition of certain underlying social and economic trends. We should note some of these trends that are not subject to short-term change: the increase in population; the increase in the proportion of the population over 65 years of age from 4% in 1900 to 9.8% in 1970 and to an expected 10–15% by the year 2000; the resulting increase in the total demand for medical care that an aging population presents; the increase in the proportion of minorities in the total population, accompanied by the pressure to equalize their income status; the increase in the proportion of women in the total population from a ratio of 106 males per 100 females in 1910 to 94 per 100 in 1970; and the steady rise in educational level as open enrollment programs bring more than 50%

---

[3] Derived from *Encyclopedia of Social Work*, p. 1602, Table 39:; *Social Security Bulletin*, current operating statistics, April 1976, Tables M18, M20, M35; and *Health U.S. 1975*, p. 27.

of the American population to a level of at least 1 year of college education, as compared to the level of eighth grade, which was the standard only 100 years ago.

Another little remarked development also contributed to the forces for change. With new medical technology, more and more Americans are being kept alive, but requiring many years of follow-up medical care and social supports. Newborn infants with high risk, those with very low birth weights or respiratory problems, represent a significant percentage of all newborn infants (as much as 6–19%); persons paralyzed from the waist or neck because of injury at work, at play, or at war can now be kept alive for decades; and the mentally retarded and the elderly, who once died relatively young from respiratory infections, now survive that hazard. The additional cost to health and welfare has not been precisely estimated, but one study found that repeated hospitalizations for the same disease accounted for more than half of hospitalizations (in four survey hospitals) and for nearly 60% of total hospital charges.[4]

Before we consider the character of present policies, it may be instructive to review the evolution of American governmental policies. The following summary does not dwell on the political drama of public policy formation, but rather it is an attempt to trace the evolution in public policy for health in order to understand better the current policy choices and to determine what guiding principles are still operative.

Emergence As A Subject Of Policy For The Federal Government: Health Insurance, 1900–1950

The easiest starting point for understanding the evolution of public policy for health is the establishment in 1912 of the American Association for Labor Legislation's social insurance committee, an action that was to stimulate state governmental activity. But it would be misleading for our purposes not to take account of the character of health policy before this period.

Before 1910 the dominant position was that the federal government had no role concerning the health of its citizens other than the prevention of disease spread through broad-scale public health activities, mainly at ports of entry, and a responsibility for two special populations: veterans and seamen. State and local governments were considered to be responsible for any aspects of health care not left to individuals, which meant that they had

---

[4] Christopher Zook, Sheila Savicks, and Francis Moore, "Repeated Hospitalization for the Same Disease: A Multiplier of National Health Costs," *Milbank Memorial Fund Quarterly/Health and Society* 58, No. 3 (Summer 1980): 454–471.

basically the same practical role as the federal government, with one important exception: Major cities took the responsibility for providing public hospital care for the poor and for those with infectious diseases. Although these hospitals were utilized primarily by poor families and especially by immigrants new to the culture, they were tax supported and therefore involved local governments in the direct administration and delivery of health care. In some eastern cities, such as New York, Philadelphia, and Boston, the city hospital networks were the pride and joy of local government; they were highly respected for the quality of care originally provided, and they were much valued by medical schools as training grounds for physicians and by the medical professions as preparation for subsequent private practice. Some cities developed extensive locally administered ambulatory outpatient clinics.

The fact that these local programs involved direct governmental administration represented a deviation from an underlying societal approach in America to government. This was stimulated in the eighteenth and nineteenth centuries, as a growing America applied the then new scientific ideas in medicine to the old almshouse treatment for the poor. This was a time when the health needs of large numbers of poor immigrants, and the protection of urban health generally, forced local government to act for the poor at a time when most middle-class persons took their medical care in their own homes and health insurance was undeveloped.

However, the deviation did not become fully developed. Between 1960 and 1974 the total number of state and local public hospital beds dropped from 953,000 to 664,000. Almost half of that figure represented special facilities for tuberculosis or for chronic or infectious diseases; large city general hospital beds represented the other half.[5] One can conclude that the underlying policy of relying upon the private marketplace showed its forcefulness and persistence as these ventures into governmental operation of some segment of the health system were attenuated and eroded.

At the federal level, the same eroding tendency can be seen in the marine hospitals. While some do struggle to survive, most of them have been replaced by giving seamen access to the private sector through financial means, rendering the marine hospitals obsolete, underutilized, and by and large neglected. Only the Veterans Administration remains as a strong example of federally administered medical care, maintaining a nationally administered network of 125 hospitals, with 96,750 beds (33,472 for mental illness), a network of outpatient clinics, and various ancillary nursing home and home-care services. This deviation from the more common pattern has been explained by the nation's sense of obligation to the veterans forced to

[5] Statistical Abstract of the U.S., 1976, Bureau of the Census (Washington, D.C.: U.S. Department of Commerce, 1976), Table 91.

devote some part of their lives to military service. But even the Veterans Administration serves predominantly a lower-income population, and over half of the acutely ill veterans with low incomes are believed to secure their medical care from normal private services rather than turning to available public programs.[6] Only services for chronic and mental illness are provided for and used by all income groups, perhaps because the crushing burden of paying for long-term care usually reduces previously affluent citizens to low-income status. But the Veterans Administration is not immune to the cumulative effect of both public and societal policies. The debate over national health insurance has raised demands that veterans along with all other citizens, be covered by such insurance which would move the Veterans Administration closer to providing fees for services rather than direct care. To date, this view has not found widespread favor.

The first advance in government policy, aside from these special cases, was introduced by the social insurance committee of the American Association for Labor Legislation in the form of a standard health insurance bill. It reduced to legislative language a plan for protection in health, and it was pressed upon various state legislators in 1915, a period when state governments were considered the primary arena for public policy in the social welfare field. This bill can be taken as an early model of public policy, even though it was not widely adopted at the time. It called for the protection of all low-income workers and provided for cash compensation in the case of injury and the payment of hospital and medical benefits to both workers and their dependents. This legislation conforms remarkably to the underlying societal policy imperatives that we have outlined. It provided for some protection of disadvantaged persons; it relied upon the marketplace for service delivery through the use of payments to individuals and providers as the element that would bring the private system and the individual into harmonious relationship.

By 1920 this effort acknowledged its failure, and the bill was never adopted as public policy. What is significant, however, is the extent to which its defeat conformed to the underlying societal policy constraints we have been discussing. At the beginning of this initiative, major constituency groups in the United States proved to be polarized, but in unexpected form. The leaders of the American Medical Association (AMA) suggested that it might eventually give official support to the movement, as did a committee of the National Association of Manufacturers (NAM). But the American Federation of Labor was vigorously opposed. For contradictory reasons over time, the members of the AMA and NAM turned against their leaders and became opposed even to this modest intervention of public policy in the

---

[6] A. Richardson, H. E. Freeman, J. Cummins, and H. Schnaper, "Use of Medical Resources for Spancos," *Milbank Memorial Fund Quarterly* 45, no. 1, pt. 1 (January 1967): Table 1.

private sector, whereas labor organizations slowly came around to supporting the movement.

In the 1920s, a period notable for its lack of governmental action in
health, a new voluntary group, the Committee on the Cost of Medical Care,
was constituted in 1927. The proposals by this citizen group once again conformed to basic constraints. It favored attempts to channel medical practice
away from the solo practitioner, but still within the private sector, meaning,
in this case, hospitals; group payment for medical care through either taxation, private insurance, or a combination of the two was proposed, but at no
time did it recommend compulsory governmental health insurance. Other
changes, such as extension of public health, the coordination of health services, and improvements in medical education, while ahead of their time,
were not fundamentally controversial.

The Committee on the Cost of Medical Care can be said to have maintained some citizens' interest in health policy, but it was not until the crisis of
the 1930s and the election of Franklin Delano Roosevelt with his New Deal
programs that the subject of policy for health finally reached the federal
government and an administration concerned with translating proposed
policies into adopted ones. For the first time, the executive branch clearly
identified itself with a policy of federal intervention for the delivery of
health services in some form. For the first time, a branch of government
adopted a policy view about health that persisted for several decades, until
the final adoption of Medicare in 1965.

The controversy over the incorporation of health insurance in the
original Social Security legislation of 1935 has been obscured by the rhetoric
of political debate. It would be mistaken to believe that a completely new
public policy for the federal government was pressed upon the nation and
defeated as a result of very reactionary forces. In fact, the executive branch,
with the delicate support of the president, moved most circumspectly, and
its final proposals conformed remarkably well to the societal policies we
have been discussing. Such strong proponents as Harry Hopkins, Eleanor
Roosevelt, and others argued in favor of health insurance as the guideline
for national policy. Other members of the executive branch, who spoke
against the proposal, were not opposed in principle but had a prior concern
with the urgency in the depths of the depression of securing the enactment
of unemployment insurance. Since the addition of health insurance to unemployment insurance would increase the number of powerfully organized
opponents, they feared that unemployment insurance as well as health insurance would be defeated.[7]

[7] For a full discussion of this period, see Peter Corning, *Evolution of Medicare;* Roy Lubove,
Struggle for Social Security; Theodore Marmor, *Politics of Medicare;* and David Hirschfield, *The
Lost Reform.*

For our purposes, however, it is significant that even the proponents considered radical at the time chose a public policy that proposed to deliver funds to individuals or to providers (vendors) bespeaking a reliance on the vigor of the private marketplace in health. Health insurance was seen as a way of assuring to all individuals minimum access to hospital and medical care by placing the financial means in their own hands. True, the policy had its radical aspects for the federal government in that it called for compulsory insurance, although on this issue, too, the proponents in the executive branch were divided and many would have accepted administration of the program through the private insurance industry as long as all persons were covered. Although the phrase "government health insurance" was commonly used in the debate, the administration remained uncommitted in the choice between a government-operated program of health insurance and a mandated compulsory system administered by the private insurance companies. However, even the most limited proposal of any form of a compulsory program appeared to open the door to potential, if not real, governmental controls, which were at the time considered unacceptable, especially in the midst of the administration fight for such major economic interests as the Social Security Act and unemployment insurance. With the decision finally to withdraw health insurance from the Social Security Act as introduced in 1935, the executive branch temporarily suspended but did not abandon its effort to secure the adoption of a different kind of federal policy in the field of health.

This initial battle at the federal level makes clear the balance of interest that must be secured to adopt a public policy of any kind, let alone one that deviates from societal policies. The American Medical Association, the private insurance industry, and the private pharmaceutical firms were organized to exercise very effective political leverage against such policy, but it can hardly be said that they dominated the controversy. Powerful congressional figures, powerful figures in the executive branch, and some constituency groups were arrayed on behalf of this mild shift in federal policy. However, what is noteworthy is that no massive support was expressed by citizens in the United States. Instead, the primacy of economic survival cast health policy in the shadow, so that in the ensuing balance of interests the proponents can hardly be said to have been either powerfully organized or for that matter powerfully interested.

This situation may have resulted from the extraordinary spread in private health insurance coverage of the population in the pre- and post-World War II era. Almost all citizens except the very poor and those on public assistance could boast of having some health insurance protection at, then, relatively low cost. Much of this coverage was stimulated by the growth of the trade unions in the late 1930s and the inclusion of health benefits as a part of their contract negotiations. The basic working population in heavy industry had been more or less protected, or so it thought. Policies covered acute care for short periods of time but gave little if any protection for long-term illness, most catastrophic conditions, mental illness, birth injuries, or any preventive health care. Still, the argument that private insurance now protected most of the population became a strong deterrent to further national efforts to enact a national health policy.

Effect of Emergency Wartime Actions on Policy Principles: EMIC

By 1943 progress in World War II made it possible once again for the executive branch to consider social policy for health. The publication in the United Kingdom of an influential proposal for a national health service, not national health insurance, provided the external stimulus to the executive branch to resume its effort to secure the adoption of a new national policy.[8] With encouragement, legislation was now introduced in the Congress.

A temporary excursion into an adopted national health policy became possible because of wartime pressures. With millions of young men in the army, with low incomes, their wives were left to manage as best they could. These wives were also young and at the prime of their childbearing years. The cost of medical care was onerous. The U.S. Children's Bureau, which had pursued since 1912, a mandate to monitor the needs of children, undertook to propose a solution for the dilemma.

The issue first assumed prominence when the medical staff for hospitals attached to Ft. Lewis, Washington, was overwhelmed by demands to provide maternity services for wives of servicemen stationed at the camp. As early as March 1942, a committee of the Association of State and Territorial Health Officers recommended that

> the state health agencies develop plans to finance from Maternal and Child Health funds (administered by the Children's Bureau) the medical and hospital care needed by wives and children of men in military service . . . and to make more readily available medical and nursing services for mothers and children in critical areas.[9]

[8] Sir William Beveridge, *Social Insurance and Allied Services* (New York: Macmillan, 1942).
[9] Nathan Sinai and Olin W. Anderson, *EMIC: A Study of Administrative Experience*, Research Series No. 3 (Ann Arbor: Bureau of Public Health Economics, School of Public Health, University of Michigan, 1948), citing hearings before the Deficiency Appropriations Subcommittee of the House Committee on Appropriations, 78th Congress, 1st session, February 11, 1943, p. 326.

The American Red Cross reported a large need for such services at 240 army posts, and inquiries by the Children's Bureau also identified widespread need for help. Funds already appropriated for maternal and child health (MCH) services, which were administered by state health departments, were totally inadequate for the new demands, because the older MCH programs were limited to narrowly defined and especially vulnerable populations, whereas the wartime situation extended to large numbers of citizens never before considered to be in the orbit of the public program. As a result, additional deficiency appropriations were sought by the Children's Bureau.

Although there was a readiness to finance emergency arrangements, numerous policy issues surfaced and had to be settled before even the emergency program could be enacted. Among them, the following questions are significant for our purposes.

1. Was the Emergency Maternity and Infant Care (EMIC) program a step toward socialized medicine or a national health program? Officials of the Children's Bureau argued that all the proposals were state programs; the federal government's only role was limited to setting minimum standards in the interest of national equity and sharing the costs. One congressman from Kansas said, "The only thing I can see about it is that it is drifting toward socialized medicine." When the chief of the Children's Bureau replied, "This is a war program and consideration of what happens next will have to be something else," the congressman responded, "It's just a leverage."[10]

After the wartime emergency passed, the Children's Bureau argued for a continuation of federal responsibility although with changes based on wartime experience.

> The Children's Bureau has been on record since 1917 as being in favor of a public program for the protection of maternity and infancy. . . . those programs should be expanded as soon as possible so that there would be available everywhere in every State, a service for the protection of the health of mothers at the time of childbirth and the health of children."[11]

It can be concluded that executive branch spokesmen, at least, supported a federal program over many years and took advantage of an emergency to try out ways for advancing proposed policies into adopted ones.

2. What should be the relationship between the federal and the state administrations? The Children's Bureau could not assert that it was running these programs nationally, but it could exercise significant influence through its obligation to supervise the expenditure of federal funds. Some congressional spokesmen were concerned that some states might deny help

[10] Ibid.
[11] Ibid, p. 35.

to some servicemen and give it to others, especially in the South, while other spokesmen were concerned lest they be forced to give any help at federal direction. The Children's Bureau policy was to set general administrative guidelines but to leave case decisions in state hands, although it agreed that it would prefer to place more stringent requirements on state administration.

3. Should cash payments be made to beneficiaries with all further responsibility left to the mother? The Children's Bureau was firm in its opposition to cash benefits arguing that

> under a plan based on cash allowances there would be no way to assure the enlisted man that care, and the amount and kind of care, will be available for either his wife or his infant. . . . The costs of care of individual sick infants would vary even more than the costs of maternity care and there would be no way to determine in advance the amount of a cash allotment necessary to meet these needs. [12]

Thus, the argument defended a system of payment tied to case-determined needs, which in the future could evolve into a system of benefits in the form of vouchers for medical care or could even move in the direction of publicly provided services.

The categorical approach was supported also on the grounds that it was the only way to assure that physicians and hospitals would in all cases receive payment, since the payments could not be diverted by the mother for other purposes. And to clinch the argument, the Children's Bureau argued that to go to a straight cash program would mean that every wife would apply and the costs would rise by 90% or more.

4. Should payment cover hospital and treatment costs? Here the Congress readily supported the Children's Bureau view that earlier programs, covering only prenatal and some postnatal costs, had to be augmented by covering the hospital and emergency treatment associated with birth itself.

5. Should the program be means tested? The final decision was clearly no, in favor of a broad entitlement based on army pay grades whereby most enlisted men (87%) but not officers became entitled to protection. Individual means testing for eligibility was considered unsuitable for a program for servicemen.

6. Should the federal government set a fixed fee for payments? The Children's Bureau was empowered to establish fee scales to set limits to what could be charged and to discourage attempts by physicians to demand payments above the EMIC payment. Some flexibility was retained to permit states to adjust fee boundaries to local conditions as part of the state plan.

---

[12] Ibid, p. 38.

By 1946, 1,222,500 maternity cases and 230,000 infant cases had been approved for benefits.

EMIC pretested six policy steps, which were later adopted as permanent characteristics for federal policy, and also probed the potential for going beyond then acceptable boundaries.

1. The guiding and regulatory influence of a federal agency was much expanded in the health field by setting guidelines for eligibility and form and amounts of benefits under a state program. These guidelines were softened by providing for various advisory mechanisms to assure cooperation of health care providers and of state agencies.
2. Beneficiaries of a federally-funded program were widened to a large segment of the population, no longer limited to the poorest and most helpless.
3. The means test was almost abolished, so that anyone falling into a clear population group was entitled to benefits without challenge. A residue of means testing was retained by excluding from benefits all servicemen above a certain rank, but the exclusions were based on rank, not on total assets, and were limited to 13% of the total possible target population of all enlisted men.
4. Payments were no longer simple patient–physician matters. Boundaries were fixed, limiting the scope of additional payments that could be demanded, and the route of payments went from government through a state agency to the provider.
5. Cost controls were introduced to private providers by the types of cost accounting procedures required by the EMIC program, if providers were to be reimbursed.
6. And, finally, modest experimental steps were taken to safeguard the quality of care provided. Standards of quality could now be overseen by a government agency and not left exclusively to the judgment of individual physicians or local medical societies.

The guiding policy of this administration was further described in the 1944 election campaign in which health policy was incorporated in an economic bill of rights. Here the administration's policy about health was defined to include "the right to adequate medical care and the opportunities to achieve and enjoy good health . . . and the right to adequate protection from the economic fears of old age, sickness, accident, and unemployment." The reference to achieving and enjoying good health can be considered one of those societal aims which have no specific policy tangibility but, when coupled with the other phrases in this campaign statement, it becomes clear that the public policy is seen as removing the economic inequities to access to medical care. This executive branch thrust was continued by President

Truman. The Wagner-Murray-Dingle Bill, among other things, retained the insurance principle but continued to seek compulsory insurance coverage without means testing. This proposed policy was once again defeated.

Redistributive and Regulatory Roles: Postwar Actions

Medicaid and Medicare

The executive branch effort was continued without much vigor until 1950, when an alternative to comprehensive compulsory national health insurance was introduced. I. S. Falk, director of the Bureau of Research and Statistics, Social Security Administration, suggested that a more modest next step might be taken by using the already enacted Social Security legislation to introduce some form of federal policy in the health field.

The Social Security Administration, rather than the Office of the President, noted that its protection for the elderly through retirement failed to protect against the single greatest cause of economic insecurity and dependency in old age: the high cost of medical care. By 1956 the executive branch introduced to the Congress proposals for health insurance only for those covered under Social Security, not for the entire population.

The nature of the policy debate did not differ materially from that of previous years. Any form of compulsory activity was opposed by some and supported by others. However, the underlying and continuing desire to do something for especially disadvantaged groups emerged when other legislation was introduced to provide some form of economic assistance for the medically indigent aged, if not for all Social Security beneficiaries. Initially, this was limited to the elderly, who might be on the margin of economic dependency and therefore not quite qualify for public relief but still need assistance with medical bills. This narrowing of the Social Security Administration's aim to extend medical protection to all the covered elderly had significant consequences.

For several years, debate continued between the executive and the legislature on two parallel lines: one pressing for medical care protection for all beneficiaries of Social Security, the other asking for protection for only those who were on the verge of indigency. The first proposal became attached to what was finally adopted as Medicare legislation, and the second was incorporated in what finally became Medicaid. On the way to adopting Medicaid legislation, an interim enactment provided medical payments for persons of very low income regardless of age. It was not until 1965 that the Social Security Act was amended to provide medical protection for all retired older persons regardless of economic status.

Much of the policy debate in this period has been interpreted as the defeat of majority will by an obdurate minority. However, many observers have suggested that in the period of the Kennedy administration, during which Medicaid but not Medicare was enacted, there was no national pressure for the wider proposals that were then urged. We cannot determine exactly how the population was divided on the issue of reform and innovation versus reduced federal spending and activity, but we can estimate that the resistance probably included half the voters.

The final enactment of both Medicaid and Medicare in 1965 together represents a remarkable agreement between government policy and societal norms as we have understood them. And yet, these two pieces of legislation also represent a real and perhaps radical addition to public policy. While the marketplace of the private vendor remains primary as far as the delivery of health care goes, access using public funds was finally mandated for most citizens.

The definition of who is to be considered vulnerable and thereby entitled to governmental protection was broadened, although it still remained circumscribed; not all citizens were granted access to funds. Those on public assistance or near the level of indigency were seen as clearly unable to purchase the health care that was by now viewed as everyone's right and therefore were considered entitled to some means for procuring it. Social Security beneficiaries may or may not need financial help for this purpose, but by and large they have limited incomes, sharply reduced from their working years, and increasing medical needs, and face escalating medical costs. This population came close to being identified in the public view as necessitous. Taken together, Medicare and Medicaid extended the authority of the federal government to about 16% of the population.[13]

We should note that these additions to public policy are concerned only with the right of the individual to purchase health care; they make no statement as to his or her right to health. They extended coverage for assistance but did not consider the nature of the delivery of medical care. The extension relied on the scientific claims made by medicine—that seeing a doctor or entering a hospital would solve major health problems. It did not provide means for altering the health status or for evaluating the results as measured by the health of the population.

Medicaid, although limited to the indigent, was seen quietly by some of its proponents as providing a model for the future. To them, Medicaid was a step toward utilization of public funds for payment for a broad variety of

[13] Based on estimated eligibility for medical care by Social Security retirees plus AFDC and SSI recipients. The *Annual Statistical Supplement, Social Security Bulletin,* published by the Social Security Administration, reports for 1976: Medicare enrollees, 20,361,000; SSI beneficiaries, 3,996,000; AFDC beneficiaries, 11,006,000; or a total of 35,363,000. The total may slightly overstate coverage, since not all AFDC or SSI beneficiaries may be able effectively to claim health benefits because of limitations in state regulations.

both medical and health-related services, such as homemakers and chore workers for the disabled. Medicare was primarily limited to payment for hospital and doctor's services. Medicaid could be seen as potentially much more comprehensive. Although it was currently limited to the poor, and therefore means tested, the legislation did open the door to extension to those not on public assistance and therefore might be considered a way of testing what would happen if a comprehensive program were extended to the entire population at some future time. Finally, Medicaid retained much more significant control than did Medicare over the objects, purposes, and directions of medical purchases. Medicare, although subject to complex billing procedures, leaves virtually all initiative to the individual consumer and his or her physician or hospital. Medicaid, by contrast, operates primarily through vendor payments that are administered by public agencies and their staffs on behalf of clients, with the payments being made by public officials to private vendors. The system thus contains the potential to modify what kinds of health services are delivered, in what volume, and in what fashion.

The fact that Medicaid has not been extended beyond its original boundaries may suggest the dangers of this extension had been recognized and avoided through a continued restriction of the program to the indigent. Nonetheless, if one takes into account the 75 years it has taken to make this slight progress, it might be considered possible that a tiny foundation brick has been laid for the future evolution of public policy beyond its present limitations.

One significant potential lies in the flexibility of the legislation, which permits, through regulation, the coverage of costs for long-term care outside of hospitals: nursing homes and home-delivered health care. These represent a social aspect of medical care that has been neglected but that through Medicaid comes to public attention as its structure is used to cover such costs. This extension came about in large part because the high cost of hospital care made insurance companies and Medicaid and Medicare officials uneasy, so pressures were introduced to discharge patients from hospitals as quickly as possible. Since most of these patients "clogging up" hospital beds unnecessarily happened to be chronically ill or elderly, their discharge depended on finding and paying for alternative forms of social care, now in nursing homes or at home. The bridge between medicine and social welfare, started by Cabot and Cannon at the Massachusetts General Hospital in Boston in the early nineteenth century, was finally extended after 1965 through imaginative use of federal programs. However, the bridge was soon used for a different kind of traffic than originally hoped for. By 1980 it was used mainly as a means to control expenditure on medical care, not as a means to enlarge social provision for that care, as is discussed below.

Facility Construction

Another example of federal actions along the redistributive axis of policy can be traced in the history of the Hospital Survey and Construction Act (popularly known as Hill-Burton after its sponsors). Construction of health facilities, except for the military, was virtually suspended during World War II. The pressure created by this backlog of construction was reinforced by the advances in medical technology stimulated by wartime discoveries. Public officials had been made aware of the startling findings of military and selective service physical examinations: A large percentage of American men fell below the minimum physical standards set by the army for its personnel. These factors combined to lead to a demand that each section of the nation be assured of a community hospital, on the assumption that such facilities would attract physicians to those parts of the country that lacked adequate medical care, especially the rural areas. A common slogan of the time was "a hospital in every county."

The demand produced the Hospital Survey and Construction Act of 1947. Under its terms, the federal government provided funds and other mortgage and construction assistance to sponsors of hospitals, to supplement funds raised locally by these sponsors. Certain standards were imposed by federal regulation as a condition for qualifying for federal aid. Among the most interesting was the requirement that the counterpart state agency for hospital construction ascertain where hospitals were needed and exercise control over the type and distribution of physical facilities. State-wide and regional councils were established through which these determinations were made. Proprietary and nonprofit groups could no longer raise their own funds and could not build where and when they wished. Governmental influence in the early years of the program was exercised to give preference to hospital construction in rural and suburban areas, while little incentive was given to build or renovate hospitals in the central core of major cities.

Over time, this legislation was amended to extend to nursing homes, to chronic disease facilities, and finally to facilities in urban areas, permitting a major rebuilding and expansion of the decaying centers of larger cities. But at its inception, the program was clearly intended to redistribute health facilities to underserved rural areas, and such a leveling of facilities did take place. Over a 30-year span some $12 billion were spent on hospital construction or modernization, 30% coming from the federal government. In 1948 some states had 2 hospital beds per 1000 population and others had as many as 6; Alabama, Mississippi, Arkansas, Georgia, and Tennessee had the lowest ratio of beds. By 1973 these states were at or above the national average of 4.9 acute beds per 1000, and some states previously having high bed ratios reduced their volume slightly. Poorer districts including rural areas, have increased their beds and now closely resemble more affluent districts.

The movement of physicians to underserved areas did not follow as even a path since factors accounting for physician location proved more complicated than suspected. The construction of facilities did not operate as a sufficient attraction in the medical marketplace to redistribute physicians. In 1973 metropolitan areas had an average of one nonfederal physician for each 500 persons, while small nonmetropolitan counties had an average of one physician for each 2000–2500 persons. Southern states still have the fewest physicians relative to population, while the north central states still have the most.

Federal Regulation: Health Planning and Professional Services Review

We have thus far considered the growth of government's role in health financing and in facility construction. There have been equally significant increases in the federal government's regulatory power in the private health provider system. Several examples will be noted, if only to indicate that regulation as well as redistribution has become a way of life in federal policy.

In 1966 Congress enacted the Comprehensive Health Planning and Public Health Services Amendments, sometimes called the Partnership for Health Act. This measure advanced federal funds to stimulate the development of health planning agencies throughout the nation. An incentive for what would otherwise remain a voluntary option was inserted by requiring, directly or indirectly, that hospitals receiving federal funds be party to some state and local planning agency of government. Such agencies, called comprehensive health planning agencies, were established in 55 states or territories. They consisted of appointed spokespeople of state and local governments, hospital associations, professional health associations, and citizens. The escalation in medical costs forced many state authorities to use these units to attempt some control over costs. A first step was the state enactment of certificate-of-need legislation, under which any new construction of hospital facilities required a certificate from an official agency certifying that the new construction was needed. Since total funds for construction were limited, this meant that the planning units would make priority choices among competing construction plans. Decisions were made through a mixture of evaluative assessment data and political influence, with planning agencies sitting nominally in judgment.

The National Health Planning and Resource Development Act of 1974 replaced the comprehensive agencies with a new form of planning—health systems agencies, which were given somewhat enlarged powers of enforcement. Their membership was enlarged to increase the role of consumers and reduce the hitherto dominant role of provider agency members in decision making. At the same time, decisions about large-scale program expansion or reduction (as well as capital expansion) and about human resources training plans became referrable to such planning units.

About the same time, federal legislation authorized a system for the regular monitoring and control of the utilization of health facilities in the hopes of preventing abuses in hospital, institutional, or physicians' services. Usually teams of physicians and other service providers establish, along with state rate-setting boards, the average lengths of hospital stay and the average modalities of treatment for major health conditions.[14] Then professional peer teams in hospitals review hospital stays and sometimes variations from average treatment modalities. Where there are charges outside the average as determined by this process, physicians and other providers are obligated to justify the variation to the satisfaction of the insurance intermediary that makes actual payments. These intermediaries are usually insurance companies operating under contract in each state. While these reviews do not actually force providers into uniform practice, they do force them to be especially conscientious about such average standards, and there is a tendency for medical practice to revolve around this average. Only in clearly exceptional cases or in the case of very strong-minded providers are deviations fought for.

With the election of a Republican administration in 1980, the entire structure of federal regulation came under attack from government as well as from the private sector. The new administration policy favored a dismantling of federal control wherever and as rapidly as possible, as a matter of principle. The financing for health planning was sharply reduced where it was not wholly abolished. In the fiscal area, however federal control continued, but in a new form and with new tools. Containment of escalating hospital costs became the slogan for the 1980s and the guiding spirit of federal action. Regulation shifted from an effort to guide or shape the nature of health care away from its earlier emphasis on assured equal access for all. Instead, federal agencies that pay hospitals and other health care providers, mainly Medicaid and Medicare, turned to reimbursement policies as a way to curtail federal expenditure for health care. Standards were developed that emphasized reduced length of stay and early hospital discharge. New guidelines were established that fixed the maximum payment a public agency can make for standardized health procedures. Diagnostic categories (DRGs or diagnostically related groups) were decided on, and average and maximum payments for each category were fixed, without regard to the individual variations in care. Instead of paying for each service rendered on a cost basis, prospective budgeting was introduced. Estimates are made of the

---

[14] In most states a public board is established that fixes rates by which hospitals and other providers are reimbursed by tax-supported programs. These rates apply mainly to Medicare or Medicaid and to public welfare reimbursements.

total payment to which any provider is entitled in a given future period. The total is determined by the mix of conditions treated (DRGs), and each provider is required to function within this capped reimbursement total, regardless of inflation, labor management negotiations, changes in patient mix, etc. Mechanisms are included to permit subsequent rate adjustments to take such changes into account, but not retrospectively. The national policy shifted from medical care to containing the costs of care. Federal influence over health care was strengthened, with fiscal not health care policies and techniques.

An Exception to the Rule

The long controversy over medical care cannot be left without noting one little appreciated anomaly in American public policy—the Veterans Administration (VA). The VA is clearly a national health *service*, administered by the federal government through full-time paid employees and linked partially to the private medical care system through collaborative relationships with medical and other professional schools. True, this system was established to provide for veterans who sustained injury as part of their military service, so that the anomaly, if it is one, reflects a sense of national obligation to its soldiers. But the system has been enlarged to provide at least in-hospital care for all veterans, whether or not their illnesses are due to military service. Ambulatory care was authorized for non-service-connected illness by the Veterans Health Expansion Act (Public Law 93–82) to reduce the need for in-hospital care. Nominally, this extension was intended for veterans who could not afford private medical care; but in reality few, if any, questions are asked about ability to pay. As an almost self-contained health system, the VA directly maintains and administers over a hundred hospitals with some 100,000 beds, as well as a network of out-patient medical clinics, nursing homes, and social services for veterans under care but living outside of a hospital. Although designed for a highly selective and limited population, in all respects it represents a model for a national health service, not insurance. The acceptance of the VA system may be the exception that proves the rule of societal constraints, but it may also be interpreted to mean that the boundaries of normal value constraints are not as rigid as the fight for compulsory health insurance has led many to believe.

The Social Effects of Policy Evolution

While no direct cause-and-effect relationship can be claimed, it seems likely that the events of the past decades have played a part in materially altering the culture of health services. Certainly, the burden of paying for medical care has been shifted. While national expenditures, both public and private, have increased more rapidly than most items in the gross national product, and while costs of medical care are now far above the common expectation of only a dozen years ago, the burden on the individual has been somewhat relieved by government assumption of financing responsibility. As has been noted, public funds grew from 13 to 40% of all health expenditures, while private expenditures dropped from 86 to 58%. When private insurance or private third-party payments are added in, the individual now pays less than a third of the total health bill out of his or her own pocket and less than 10% of all hospital payments. This has been true not only for the aged, although their benefits are more marked. Between 1966 and 1972, the proportion of personal health expenditures paid by the aged directly dropped from 53 to 28% while government's share rose from 30 to 66%. For those under 65, government payments rose only from 20 to 26% and direct payments dropped from 51 to 38%, but private insurance (reflecting in part industrial labor health contracts) rose from 27 to 34%.[15]

There has been some redistribution of health resources. Facilities have been distributed throughout all parts of the country, poor and rich, rural and urban.

Very little can be said about the effects on the health of the population stemming from such a slow evolution of policy. But in one respect, at least, the long battle has had significant results from the point of view of both human beings and public policy. The federal policy of redistribution of access and monitoring distribution is now clearly established. Medicare and Medicaid are the sources of a perceptible shift in the distribution of health services. The elderly and poor receive more medical care and pay less of the cost than was formerly the case. The elderly have benefited most dramatically, at least in terms of access to health services. While persons between the ages of 19 and 64 meet 71% of the cost of medical care from private sources, including private insurance, the elderly pay only 40%.

This shift in distribution has been subject to counterattack, with the result that after 1970 the Medicare proportion of payments for the elderly dropped overall from 44 to 38% and its share of physician costs dropped from 60 to 52%. The reversal was due in part to increases in the coinsurance or deductible amount for which the insured are held personally liable and even more to a sharp drop in the number of physicians willing to accept Medicare fees as their total charges. Between 1969 and 1973, the proportion of physicians willing to accept full assignment of their fees to Medicare dropped from 61 to 52%.

Beginning with 1980, costs to consumers began to increase and reach

---

[15] Barbara Cooper and Nancy Worthington, "Age Differences in Medical Care Spending 1972," *Social Security Bulletin* 36, no. 5 (May 1973): 3.

40% of the total. The total out-of-pocket expenditure of individuals has continued to increase, as the total medical cost has escalated; coinsurance and deductible provisions in both private insurance and under Medicare have also continued to increase. The cost of care is increasingly visible to consumers, and their proportionate share of the medical bill is likely to increase even more as long as national policy is to reduce the share that government pays for health care.

However, it was clear in 1966, and it remains substantially true today, that the elderly have been the beneficiary of a significant redistribution. In 1966 the hospital-days care for the aged rose by 25%, and even more vital, they were less dependent upon charity. Before Medicare 17% of hospital-days care for the aged were without charge, meaning they were treated as charity cases; after Medicare this figure fell to 3%.

The poor, among whom the aged constitute a large proportion, have also benefited, but not as dramatically. A full analysis would have to take into account regional variations, race, and urban location. However, we can draw a few conclusions suggesting how far these policies have directly benefited the poor in terms of access to medical care. Medicare and Medicaid meet 57% of all the expenses of personal health care for families with incomes under $2000 and 84% for families with incomes under $5000. If a near-poverty level for a family of four is taken to be $5700, then government sources meet 46% of health costs for those below this level, but only 15% for those above it. [16]

If we turn to use of physician services, we find that in 1964 nearly 28% of all poor families and 33% of nonwhite poor families had not seen a doctor for 2 years. In 1973 these percentages dropped to 17% of all poor and 18% of nonwhite poor, almost equalizing the relationship by color. [17] Interestingly, in the same period 17% of the nonpoor white population did not see a doctor for 2 years and this figure fell in 1973 to 13.4%. For nonwhite, nonpoor families, this proportion dropped from 24.7 to 15.3%. Thus, the differential by physician access has been, in an aggregate sense, almost abolished.

By another measure, that of number of physician visits per year, the poor have fared a lot better. Between 1964 and 1973, the average number of visits per person per year for poor families rose from 4.3 to 5.6, while for the nonpoor the number rose from 4.6 to 4.9. The lower average number of visits by the nonpoor is probably related to their lower incidence of illness; this measure can tell us little about whether the amount of medical care received was appropriate for the amount required.

Although these data suggest that some leveling of access has occurred,

---

[16] Data in this section from *Health U.S. 1975.* op.cit.

[17] In 1964 nonpoor families were defined as those with incomes under $3000; in 1973 the figure used was $6000.

others indicate the persistence of unequal access. Thus in 1973, only 5% of medical visits by whites were to a hospital outpatient clinic, while 16.4% of visits by nonwhites were to clinics.

If slight, rather than dramatic, changes have been produced for individuals, the same can be said regarding the system of medical care itself. Except for hospital facility distribution and financing, the system has been remarkably unaltered. In the financing of hospital care, significant changes have occurred, but still in the direction of shifting the cost burden rather than altering the practice of medical care delivery.

There has also been a redistribution in an unintended direction, because hospitals and physicians have benefited significantly through an increase in incomes. Hospitals are less likely to operate at a deficit, meaning that private philanthropic funds are used less to meet hospital deficits. In a sense, conventional wealthy contributors have benefited by being relieved of an obligation. The income of physicians has increased and in some categories has increased enormously, as in the substantial improvement in the relative position of radiologists, pathologists, and anesthetists as a direct consequence of reimbursement policies.

To illustrate the effect on the hospital system, between 1961 and 1965 (before Medicare) revenues increased annually by 10.4%, but between 1965 and 1976 revenues increased 16.4%. In the same periods, semiprivate room charges increased by 5.6% and 13%, respectively.[18] Also in this period, all consumer prices rose, but not as rapidly. Part of the increase in hospital charges can be attributed to higher wages for nonprofessional workers, to a shorter work week, and to increases in the cost of equipment and drugs. The ratio of staff to patient census went up from 240 per 100 in 1961 to 301 in 1971, and average earnings rose from $3371 to $6028. However, private payments dropped from 27 to 11% of all income, and public payments rose from 8 to 39%, suggesting some correlation between funds pumped into medical care and rising costs. Between 1961 and 1971, private hospitals doubled the ratio of net income to plant assets from 1.4 to 3%.

There have been other social effects as well. Medical care has been more and more institutionalized and is now predominantly delivered in hospitals. Home visits and the delivery of medical care in any form to the patient's home has been significantly reduced. Hospitals have become larger and often less personal. Physicians' offices are often crowded and replace outpatient clinics of earlier times. The prescription of drugs and chemical therapies have increased enormously, with both great benefits and possible damage. With the rapid expansion in scientific means made possible in part by public support for the purchase of services or payment for research, the

[18] Julian Pettergill, "The Financial Positions of Private Community Hospitals, 1961–71," *Social Security Bulletin* 36, no. 11 (November 1973): 3.

capacity to monitor and control the use of noxious or dangerous medicines has diminished. Attention to preventive health methods has declined as hospitals and physicians' offices have become the dominant focus of health services, while public health, sanitation, and supervision of water supply have diminished in importance in health policy. It appears that environmental protection efforts may someday assume the prominent position that public health once held in this field. Finally, medicine's concentration on scientific and technical cure has outgrown its attention to life-styles and patterns of living as contributors to disease. At the present time, arguments about the illness-producing effects of basic life-styles are raised by private voices and have not yet become a part of national policy. Complaints that our illnesses are due to poor diet, speed, tension, and lack of exercise are not yet on a public policy agenda.

Thus, while the preamble of health legislation has argued that the purpose of the public policies adopted has been to improve and maintain the health of the people, the policies in effect have concentrated only on giving the population access to whatever services have been developed by the private providers—hospitals, physicians, the pharmaceutical companies, and so on.

By 1980 another set of trends had begun to emerge. The most significant has been the increasing corporatization, or privatization, of health care. More and more of health care is dominated by either a profit-making structure or by fiscal rather than service-oriented techniques. About 10% of general hospitals are profit making, but this sector is the fastest growing. Not only are hospital beds increasingly owned by investor companies, not community nonprofit boards, but more and more nonprofit hospitals are turning over the management of their hospitals to national management companies whose emphasis is on turning a profit, operating out of the black, controlling costs, and manipulating patient services to produce these results. The number of hospitals so owned or managed almost doubled between 1977 and 1982, from 725 to 1040. The justification for this trend is found in a claim that business management is more efficient. Much of this "efficiency" may be due more to a business manager's ability to maximize insurance revenue than to ability to reduce unnecessary expenditures. One study of 280 profit and nonprofit hospitals concluded that operating expenses per patient-day are 6% higher in the investor-owned companies.[19] However, the appeal of enhancing income now clearly contends with community service as a guiding principle in the health field.

This trend is encouraged by public policy in several ways, but the treat-

[19] See "Treating the Balance Sheet," *The Economist*, August 20, 1983, pp. 26–27; and N.R. Kleinfield, "Operating for a Profit at Hospital Corp.," *New York Times*, May 29, 1983, Section 3, p. 1.

ment of capital costs in calculating reimbursement by public agencies may be as influential as the desire of an affluent middle class to have its own distinctive medical facilities. Public reimbursement includes the cost of securing money to build medical facilities under a formula that assures private developers between a 15 and 20% return on invested capital. This has been justified as a way to stimulate private construction but is obviously a way also to subsidize that construction. Nonprofit organizations do not benefit from equivalent treatment, although they have received matching public dollars under the Hill-Burton Hospital Construction Act.

A second development is the steady squeezing out of small inner-city community hospitals as populations move to the suburbs and as the complexity of financing hospital care increases. The burden of rising costs and serving a low-income population has led to the disappearance of many inner-city hospitals. Large teaching hospitals remain in central cities, which means that the most costly of hospitals are used to provide care that once was given in less costly community facilities. In addition, hospital care has become less accessible to the poor remaining in the city who have to travel farther.[20]

A final consequence of the attempts to cap or control hospital costs is only beginning to emerge in the mid 1980s as an unplanned, but not unexpected, result of budgetary control. More and more day surgery is being performed without overnight stay. More surgical and medical care is being offered at full fee by doctors in street-front walk-in clinics, outside of hospitals where such care once concentrated. Such clinics are based on new technology plus economic gain, not on community service, except indirectly as an example of a marketplace health system. Whether the poor or those with difficult health conditions will be well served remains to be seen. It is quite possible that medical care will once again become a two-level system, one for the poorest and another for the better off.

A counter development is the restructuring of hospital activity itself. Some hospitals are diversifying their efforts. They staff nursing homes outside their walls, staff and operate neighborhood health centers, and take over home health agencies. Paralleling this is a tendency for home health agencies to consolidate and merge into larger and larger organizations to compete effectively with proprietary providers of home care, which are now fully reimbursable from public funds.

In 1980 the organization of the health system began a major shake-up induced by public concern over costs of care. Numerous interests and issues are involved in the shake-up: the future of teaching and medical research, care for the poor and the chronically or long-term sick, control over medical

[20] Alan Soger, "Why Urban Hospitals Close," *Health Services Research*, 18, no. 3. (Fall 1983): 451–475.

facilities, and preventive or public health. Public policy has set the shake-up in motion, but as of 1983, it did not offer guidance about the shape desired for medical care by the American people or by the health professions. The outcome may be studied as a test of the Republican administration's commitment to the marketplace, letting some unseen hand determine the final outcome. Two main alternatives for health seem to lie ahead: a successful reorganization in the market, or more likely, a period of chaos and confusion followed by a determined new effort at public policy construction of health care through either a national health insurance system or some other form of health services. The history of public policy to shape health care is not yet completed.

A New Stage for Health Policy

What conclusions can be drawn from this long and painful struggle to achieve what may, in policy terms, seem to be rather minor advances? Whatever one may think of its merits, government officials have promoted one policy with persistence since 1935 and have produced perceptible changes in the way society assures the health of its citizens, doing so beyond the constraints that our society has imposed on public policy.

True, the fidelity with which public policy conforms to societal norms has been clearly demonstrated, but public policy can, albeit with enormous difficulty, lead the way to a change in societal policy through the slow, incremental enactment of specific pieces of public policy. In this example, the use of the federal government to influence the distributive effects in the health field has been enlarged. But the foundation has also been laid for future government action affecting the organization and structure of health care more radically than in the past. The unexpected consequences of actions made possible to date—that is, increasing government payment—may pull public policy further and further down the road of active intervention in the private sector. As interested groups and voters have come to expect more health assurance through their continued reliance upon science and more protection without direct personal cost, the more government expenditure for health services has increased. This in turn has produced anxiety about the scope of the cost and the possibility of containing it, which in its turn has forced some attention to ways to modify the delivery of services. A new plateau of public policy has thus been reached. It is no longer a question of whether government should act, but of how much and in what direction.

Direct intervention to modify the delivery system lies in the future, since any consideration of a national health service has not yet been introduced into the American debate. The minor experiments in governmental administration—city hospitals and clinics, EMIC, and the Veterans Administration—even appear to have lost ground in favor of a privately organized set of services.

But these dynamics have already produced a variety of governmental controls over the functioning of the health system that may some day justify reassessment from the point of view of their overall impact. Federal policy by and large determines what hospital and nursing home facilities will be built and where. This has been exercised cumulatively and incrementally, first, by the enactment of the Hill-Burton law, which provided for federal contributions to the support of hospitals, with priorities to assure that all geographic sectors of the country, even the most rural, have hospital facilities. More recently, this has been extended to the concept of certificate of need, whereby health systems agencies are entitled to question further expansion of hospital facilities and their location. Many states have the capacity to deny a certificate of need, which effectively halts capital expansion, although it does not yet positively direct construction in underserved areas.

The character of services provided is now mildly challenged by the requirement that all medical facilities subject the practices of their physicians to professional review bodies, in order to assure that there are no wide variations in the practices of physicians. True, this control is exercised on a peer basis, physician over physician, but it is mandated by national policy.

The Health Manpower Act of 1975 now largely determines the volume and type of medical education. While in the past, this has been a reflexive policy, responding to the choices made by the medical professions and medical schools, recent enlargement of the policy provides for national priorities to be established by quasi-governmental bodies governing the types of health personnel required and their distribution. The priority guides will in the future govern the allocation of manpower training resources, which in their turn will govern the production of health personnel.

Finally, review standards and control by fiscal intermediaries, such as Blue Cross associations, now determine what health services will in fact be paid for out of the more than 35% of the health bill met by public funds. Since hospitals, nursing homes, and, to an increasing extent, physicians are dependent upon these funds for their incomes, this capacity in an administrative mechanism to determine what will be paid for in health care can become decisive. To date, these choices have largely been left in the private sector, either in the hands of physicians to determine their average billings or in the hands of private insurance companies, but the principle at least has been established that the requirement can be federally mandated.

It thus appears that the operations of limited societal policies may produce an accumulation of small effects that can in time lead to a radical renovation of the health delivery system. But it is important to emphasize that radical change is not yet in sight.

The Character of Current Public Policy Issues

The current state of development of the national government's health policy leaves the following issues unsettled, and it is difficult to state with any certainty whether a national policy on these subjects does exist.

Should financing access to health services be extended from those special categories now covered to the entire population? This in effect would involve an attempt, not as much to redistribute health services to benefit the entire population, as to remove from individuals the illusion that they do not have to bear some of the burden of medical costs and that these costs can be shifted to someone else. If all persons are covered and if demand continues to grow as it has, it seems inescapable that either the costs will increase or controls on utilization and on the nature of provision will have to be introduced. Can such controls distribute a highly valued commodity—medical care—to persons equally, regardless of income?

With or without an extension of financial coverage, what, if any, shall be the federal policy to control the escalating costs of medical care, which have so exceeded increases in the GNP and cost of living? Specific pieces of legislation have been introduced, but there seems to be no indication that the national government has at any stage adopted a policy of systematically controlling the cost of medical care when, by this phrase, one means controlling the charges made by all medical providers. Some control exists in programs that set fee scales, but this is limited to use of the public dollar. Private payments are still the greater part (60%) of the total expenditure for medical care, and there is no indication that a national policy to control the imposition of charges to the private consumer is anywhere in sight. The only controls in the past have been negative in the sense that they are imposed only on aspects of medical care that are paid for by public funds. Can controls act in a positive sense to direct the delivery system to do more of some things (e.g., ambulatory care in ghettos) and less of others (say, cardiac bypass operations)?

What are desired forms of organizing health services? If any answer is to be given to such a question as a matter of national policy, it is essential that a judgment be made between the present private system and some alternative form. There have been modest experimental probes into alternatives. For example, encouragement of the creation of group practices was embodied in national legislation, and a few health maintenance organizations did result. However, the legislation did not require prepayment, and health maintenance organizations have been financially supported only on a small, experimental basis and without substantial continuity. Some alteration in the balance between hospital and primary care (the services of a doctor in an individual's community) has also been attempted, but without any clear national choice as to direction. The primary flow of support continues toward payment in the hospital. Modest sums have been expended to encourage the education of physicians prepared to practice family medicine, and some emergency funds have been used to underwrite the development of neighborhood health clinics in ghetto areas. But neither of these represents a permanent national commitment to assure the delivery of primary care services by family doctors or through neighborhood health centers.

At the extreme, we may someday have to decide whether to abandon our primary reliance upon a system of insurance and financing and substitute a program of health services. The model best known in the United States is the British National Health Service.[21] The British government acquired all the hospitals and placed their administration in the hands of regional hospital boards; the boards operate on behalf of the national government, but with a large measure of freedom, subject only to total funding provided by the national treasury. Physicians are paid by tax funds, either as specialists on hospital staffs or as general practitioners with their own lists of patients, for each of whom the physician is paid an annual per capita sum. Physicians are free also to develop private fee-for-service practices within set limits. Physicians' levels of payment are negotiated with professional associations, all persons have a physician of their choice, virtually no charges are made for any medical attention or hospital care, and small sums are charged for common medicines. The system is complex, but its main features are the assurance of a minimum of physician attention to all, no cost barrier to medical care, and no fee-for-service complexities.

Many arguments have been raised for and against such a system. It exists in other countries in some form, but mainly in socialist or communist nations. The substitution of a health service for a health insurance has not yet been raised in general policy debate.

How will the purposes of the national health policy (other than the global purpose of assuring access) be defined? Small-scale programs are supported to provide presumably preventive health services for mothers of newborn infants, to provide special centers to concentrate on the needs of geriatric patients, or to pay for the care of industrially injured workers,

---

[21] For a full discussion, see Gordon Forsyth, *Doctors and State Medicine: A Study of the British Health Service* (Old Woking, Surrey: Open University Set Book, Pitman Medical, 1966); and I. Douglas-Wilson and Gordon McLachlan, eds., *Health Service Prospects* (Boston: Little, Brown, 1973).

such as miners. The occupational health legislation has provided modest sums in an effort to reduce health hazards in industry. And a program of environmental protection has been launched in an effort to clean up the water supply and reduce industrial pollution.

In one sense, these national programs appear, when taken together, to amount to a federal policy to have both butter and guns. Primary reliance is still placed upon private providers and the curative miracles of modern science, which claim the bulk of public expenditure and human resources. On the other hand, parallel activities are also initiated with much less money and personnel to tackle great environmental health hazards. And even smaller sums are made available to private groups to experiment with alternative forms of delivery organization, such as group practices. But none of these can be considered more than small-scale testing experiments by contrast to the major policy of trusting the private system to function reasonably well for itself and government to step in to correct the most glaring inequities. However, as has been stated before, the volume and scope of the public investment in this policy are now sufficiently great and the contradictions and tensions that have ensued from it are sufficiently disturbing to open up the possibility that the field of health policy will continue to grow and to be controversial. There may be a stage when the nature of health services themselves will be altered or planned by government action, but such a shift in public policy to alter societal policies remains in the future. For the time being, the legislation most likely to be enacted remains rooted in the past—insurance to cover costs, with an increase in government regulation.

The subject of serious disability may prove to be as powerful a force to move government into new roles as is the anxiety over the cost of our present medical and health system. Federal policies of relying upon payment mechanisms alone have created within 30 years a vast addition to the health system, that of proprietary nursing homes that manage more beds than do all our hospitals. At the same time, the prevalence of severe disability increased. Between 1960 and 1970, the proportion of adults covered by Social Security who qualified for permanent disability benefits increased by 225%.[22] The elderly over 75 years of age are especially prone to severe disability, which makes living at home difficult without some supportive personal services. And the proportion of older people is the fastest growing in the population. Serious auto and sport injuries are increasing in prevalence and possibly in incidence, so that there is an increasing proportion of young adults with lifetime disability. Medical science now keeps alive large numbers of children who once died in the early years of life because of congenital disease or injury, but who now survive for long lifetimes of

---

[22] P. R. Lerner, *Social Security Disability Applicant Study, 1970* (Washington, D.C.: Social Security Administration, U.S Department of Health, Education, and Welfare, 1974).

severe incapacity. To these must be added the apparent increase in cases of alcoholism, drug abuse, and mental illness, all of which are long-term conditions that impair functioning.

Our health system is focused on curing those conditions that it knows how to cure; it has little competence yet and even less interest in taking care of a growing population of disabled persons. But inattention to their needs does not spare the health system, because for lack of proper attention these patients return often to acute hospitals, which can do little for them, or they unnecessarily end up in nursing homes, for which the health system must pay.

It is possible that the strain that this phenomenon introduces may force an alteration of the system, although the type of change cannot be clearly outlined. It is likely that some shift may have to occur in the proportionate amount of attention given to the chronically ill, which would demand in turn major changes in the training and practices of physicians, nurses, and hospitals. Such a shift is not likely to be welcomed nor is it likely to be introduced by present providers acting on their own initiative. An alternative to this type of shift in emphasis might be a new system for caring for this population, combining nursing homes and various homecare and personal services. The financing of such a parallel system would necessarily become competitive with the health system and increase the total of the nation's income spent on health matters.

In this still unsettled period, the future structure of America's health system will depend on whether the current reliance on the marketplace will ultimately give way to more socially oriented and service-focused control over health care. Whichever course is finally followed, it remains reasonably certain that the investment of tax dollars will play a major role, and that in turn insures that federal control will increase. The open issue is whether its role will be guided by service or by fiscal policy considerations alone.

Additional Readings

Anderson, Odin. Health Services in a Land of Plenty. Chicago: University of Chicago Press, 1968.

Corning, Peter. Evolution of Medicare. Washington, D.C.: Office of Research and Statistics, Social Security Administration, U.S. Department of Health, Education, and Welfare, 1969.

Donabedian, Avedis. Benefits in Medical Care Programs. Cambridge, Mass.: Harvard University Press, 1976.

Health Policy Advisory Committee (Health-PAC), ed. America's Health Empire. New York: Random House, 1971.

Marmor, Theodore. The Politics of Medicare. Chicago: Aldine, 1973.

Sheps, Cecil, and Lewis, Irving. The Sick Citadel. Cambridge, Mass.: Oelgeschlager, Gunn and Hain, 1983.

Somers, Herman, and Somers, Anne. *Doctors, Patients, and Health Insurance.* Washington, D.C.:
    Brookings Institution, 1961.
Starr, Paul. *The Social Transformation of American Medicine.* New York: Basic Books, 1982.
Stevens, Robert, and Stevens, Rosemary. *Welfare Medicine in America.* New York: Free
    Press, 1974.

Housing

Enlarged Aims— Minimum Results

5

Providing shelter is another dimension of existence in which federal govern-mental obligations have expanded significantly. The expansion accelerated in the 1960s and reversed in the 1970s. The breadth of social concerns has been remarkable. Government concern about shelter was originally local and limited to the income and economic provisions already discussed. But the growth of urban concentration focused attention on minimal regulation of land use and on standards for construction through local zoning and building codes and, to a lesser extent, on the provision of housing for poor families. In an unusual manner, housing policy seems to have completed a full circle. In its origins, at the level of local government, public concerns were deeply infused with a social purpose—concern for a deprived popula-tion, adequacy of space, reduction of overcrowding, relative value of high versus low densities, and provision of essential amenities, then defined as ac-cess to running water, indoor sanitation, and air. The relationship between housing arrangements and population dispersion was even considered in the early debates in New York State. This early breadth of approach was followed by a long period in which the concentration of policy was on physical construction, stimulation of the private housing market, modest public construction for low-income families, and regulation of land use. By the 1960s, however, concern for the entire range of social as well as physical environments reemerged only to lapse by 1980 to a constricting economic and political environment.

Physical Housing as Policy Objective

Origins of Governmental Intervention

Much of the pioneer activity by local government took place in older eastern seaboard cities, such as New York. In the 1890s, the needs of new immigrants and the jerry-built private-market, profit-making construction of housing with a short-term outlook produced an intolerable market situation: high density of population, the spread of disease, and the complete absence of minimum amenities in what was then considered decent housing.[1] A New York survey exposing such conditions found nearly 3000 individuals in one block of 39 tenements, with only 264 water closets, with 40 units of hot running water, and a high incidence of tuberculosis.

Findings such as these gave rise to widespread civic action and conflict with local political and construction interests. The reform movement prevailed, however, and state legislation was enacted providing for the establishment of a tenement commission to tackle the host of interrelated problems that this information revealed. Implicit was a concern for physical and social relationships affecting large numbers of human beings, but the terms of reference and the premises of the commission and its leaders concentrated primarily on physical and regulatory solutions.

It was believed that regulation of private construction by government was much preferable to public construction or administration of housing, and there was little confidence that government could effectively administer housing programs. This skepticism prevailed in a period when the corruption of local government processes was widely publicized. It was believed that strong regulation by a tough-minded administration could produce better physical standards in new and old housing. Such improvements were expected in themselves to provide the kind of "decent environment" that would resolve all other difficulties: Reduced population density and access to air and sanitary facilities would be sufficient. It is even possible to perceive some early glimmerings of concern about concentrations of poor families in segregated sections of the cities, the slums. The distressing conditions in which poor families found themselves and the concentration of low-income families in congested segments of the city were all blamed upon the profit-making motive to secure the maximum return from the minimum investment and the maximum use of the least amount of space. Since these circumstances were controlled by builders, it was presumed that tight regulation of standards might lead to an elimination or reduction of slums.

---

[1]For a valuable summary of the origins of governmental intervention, see Roy Lubove, *The Progressives and the Slums* (Pittsburgh: University of Pittsburgh Press, 1962), especially Chap. 5 on Tenement House Commission of 1900.

Beginnings of Reform

A major step toward federal policy was taken when the Housing Act of 1937 was passed as part of the New Deal momentum of the depression years. The act provided the first federal subsidy for housing. Programs of the 1930s produced public construction and administration of low-income housing, with federal support of locally initiated plans. During this period, New York City provided housing for upwards of 500,000 persons—an entire city, produced with federal help, but planned, built, and managed by the local housing authority. Public housing elsewhere was undertaken, but not on such a large scale, and much of the programming was concerned only with basic physical structure—that is, the construction of safe, solid, unimaginative housing capable of being rented at a very low figure.

Proliferation of Programs

The housing shortage created by the halt in construction during the war years and the rush of discharged veterans to establish independent households was an important area of concern in the late 1940s. In 1949 amendments to the Housing Act of 1937 authorized a program of publicly administered and constructed housing, creating 135,000 units annually for 6 years. In addition, separate categorical programs were directed at slum clearance and urban redevelopment. The Federal Housing Act of 1949 contained as one of its goals the provision of a decent home and a suitable living environment for every American family. This objective has been more or less maintained in all succeeding administrations. However, such an ambitious objective needs to be examined more closely in light of the specific policies adopted in federal programs. By and large, the practical policies as distinguished from the stated aspirations conformed to the basic societal guidelines that have affected other programs—a reliance upon the private market, with government in a subsidiary or supplementary role, and some preoccupation with especially disadvantaged groups.

Within this framework, a federal executive agency had by 1968 proposed the construction of 26 million new homes over a 10-year span in order to provide adequate shelter, to improve substandard housing, to replace substandard units, and to accommodate newly established families in a period of rapid family formation. This goal was to be achieved primarily by stimulation and incentive for the private construction market, and in fact, by the late 1960s that market was producing about 1.5 million units annually. However, these new constructions did not necessarily address themselves to removing substandard units or to meeting the needs of families with low income.

A significant array of administrative agencies was established, including the Housing and Home Finance Agency, the Federal Housing Administration, and the Urban Renewal Authority. The most influential of these, the Housing and Home Finance Agency, functioned primarily through mortgage and construction guarantees. The incentives for the private market were directed primarily toward housing for middle- and upper-income families, on the assumption families with lower incomes could occupy the housing left behind by the higher income families, and thus the interests of all groups would be served.

A succession of complaints and pressures led to the enactment of a variety of specialized programs without fundamentally altering this approach. Large concentrations of the poor in low-cost public housing produced concentrations of social difficulty and distress and established that the simple replacement of substandard housing by sterile, sanitary housing exacerbated rather than ameliorated social difficulties, especially when such construction did not take into account the whole range of problems of social and group relationships and the decayed environments outside of the apartments. Urban renewal, the attempt to get rid of slums by bulldozing them, led to the charge that many of these programs were attempting to revitalize the inner city by attracting middle- and upper-income families to better housing, but without taking care of the families thus displaced from slum areas. In the period between 1949 and 1963, it has been estimated that the urban renewal program alone removed about 177,000 family dwelling units and 66,000 individual family units from the market and replaced them with only 68,000 dwelling units, of which only 20,000 were for low-income families. This led to the accusation that urban renewal, with the expenditure of several billions of dollars, succeeded in reducing the supply of housing for persons of low income rather than increasing it. Not only were families displaced by these programs not provided with replacement housing anywhere, but in the period of disruption that ensued, families with limited means were forced to move into higher rental housing without any assistance for making the transition.[2] Old neighborhoods and whatever supportive network of social relationships they contained were destroyed with the dispersion of previously more or less class-homogeneous populations into new and strange areas.

By 1966, the year in which the Demonstration Cities and Metropolitan Development Act (Model Cities) was enacted, the growth of federal commitment measured in dollar terms became dramatic. In 1940 and in 1950, it was estimated that federal grants to state and local jurisdictions averaged about $2 billion per year. In 1960 this figure increased to $7 billion, and by 1966 it was estimated that approximately $16 billion were expended in federal

[2] Bernard Frieden, *The Future of Old Neighborhoods* (Cambridge, Mass.: MIT Press, 1964); Scott Greer, *Urban Renewal and American Cities* (Indianapolis: Bobbs-Merrill, 1965).

grants, plus some $12 billion were available for residential mortgage guarantees. At this time, the Presidential Commission on Intergovernmental Relationships (the Kastenbaum Commission), appointed by President Eisenhower, reported that "federal grants, represented in the variety of categorical programs, did not constitute a system. The program has had such varied characteristics, and diverse objectives, and piecemeal organization, that this could lead to not only confusion but cross-purpose program development."[3]

By this time and continuing at an accelerated rate until the 1970s, the congeries of federal programs had become so intertwined with the private construction of housing for persons of all income classes that the old boundaries that constrained federal responsibility were no longer applicable. Policy was no longer concerned with the disadvantaged alone or with one-time emergency measures as in the postwar period. Federal policy continued to be an accumulation of independent programs out of which it is difficult to extract a clear set of policy directions. In 1966, when various programs were consolidated in one super federal agency, the Department of Housing and Urban Development (HUD), the federal programs were roughly clustered into four categories defined by objective:

1. Urban renewal programs intended to improve central city environments, a program used in most cities to construct middle-class housing, to tear down slums, to alter the mix of population in the inner city, and to improve the environment through such means as nonpolluting transportation
2. Mortgage guarantee programs for all income classes, which strongly stimulated the construction of housing in suburban areas and even the experimental construction of new cities, both of which stimulated the dispersion of populations from the inner city, but without strong enough incentives to increase significantly the volume of housing, especially for the poor
3. Programs to provide dwelling units at low cost to a limited extent through publicly administered housing and increasingly through various subsidy devices for builders, such as low interest rates, tax write-downs, and incentives in the acquisition of land, intended to reduce ultimate rental or sale price for the consumer
4. Modest programs for special groups, especially the aged and the disabled

While these programs were in some respects addressed to certain social problems of certain special groups (the poor and the elderly), the definition

---

[3] U.S. Commission on Intergovernmental Relations, *Message from The President of the United States. Transmitting the Final Report to the 84th Congress*, 1st session, House Document No. 198, 1955, pp. 118, 139.

of policy objectives remained general: to improve the physical quarters of all persons living in substandard housing. The focus on the objective of physical housing ignored the social consequences of the actual results of the programs: conflicting claims upon the distribution of income by different economic groups, the disruption of groups with more or less homogeneous economic-class conditions, the relocation of persons of different status to common neighborhoods in the inner city, and the segregation of populations by income class in suburban areas.

Emergence of Concern for the Social Environment: The Model Cities Experiment

The clear worsening of the condition of low-income families was for a time obscured by the value definition of *substandard*. Between 1950 and 1959, for example, the percentage of unsound housing occupied by whites dropped from 18 to 14% and by nonwhites from 60 to 46%; the percentage of overcrowded units declined for whites from 12 to 8% and for blacks from 30 to 25%. But the definitions of *unsound* were not very tough; the gross disparity between white and nonwhite conditions could not be concealed for long, and the pressures for attention to minorities and low-income families segregated or hemmed into large city centers became irresistible.[4] Housing policy was no longer a matter of simply stimulating construction or of giving attention to physically unsound housing. It had also to give attention to very troublesome problems of class and social relationships and to the dilemmas of population concentration and dispersion.

The consequences of previous policies that led to the concentration of poor, usually public assistance families, in densely concentrated high-rise units, forced attention to the host of social problems with which low-income families are plagued. Federal programs by and large made no provision for tenant services that this population urgently required, and the running sore of low-income housing was difficult to ignore. The New York City Housing Authority was forced to establish a division of community services to consolidate its own activities and those of a variety of private agencies with a services budget of some $20 million per year, in order to attend to the most minimal social needs of the 500,000 people living in Housing Authority units. Recreational activities, vocational preparation, legal aid, homemaking services, literacy training centers, study centers, and the like had to be pro-

---

[4] Bernard Frieden, "Housing," in *Encyclopedia of Social Work* (New York: National Association of Social Workers, 1977), 17th ed., pp. 639–651.

vided as a palliative if not as a serious solution to the problems of living faced by low-income families in the city.

Pressures such as these found expression in the expansion of social programs of the middle 1960s. One of the interesting forward steps in federal social policy was embodied in the Model Cities legislation of 1965. A presidentially appointed task force reviewed the explosive situation in low-income and urban areas and proposed the testing of a new national approach to cope with these difficulties. The policy of the new program was to include concentration of federal resources in order to assure a critical mass of effort directed at clear-cut objectives; coordination of the disparate and often contradictory federal program activities in the direction of this objective; and mobilization of local leadership, especially from low-income populations, in the direction of joint action on the problems of urban housing and environment. The legislation as drafted by the president's office proposed that the new approach would be tested in 50 cities, be financed entirely by federal appropriations, and introduce into each demonstration city a federal administrator to provide an active influence rather than a simple monitor of the ways in which these federal funds were used to further the objectives of the program. The legislation was clearly redistributive in its intent and clear about its constituency. Its preamble states:

> The Congress hereby finds and declares that improving the quality of urban life is the most critical domestic problem facing the United States. The persistence of widespread urban slums and blight, the concentration of persons of low income in older urban areas, and the unmet needs for additional housing and community facilities and services arising from rapid expansion of our urban population have resulted in the marked deterioration in the environment of large numbers of our people while the nation as a whole prospers.[5]

The legislation was intended not only to provide direct assistance but also to help the cities coordinate their other welfare activities aided by other federal social programs to encourage an economical use of all federal, state, and local efforts to improve the quality of urban life. The bill was intended to provide a demonstration of the effectiveness of a massive, comprehensive effort to rebuild or restore entire sections and neighborhoods of slum and blighted areas.

The Congress was unenthusiastic about many aspects of this proposal and finally adopted a much more vague statement of purpose: "maximum opportunities in the choice of housing accommodations for all citizens and of all income levels." This phrasing replaced administration proposals that

---

[5] U.S. Congress, House Subcommittee on Housing, *Hearings on Demonstration Cities, Housing, and Urban Development*, 89th Congress, 2d session, 1966, p. 1.

included such language as "counteract the segregation of housing by race or income." The Congress also weakened the draft legislation in a number of ways. It removed the proposal for a federal coordinator to be located in each demonstration and substituted funding for technical assistance from the various federal agencies whose programs affected urban housing. It also doubled the number of cities to be included in the Model Cities experiment and thus reduced the total sum of money available to any one. Finally, it removed the provision that all other federal programs relevant to urban housing give priority to the Model Cities areas and called instead for simple coordination of activities through HUD. The administration sought to increase slightly the margin of federal authority, and the Congress cut it back to ensure the more conventional understanding of partnership between federal, state, and local governments and private industry. At the time that Model Cities legislation authorized appropriations of approximately $2.3 billion plus $412 million of earmarked urban renewal funds, the Congress retained the antecedent categorical programs and funded them at the level of some $12 billion, without any provision that these programs give priority attention to the purposes of Model Cities. These differences in concepts held by the executive and the Congress persisted throughout the 1960s.

The total effect of the administration's attempt to focus federal policy was thus reduced to only an addition to the accumulation of diverse, limited, and ineffective programs. The adopted national policy of the federal government (meaning both the executive and the legislative branches in agreement) succeeded in giving supplementary attention to especially difficult areas without significantly altering the traditional reliance upon the private marketplace to deal with the social dilemmas of housing. It has been estimated that by 1971 federal spending in urban areas ranged as high as $44 billion, including loan insurance and guarantees.[6] A more realistic figure, which excludes loan insurance and guarantees, would still approximate $10 billion, spent specifically for these focused urban needs. Out of this total, the Model Cities program secured annual appropriations of approximately $390 million per year, or about 15% of the total for HUD's urban programs, about $2.6 billion.

With the coming of a Republican administration in 1968, the Model Cities program was not immediately dismantled, but the whole thrust of federal policy began to shift in the direction of the new federalism and the experimentation with general revenue sharing. General revenue sharing not only provided for a more generous distribution of funds, some $5.3 billion in

[6] See U.S. Congress, Senate Subcommittee on Executive Reorganization, *Hearings on the Federal Role in Urban Affairs*, 89th Congress, 2d session, August 15–16, 1966, pt. 1, pp. 178–181; Staff Paper, Office of the Assistant Secretary for Model Cities, *The Basis for Analysis of Federal Aid Programs for Urban Impact*, 1971.

the first year, but shifted major responsibility for choice making from the hands of the federal government back to the local government and the local interplay of political forces. On the average, revenue-sharing allocations were double that of Model Cities funding, and local pressures significantly reduced the saliency and priority position of low-income areas, which, on the average, represented less than 10% of urban populations. By 1972 adopted federal policy continued to represent a limited attention to poverty areas or to their complex network of social as well as housing problems. But although the effort remained modest by comparison with the thrust of other federal programs, it did persist as a beachhead of federal policy far beyond that of previous years.

The impact of the national policy in this decade of strong effort and altered priority making has been summarized by Frieden and Kaplan.[7] These analysts conclude that dramatic improvements in living conditions did not take place through Model Cities largely because only a small share of all urban aid was devoted to Model Cities and there was a low level of overall national commitment to the cities over the decade. The 6 million residents receiving grants in the final round of Model Cities programs received proportionately less than other populations in urban areas benefiting from other federal housing programs.

One other conclusion can be drawn from the Model Cities experiment that has importance if one wishes to consider the public policy role of the federal government. Local governments, even where they vigorously supported Model Cities planning, had great difficulty in actually securing and spending much increased sums on improving the conditions in their Model Cities areas in the time available. This raises the question of whether cities can spend federal funds effectively on the problems of poverty areas, given the modest scale of this experimental approach. Roland Warren found that

the agencies concerned themselves with Model Cities principally for two related purposes: to prevent any threat to their own domains and their own viability and, where possible, to benefit from the program by increasing their budgets or enlarging their domains.... if we had been serious about it, we would have needed a budget at least four times as large.[8]

Frieden and Kaplan state that

no simple conclusion can be reached about the ability of cities to spend federal funds effectively. Large numbers of them applied to participate in the Model

[7] Bernard Frieden and Marshall Kaplan, *The Politics of Neglect: Urban Aid from Model Cities to Revenue Sharing* (Cambridge, Mass.: MIT Press, 1975).

[8] Roland Warren, "The Model Cities Program, An Assessment," in *The Social Welfare Forum, 1971* (New York: Columbia University Press, 1971), pp. 153–154.

Cities program; both their plans and their planning arrangements were consistent with the purposes of the program. Along the way, the mayors endured many local controversies with citizen groups and undoubtedly paid a political price for their support of the program . . . but their commitment was slow to produce tangible results. The cities, like the federal government, and partly because of the federal government could not reorient their own agencies quickly enough.[9]

Assessment of Federal Policy

The lesson is a sobering one. Once housing programs are institutionalized in any agency structure, be it governmental or voluntary, the process of changing the direction and thrust of those programs and agencies is slow and difficult to bring about. It apparently requires a significant, directed effort conducted over several years and with more substantial resources than are usually committed to assure that policy aims move programs and governments in new directions.

It is difficult to make a final assessment about the effects of federal policy, given the characteristics thus described. If one takes as a measure the removal of substandard housing—meaning housing with measurable overcrowding, without running water, and with measurable fire hazard—it can be said that federal policy has reduced, but not eliminated, the volume of substandard housing for both white and minority populations.

A somewhat more rigorous and socially oriented measure would include not only housing condition and overcrowding but the ability of the occupants to afford adequate units. Such a measure is one of the interesting and significant examples of a social measurement that results from examining the crossover relationship between several human activities—in this case, physical housing, family income, and the economy. By this measure, in 1970 there were at least 13 million housing-poor households in the United States. Of this total, 6.9 million households lived in physically inadequate units, and an additional 6.2 million were living either in housing of excessive cost in relation to income or of inadequate size.[10]

Have conditions changed against such an enlarged framework? A clear answer is not possible. According to the 1960 census, 8.5 million families were living in substandard (meaning dilapidated) housing and an additional 6.1 million were living in overcrowded conditions, but it is not known how much overlap (meaning families living in both overcrowded and sub-

---

[9] Frieden and Kaplan, *Politics of Neglect*, p. 230.

[10] David Birch et al., *America's Housing Needs 1970–1980* (Cambridge, Mass.: Joint Center for Urban Studies, MIT-Harvard University, 1973).

standard housing) there was. If we were to limit ourselves to dilapidated housing conditions alone, it would appear that there has been more change as a result of all the programs now at work, from 8.5 million in 1960 to 6.9 million in 1970, as estimated by a report of the Joint Center for Urban Studies at MIT and Harvard University. Over a longer time span, 1940–1977, housing inadequate because of plumbing or other major deficiencies declined from 49% of the total housing stock to 9%; deficiencies resulting from overcrowding, meaning more than one person to a room, declined from 20.2 to 4.4%.[11]

If one considers the larger issue of availability of adequate housing congruent with income, several categorical programs have been introduced and funded, but these are small in comparison with the much more significant federal intervention in housing to stimulate construction and financing for middle- and upper-income families, or to stimulate commercial and urban development. By way of illustration, in 1979 all mortgage and loan support by federal agencies (home mortgage loans and guarantees, project mortgage support, and home improvement aid) totaled $22.8 billion. This supported and stimulated commercial and residential housing for populations able to repay loans. This has grown, cumulatively, from $4.4 billion in 1950, doubling each decade. By contrast, in 1979, $3.65 million in block grants for community development yielded only 1.1% for rehabilitation of public residential property, reflecting the priorities of local planning, which emphasized facility construction (waste removal, water supply, roads, etc.). Under an urban development program, $385 million produced 27,531 housing units in 1979, of which 14,483 were identified for low-income families. Under Section 203 of the Housing Act, 3.3% of funds for construction of single-family homes went to families with incomes under $15,000 a year, a dramatic drop from 94.7% in 1960. Under Section 236 of the same act, 56,487 single-family homes were financed for families with incomes under $15,000, the median income being $6885. Rent supplements for families with incomes under $10,000 went to 18,260 units. And in 1979, 44,019 low-income public housing units became available for occupancy, many of them limited to the elderly.[12]

Up to 1980, federal policy has been to stimulate the private housing market but also to intervene in a minor way through a variety of specialized programs to help people who are too poor to benefit from general housing opportunities. The array of such socially directed programs is sometimes confusing: mortgage help for specified low-income owners, mortgage help

[11] *U.S. Statistical Abstract, 1981*, Table 1378 (Washington, D.C.: U.S. Government Printing Office, 1981).
[12] U.S. Department of Housing and Urban Development, *1979 Statistical Yearbook* (Washington, D.C.: U.S. Government Printing Office, 1979).

to builders to produce for a low-income market, rental subsidies to either investors or individual renters, construction aid for housing for low-income elderly, and help for low-income public housing. Since 1980, funding for such targeted purposes has been reduced and the housing construction industry has been in a deep decline: Housing starts declined by 16.6% in 1960, 2.1% in 1970, and 25.4% in 1980. Meantime, the population has continued to grow, slowly; more families are forming; and more individuals continue to establish independent homes rather than doubling up with relatives. Vacancy rates in rental housing dropped from 6% in 1975 to 5% in 1978, recovering marginally to 5.4% in 1980.[13] These trends, along with 10% unemployment in the early 1980s, created housing pressures that outstripped the relatively minor, if well intended, efforts to use federal action to relieve that pressure. The marketplace has not effectively responded to these pressures.[14]

Up to 1980, there was confidence that national understanding of a social problem such as lack of adequate housing for all citizens would lead in time, and with experimentation, to constantly improved national social policies and even to new directions. But whatever the details of the longtime trend, it is at least clear that the reduction in substandard housing has proceeded very slowly indeed.

The introduction of the concept that excessive rental or home purchase charges constitute a factor in defining substandard housing shifts the possible direction of public policy in a completely new direction. It is doubtful whether regulation and incentive to private suppliers of public housing will alone be sufficient to overcome this aspect of deprivation. But will our underlying societal policy norms permit an extension of federal responsibility to this extent? There has been reasonable support for the idea that the federal government should in some way participate in reducing the volume of substandard housing measured in physical terms. The chosen instrument has been the private marketplace, which has functioned slowly, with subsidy, to accomplish the end desired. Regulation seems to be moderately useful, but its effect has been to increase the cost of housing, when added to other inflationary tendencies. The broader definition of deprivation led the federal government to income distribution as much as to housing policy. Traditionally, if a population is considered at a serious disadvantage, there is support for federal intervention. But the point has not yet been reached where a strong federal attack on substandard housing as more broadly defined is supported. The enlargement of mortgage support, with the concomitant legislative difficulty in securing support for additional public pro-

---

[13] U.S. Statistical Abstract.
[14] See Frieden and Kaplan, David Birch op. cit.

grams that can attack the other dimensions of deprivation and housing, would suggest that the time is not yet ripe.

The outlook, though, is not all bad. Some smaller-scale areas of social policy have begun to emerge so that the outlook may not be entirely bleak regarding federal responsibility for the social dimension of housing. What follows below may be said to represent the 1975 inventory of federal aid. These programs continued to grow until 1980, not only in dollar value but in variety, so that the tools that can ultimately be used to shape federal social policy in housing are probably stronger than ever before. The programs are still in place and what is lacking is a sense of direction to be given this variety of programs from the standpoint of federal policy. Adequate financing depends on a shift in federal policy to focus on assurance of housing specifically for those with low income or incomes too low for an inflated housing market with high interest rates.

Provision of Income to the Poor

Public assistance may be said to be one of the largest underwriters of substandard housing in the country, because the level of public assistance is usually so low that families can afford only the lowest level of housing adequacy. Federal income policy as previously discussed has been made more uniform through Supplementary Security Income programs, at least for the elderly, the blind, and the disabled, and the executive branch continues to search for the means to reform income maintenance on behalf of other populations (families with dependent children and the unemployed). Federal and state reduction in financing for AFDC or erosion of AFDC income by price inflation (in the absence of regular indexing) since the middle 1970s has exacerbated the housing dilemmas of single-parent families, which include some 10 million minor children.

The federal government has instituted some pilot programs to experiment in the use of direct cash subsidies for housing expenses. Such subsidy programs provide eligible families with supplementary payments usable only for housing to guarantee that their private payment for housing out of earned income does not exceed 25% of total income. Presumably, this addition to the income of low-income families who are forced to compete in a high rental market gives them more access to better housing. In 1975 these housing allowances were extended experimentally to 24,000 families; $160 million were authorized.[15]

---

[15] *Experimental Housing Allowance Program: Initial Observations* (Washington, D.C.: U.S. Department of Housing and Urban Development, 1975).

General Revenue Sharing

This program can be used by local governments to supplement housing income for poor families, to mount other programs to reduce the cost of housing to the poor, to improve the conditions of housing stock through direct public programs or through the stimulation of local low-cost construction, or to reduce tax burdens. Such action requires pressure from local citizens to alter the priorities governing use of this federal income. Revenue shared dollars rose from $6.9 billion in 1974 to $9.6 billion in 1978 but fell to $6.8 billion in 1981 as a result of new federal decisions to reduce the scale of federal involvement in social programs.

Block Grants for Community Development

Special-purpose revenue sharing for community development programs could encompass Model Cities, urban renewal, and grants for water and sewer projects, open space, beautification, neighborhood facilities, and housing rehabilitation. Whether or not a consolidated grant program to local governments, without the constraints of numerous federal categories, would be directed toward low-income populations or to especially troublesome social needs remains to be tested. Such a special revenue program introduces predictable future income so that long-term planning can be done. However, the level of funding in 1975 was only the level of current expenditures, which means that available funds are eroded annually as inflation proceeds. Such specialized revenue sharing is intended to concentrate on metropolitan areas (central cities and others with a population of 50,000 or more) and some urban counties, rather than being spread across all 38,000 units of state and local governments. Since the formula proposed for distribution would take into account population, overcrowding, and poverty, the cities in greatest need might be expected to secure proportionately larger funds, whereas others ranking lower on these criteria might receive less.

The Housing and Community Development Act of 1974 makes a modest start along these lines.[16] But in 1977 the formula for allocating $2.5 billion in appropriated funds was already sharply challenged. Older cities with severe blight and unemployment were getting reduced allocations under a formula intended to help the economically depressed areas, while more affluent suburban and southwestern cities were getting increased allocations. A mechanical economic formula has not yet been fine tuned sufficiently to fit local problems.

The major effect of block grants, aside from the fiscal relief given to

[16] See William Frej and H. Specht, "Analysis of the Housing and Community Development Act of 1974," *Social Service Review* 50, no. 2 (June 1976): 275–292.

localities, is to shift policy action from Washington to state and local govern-ments. It is at those levels that the rules are shaped that decide the purposes to which block grant dollars will be put and the populations that will benefit. Welfare advocates are not as well equipped to play an active role at these lo-cal levels as they have been at the national level.

Continuation of Categorical Programs

If special revenue sharing for community development is not enlarged and extended, the preexisting categorical programs would undoubtedly con-tinue: urban renewal, mortgage guarantee support, and the like. Among these are:

1. Mortgage construction support both for one- and two-family hous-ing and for apartment housing
2. Subsidized mortgage arrangements so that interest paid on mort-gages is reduced
3. Turnkey programs whereby contracts are entered into with private contractors to construct housing according to public specifications spelled out in contracts that, when completed, are purchased by lo-cal governments and rented to families eligible for public housing; these have led to the construction of somewhat smaller housing units
4. Sections of the Housing and Urban Development Act that reduce the interest families pay on mortgage loans insured by the Federal Housing Authority or that provide subsidy to the mortgage holder, who in turn will be enabled to charge lower rentals and still operate the property profitably; in 1969 a total of only 38,000 families re-ceived assistance through one of these means
5. The National Housing Act, which provides very modest levels of financial assistance to such nonprofit corporations as labor unions, churches, and fraternal associations that seek to construct low-cost housing on a nonprofit basis; this operates through interest-free loans and technical assistance
6. The National Housing Corporation, a consortium of industrial and financial companies, which raises seed money through selling its stock to corporations

A result of economic recession and the 1980 elections was the New Towns or experimental cities legislation. Incentive funds were temporarily allocated to stimulate developers to design and build new towns. A few New Towns have actually been constructed in part, and others are still struggling to find economic viability. One of the major aims of these New Towns pro-grams has been to test the kinds of living environments possible with the application of modern technology. Incidentally, they also test the feasibility of thinning out urban concentrations through planned construction of new environments outside or on the periphery of large metropolitan areas. The New Towns legislation provided minimal federal support to private developers' experimentation in creating better comprehensive environments for living that go beyond the simple construction of housing units. New cities presumably are planned to take into account the social, cultural, educational, and health along with the population and housing requirements of the resident populations. Unfortunately, the discontinuity in support for this program, economic stagnation, decline in the building industry, inflation, and political competition brought this effort at large-scale urban planning to an end by 1980.

It would appear from the foregoing review that federal policy has remained within the constraints of social norms with one vital exception: the extension of government into actions that affect housing for all income classes, not only the poor. The extensiveness and breadth of federal involvement has now become sufficiently great for it to be difficult to visualize any retreat. The goal of social policy concerning the poor is still very limited and concentrated on improving the physical environmental conditions, but supplementary efforts to support beautification, to improve air and water standards, and to alter densities are all moves in the direction of wider social responsibility by federal action. The worst that can be said of the nominal steps taken thus far is that they are just that: They represent tentative probes and experiments with continuity, but limited financial support. They fail to remedy the market's inability to produce low-cost housing. Nonetheless, they represent steps in a clear direction.

Residential Segregation

In one respect, it can be said that the federal government has become significantly enmeshed in an almost completely social aspect—that of a housing mix. Federal intervention in housing has generally moved along the paths of market preference, which appear to have followed the constant mobility of populations and the self-segregation by economic class and racial preferences. But marketplace preferences and national policy have encountered another national policy, one enforced by federal court decisions and congressional civil rights legislation. Together, these give the federal government the instruments for modifying the natural distribution of populations in the market. Model Cities represented a small attempt to redistribute the federal effort in favor of low-income groups in cities that are heavily dominated by the dilemmas of racial minorities. Civil rights legislation and court decisions impinge upon state and local tradition and law, undermining land-use policies that discriminate against racial minorities and discourage their moving into hitherto white communities.

Finally, a continuing demand for attention to the social needs attached to housing—recreational space, beautification, reduction of congestion, and access to health, shopping, and social services—suggests that federal support is present to assure the presence of these amenities that were once considered privileges and are rapidly becoming matters of necessity. In the late 1970s, environmental pollution became so explosive an issue that a new federal agency was established, shifting some federal interest in the environment from the socioeconomic aspects of housing to physical aspects of environment.

Issues Concerning Age, Race, and Economic Class

If one moves beyond these components of social policy, other considerations emerge. An achievable aspect of federal social policy can be seen in the field of aging. A long accumulation of behavioral studies indicate that the elderly prefer to maintain their own housing, but in close proximity to families; that they seek relatively safe neighborhoods; that they require easy access to health, shopping, and social services; that their morale is improved when there is some concentration of the elderly so that shared interests can be mutually reinforcing, but that they do not like age-segregated housing. Rosow and others have indicated the rich supply of mutual aid and support that the elderly give each other when they live near their peers but also in a viable environment with other age groups as well.[17] Certain kinds of federally supported programs for housing provide that at least 5% of the constructed units be available and suitable for the elderly, but if these 5% are not subscribed to, other uses are usually sanctioned. There is nothing in present public policy that consistently uses such federal housing support to stimulate actively the construction of housing environments based upon this principle. Initiative is left to local sponsors. Federal support for the construction of special units for the aged has thus dealt with half of the policy potential—that of providing incentive for clusters of housing occupied solely by the elderly. Whether these units have appropriate access to other populations and to services has not been thoroughly investigated.

Modest federal support for the construction of service facilities, space for recreation, and the tentative explorations through new cities also represents a nascent federal concern with the wider environment that is being created. But this remains consistently at the level of experiments without strong federal support or direction. The shaping of environments remains, on the whole, in the hands of local and state governments through city planning and urban-use legislation or regulation. Federal policies on healthy en-

---

[17] Irving Rosow, *Social Integration of the Aged* (New York: Free Press, 1967).

vironments—defined to mean air, water, and sewage predominantly—deal with growth but not the social aspects of the environment. Nonetheless, the activities resulting from these federal interests represent the development of tools that might be used systematically under the guidance of policies to influence the environments in which populations live.

Perhaps the most powerful issue that demands the attention of social policy now and in the near future is race relations. Many neighborhoods are relatively homogeneous in race or economic class as a result of tradition and history. Should these neighborhoods be systematically altered in order to bring about more heterogeneous neighborhoods and communities? Thus far, tools to alter the present balance or mix of populations have been made available to minority groups through civil rights legislation and occasional housing regulations. The most powerful of these may prove to be the school desegregation orders of the courts, with their consequent testing of forced busing as an instrument of change.

However, it cannot be said that a systematic national policy has yet emerged committing the national government to strong positive action for one or the other policy—homogeneous or heterogeneous neighborhoods and communities. Many federal programs are contradictory or act at cross-purposes.

The adoption of a clear policy in this troublesome area is made especially difficult and unlikely because of the conflicting views held by segments of the American population. Various studies of populations' preferences indicate that few consistent agreements can be found among consumers of housing, although their behavior does fall into certain rough patterns.[18] Some minorities seek to remain in homogeneous communities, while others prefer to move outward into areas populated by different groups. Some persons prefer apartment living in high-density areas of the cities, while others prefer open space. All income and racial groups have the same basic concept of what they want in housing—it should be decent and comfortable—but the definition of decent and comfortable varies in our large and diversified population, not by race, but by culture and income.

Minimalist Government and the 1980s

By 1980 the effects of federal housing policies became clear. The dominating role of marketplace construction and housing supply, along with minor

---

[18] Birch et al., *America's Housing Needs;* William Michaelson, "Social Adjustment to the Environment," in *Encyclopedia of Social Work,* 16th ed. (New York: National Association of Social Workers, 1971), pp. 291 ff.

public programs to rectify disparities in housing, solidified the pattern of housing in most communities. Private production of housing fluctuated widely as economic conditions in general, and those in the housing industry in particular, rose and fell. In 1974 the housing slump was the most severe since 1940, exceeding those of 1960, 1964, 1966, and 1969. Rising interest rates proved disastrous to housing, and in the 1980s, the slump was greater than ever. Such housing as was built was either for the affluent, as the cost of a new home rose dramatically, or, in a limited way, for the elderly, where subsidized housing still produced some units offered at low rental. Subsidized housing, which produced over a fifth of U.S. construction in 1970–1971, almost disappeared as the federal program was phased down.

Federal policy affected housing through fiscal and tax effort. The mortgage loan market continues to be controlled through management of interest rates, and the attempts to control inflation led to such high interest rates that housing continued to decline. On the other hand, families that could afford to purchase homes benefited by generous indirect subsidies through income tax deductions. In 1974 these subsidies amounted to $9.7 billion, and an additional $2 billion annually went to investors in housing construction.[19]

In addition to inflation, such factors as energy and oil shortages, the reduction in the size of families, and the increase in single-person households and in employment of married women altered the pattern of urban living. Condominiums became a popular housing choice in the 1980s, but for a middle and upper-middle class. Rental housing in major cities converted to condominiums, reducing the volume of accommodations available for low-income families; the drop in housing vacancy rates proved disastrous for these families in many cities. In some areas, prebuilt mobile homes became the major housing resource.

Racial minorities began to move into the suburbs, but at a slow rate, and usually these were middle-class, successful families able to overcome traditional hostilities. Between 1970 and 1980 the proportion of minority citizens living in suburban areas rose from 12.3% to 24.6% and declined in central cities from 56.5% to 54%.[20]

The result of such basic changes in society and the private market orientation of federal policy produced a situation in which, by 1982, middle-class families fared modestly well, at a rising cost for shelter, while poor families found themselves in the most difficult circumstances since the depression years.

[19] U.S. Department of Housing and Urban Development.
[20] Statistical Abstract of the U.S. 1982–83 (Washington, D.C.: U.S. Bureau of the Census, Statistical Abstract 1982–83), Table 24, p. 21.

The Future of Federal Involvement

Given such trends, the most that can be expected of federal policy in housing
is a future renewal of programs directed at specific and specialized problems—construction of neighborhood facilities, housing renovation, special
subsidy for housing expenses for low-income families—and some policies
designed to limit the most extreme arbitrary segregation in local actions. It
can be expected that the development of new environments will proceed as
a result of innumerable local decisions, rather than under the direction of
national policy. Property developers, both national and local, are likely to
dominate policy at the local level for some time to come, although the 1983
city elections revealed a new vitality for neighborhood citizen action groups,
which may be able to direct more attention to neighborhood housing rather
than to commercial center-city growth.

Confusion in the development of clear-cut federal policies, other than
along the dimensions already outlined, can be explained in part by the displacement of earlier views about the power of desirable environments. At
the turn of the century, there was a widespread belief that changing the
physical environment would improve people's lives. Subsequent experience
showed that the intended effects were not secured. Concentration on
physical housing did not necessarily improve either home or neighborhood
environments, or at least not for very long. The replacement of dilapidated
housing frequently resulted in less spacious units and an even greater population density. The historic accumulation of neighborhood informal reinforcing services were frequently destroyed, and new forms of construction
and building did not provide replacements except at a great cost and from a
distance.

It has been established that changes in the physical environment produce improvement in the quality of the lives of the poor only when grossly
substandard housing is replaced by constructions with reasonably good
standards. As a result, the belief has emerged that social surroundings are
more important than housing in what determines the lives of human beings.
In the 1960s race and poverty were major social issues, while housing was
less of an issue. However, whatever conclusions are reached about the best,
ultimate solution, the existence now of substandard housing and the concentration of racial minorities in that housing must be confronted, so the
two views are still in conflict.

For a time, the Green Belt prospect and open housing (defined as small
concentrations and small densities in suburbia) have also proven to be less
than completely satisfactory. Suburban expansion has provided an opportunity for physical innovation and population mobility, but families by and
large have been found to bring with them their inherited cultural patterns,
simply transplanting them to a new physical environment.

None of this is to argue that the physical environment is unimportant, but the nexus of socioeconomic relationships is now at the center of public concern. However, we must still deal with the physical fact of substandard housing; we must still confront the issue of concentration or segregation of racial and economic groups; and we must accept that we still know little about the intricate workings of social relationships. These factors make it extremely difficult to plan national policies in much detail, except at the rather primitive levels we have discussed thus far.

The following issues can be identified as governing exploration and search for federal policies in the future.

High-Density Concentration

Given the historic development of population distribution and the urban base of our economic system, it seems unlikely that high-density concentration of residences will thin out.[21] Crowding in densities at some level does have undesirable consequences, but individuals and groups differ widely in how they balance the disadvantages against what they feel is desirable. The demands of available space and the economics of housing construction have stimulated high-rise apartment living in urban areas. The high costs of transportation, water, and sewerage over a large area have encouraged the recent emergence of high-rise apartment house construction even in suburban areas once considered to be the primary domain of single residences. While many families have difficulties with high-rise living, many seem to prefer it because of the ease of access to urban resources, the security, or other social and practical amenities that are provided. It is possible that over time high-rise living may be found most acceptable for young families and those at the beginning of their careers, for single persons, and for the elderly, but this has not yet been established as a basis of policy.

Elimination of Slums

The issue of renovation of dilapidated housing and elimination of slums has not been resolved. There is accumulating evidence that some persons prefer to stay in what was once considered a slum area, provided the quality of the housing there can be upgraded. Improving housing and amenities in such areas seems to be a major frontier for continuing public policy. The Model Cities experiment represented a promising initiative at the level of federal government, but it did not receive sufficient support. Instead, major cities have revitalized their centers by using federal aid for commercial and luxury housing construction in an effort to raise the inner-city tax base. The

---

[21] Michelson, "Social Adjustment."

justification has been that such a tax base increase is essential if cities are to do more for citizen housing, education, and social welfare.

Integration of Social and Ethnic Classes

Public actions to date have by and large served to break up ethnic segregation but without positive steps to limit the reestablishment of homogeneous communities by suburban land use control and urban development procedures. Even less tested are housing actions to promote a mix of social and economic classes living in the same neighborhood. The growth of a middle class among black and Hispanic minorities, slow as it has been, may one day break down residential segregation, but economic and civil rights policy will influence this evolution more than will housing policy.

Integration of Age Groups

The progressive aging of the American population produces the need for some ultimate attention to the pattern of living to be provided for the elderly. For those who are physically vigorous, the varieties of cultural and economic choices already alluded to probably preclude a systematic national policy in favor of any particular pattern. However, when enfeeblement sets in, the social issues become dominant. Shall the public thrust be in the direction of institutionalization (as discussed in the chapter on health) or toward the production of supportive services to enable the elderly to remain in private residences? And what kind of private residences? As will be discussed in Chapter 7, it is likely that public policy will in time settle down to a clearcut direction regarding this subgroup of the elderly population. But for all the others, it can be assumed that the federal government's action will be to permit the market of choices to determine the nature of relationships ultimately to be established.

Minimalist Government and Housing

The 1980 elections reversed the previous 50 years' acceptance of a major role for the national government in shaping the housing of Americans. In its place, the idea of a minimalist role for government has been substituted. Although the working out of such a policy approach is still uncertain—political shifts may intervene—a few clues have appeared. For welfare, the most significant is the retreat of the federal government from a focused concern for the poor. The budget proposed for 1984 cuts money for assisted housing from $26 billion, the 1980 figure, to $10 billion, and the proportion of income the poor must allocate to housing is planned to rise from 25 to 30% of total income before eligibility for any housing assistance is established. Efforts to target programs to these populations have remained minor, funded in minor ways. At the same time, federal support for across-the-board housing has continued to increase through mortgage support. The basic policy thrust of successive administrations has been to encourage housing for all, letting the poor benefit from an overall increase in housing stock. The able-bodied poor are left to take their chances in the marketplace, but housing for one sector, the aged, has been supported. The effect has been to move policy choice back to state and local governments, where decisions are made about the purposes to which community development funds will be put.

Additional Readings

Aaron, Henry J. *Shelter Subsidies: Who Benefits from Federal Housing Policies.* Washington, D.C.: Brookings Institution, 1972.
Fisher, Robert. *Twenty Years of Public Housing.* New York: Harper & Row, 1959.
Frieden, Bernard. *Metropolitan America: Challenge to Federalism.* Washington, D.C.: Advisory Commission on Intergovernmental Relations, 1966.
Frieden, Bernard, and Kaplan, Marshall. *The Politics of Neglect.* Cambridge, Mass.: MIT Press, 1975.
Gorham, William, and Glazer, Nathan. *The Urban Predicament.* Washington, D.C.: Urban Institute, 1976.
Grigsby, William G., and Rosenburg, Louis. *Urban Housing Policy.* New York: APS Publications, 1975.
Stegman, Michael. *Housing and Economics: The American Dilemma.* Cambridge, Mass.: MIT Press, 1971.

Toward a Personal Social Services System

The Unplanned Emergence of a Federal Policy

6

Thus far, we have been considering examples of the developments in federal social policy that are within the commonly accepted view of what constitutes social welfare—income, housing, and health. But ever since the 1930s, a little publicized but persistent evolution has taken place to broaden the conception of what constitutes social welfare as an appropriate area of federal responsibility.

Dimensions of Personal Social Services

Public policy actions in social welfare were traditionally concerned with the provision of minimum income; the guaranteed access to health, housing, and educational services; and the management of a correctional system. This view of what is subsumed under the general heading of social welfare was enlarged in 1920 with the enactment of the first Vocational Rehabilitation Act. The act was initially seen as an adjunct to the existing educational and medical services to fill the recognized gap in social provision for military personnel. Vocational training programs to equip manpower for economic careers were seized upon as a foundation for the development of special services for those disabled either in industry or in military service. In the succeeding 50 years, rehabilitation grew until it assumed a minor but established place in the spectrum of welfare services. A federal bureau was established; a network of relationships between federal, state, local, and private organizations was formed; a new profession of vocational counseling developed; and annual funding was assured year by year, rising in 1975 to over $750 million per year. Following World War II, the concept of rehabilitation was broadened significantly by an expansion of medical rehabilitation technology that added to the established vocational medical procedures for the physiological and psychological restoration of function.

While this evolution was taking place, a more subtle evolution also occurred, involving an area of welfare activity ambiguously identified as the social services or social work. In the following pages, the phrase *personal social service* will be used in place of the common but confusing terms *social work* (as a profession of counseling) and *social service* (as a basic and established set of programs).

This new profession gradually assumed a dual position. Social workers were employed in all the other social programs. In addition to other, more tangible tasks noted below, they performed a variety of counseling and guidance functions to help individuals deal with troublesome situations. This evolution can in part be traced back to the historical view that individuals who cannot manage their income, health, housing, and educational needs independently are somehow weaker than the average person and require specialists' assistance.

This concept of a social service adds a new area to the conventional welfare responsibilities we have discussed—income maintenance and the provision of health, housing, education, corrections, and (later) rehabilitation. These have been the publicly underwritten areas of modern life that require governmental sanction and support and that are addressed to the needs of individuals, especially individuals who require some special attention in the interests of equity and public conscience.

In this chapter, two aspects will be explored: (1) the evolution of a policy about personal social services; and (2) the evolution of an integrative policy about the "basic" services.

In England, where income, health, housing, and education had long been taken to represent the social services, a fifth social service of equal stature was added, known as "personal social services." One function of the personal social services was to provide and manage a residue of concrete services that special groups required but that were not conventionally provided by the older social programs. Examples are (1) the provision of day care for children of working mothers or of single-parent families (where the head of the family must work while minor children are left at home); (2) the provision of homemaker services in cases of either long- or short-term illness or disability; (3) the management of day-care programs for isolated or disadvantaged persons; (4) the management of intersystem information and referral activities that would link together several programs for individuals with multiple requirements or reduce the overlap of functions among services.

A second function was to provide psychological counseling. The anxieties, ambiguities, and distresses of modern urban life were perceived as being great enough to require a publicly supported counseling service to help individuals cope more satisfactorily with them.

In addition, the rigidities of such other basic services as income, housing, and health became severe as they involved larger and larger bureaucracies, so that an external and independent advocate on behalf of disadvantaged groups became increasingly necessary. The personal social services assumed this advocacy function to alter or moderate the rigidities of the basic systems so that they would be more responsive to individual needs.

As social workers pursued these functions, it began to be felt that, not only the disadvantaged, but all citizens might need or benefit from the services. For examples, all families might benefit from access to day-care facilities and all children might benefit from the preschool experience. Thus, the concept of special services for special groups has been broadened to the view that all families should have access to the personal social services, much as they do to education.

Despite these uncertainties as to what the personal social services really consist of, there has been a fairly consistent evolution in federal programs that take on the character of a federal policy. Defined one way, this evolving policy has been a federal determination to work continuously on the reorganization and rationalization of the complex of public activities loosely defined as the "basic social services." This policy of rationalizing established public functions has required either the creation of a personal social services system (as the fifth basic social service) or a more effective distribution through all the basic systems of administrative and professional social workers. The evolution of this policy, if it is one, toward welfare rationalization illustrates the unwitting emergence of policy without a firm conceptual basis of the subject matter to be affected. Is the policy to be one of integrating well-established social systems? Is it to be the creation of a new personal social service system to join the others? Or is it to be the federal underwriting of an emerging profession, as in the case of vocational rehabilitation, to staff service systems?

The course of evolution has been one of constant change. The dimensions of the public action and its purposes have both been modified with amazing frequency. Sometimes it has appeared that the policy has been one of strengthening family life, and at other times, it has reflected a sole preoccupation with the reduction of relief dependency.

Evolution of a Personal Social Services Policy

Expanded Concept of Social Welfare: 1935–1972

The roots of this development can be identified as early as the 1930s, when the federal government first entered into the area of economic security of persons through emergency relief legislation. Several of the emergency relief programs, intended solely to give economic means of subsistence, also provided small units of specially trained social workers to deal with social problems on a case and clinical basis. Part of the motivation was to help especially troubled individuals to surmount economic dependence, but another part of the motivation was the pioneering development of a tax-supported, personal service counseling program to give help beyond economic support to individuals with a variety of personal difficulties.

In the years following the enactment of the Social Security Act, the Bureau of Public Assistance incorporated the antecedent private charitable beliefs that social workers were needed in the administration of public assistance programs to identify individual family variation in requirements, to formulate a plan of action, and to carry through that plan of action. These functions were for many years tied to the administration of relief payments.

In 1956, however, following long, persistent encouragement from the Social Security Administration, the Congress finally amended the Social Security Act to give statutory recognition to the provision of social services to families on relief. Social services were for the first time defined as something different from the administration of relief payments themselves, at least with respect to an adopted federal policy. In the initial years, the federal government undertook to match local funds for the payment for these social services. This represented the federal government's first statutory acceptance of the idea that a personal social service beyond income provision merited federal support.

In 1962 the federal share was increased from 50 to 75% in order to stimulate the states to develop such services more rapidly. The objective of these amendments was to reorient the cash transfer program to one that also stressed the rehabilitation of persons on relief. In a new departure, the staff was also to be used to prevent other vulnerable persons threatened with financial instability from becoming economically dependent. Unmarried parents, deserted families, families with adults potentially able to support themselves but currently not doing so, children with special problems, and the aged or disabled were cited as categories of persons justifying the attention of these newly sanctioned services. They were intended to help parents, improve home conditions, assume wider responsibility for the guidance of their children, and improve the management of their financial resources. As a token of this shift in emphasis, the Bureau of Public Assistance was renamed the Bureau of Family Services.

This broadly gauged program did not develop very rapidly. In 1967 the structure of the Department of Health, Education, and Welfare (HEW) was modified. Public assistance rolls and claimants were increasing rapidly despite the preventive promises of the 1962 amendments. The personal social services responsibilities already identified were separated from the administration of income maintenance programs. They were redistributed to a variety of other bureaus within HEW, including the Administration on Aging, the Rehabilitation Services Administration, and the Children's Bureau. These three were bound together for coordination and management purposes in an overriding Social and Rehabilitation Service.

Meanwhile, the reorganization in large part under pressure from the Congress, introduced a new work incentive program that shifted the emphasis of the personal social services away from prevention and toward a concentrated effort to move dependent families off the relief rolls. A great deal of staff effort was redirected toward the procurement of job retraining services, and funds were mandated for the provision of day-care services for the children of working mothers in single-parent families. At this time, although the bulk of the personal social services was directed to persons on relief and could thus be considered simply as a part of the administration of an income maintenance program, the day-care services were legally extended to families in certain geographic areas that included families of low income in danger of becoming economically dependent, even though they were not yet on relief.

The separation of the personal social services from income maintenance signaled a major departure in public policy in the direction of a public service program unconnected with economic dependency. In the past, economic dependency was assumed to have some association with personal deficiency or weakness on the part of recipients, but in the new conception, income maintenance was assumed to be a consequence of defects in the economic order and entitlement a matter of right not requiring any specialized professional administration. Where relief recipients had personal problems requiring attention, these might be provided under public auspices, since these families presumably could not purchase relevant counseling services from other sources.

This evolution, however, required some attention to the definition of boundaries for the new personal social services. One report of the secretary of HEW defined these services simply as "those human services rendered to individuals and families under societal auspices."[1] It was assumed that health, education, housing, and income maintenance served the general public as people sought self-development, whereas the social services were

[1] Jack Wedemeyer, *Policy Issues in Service Delivery* (Sacramento: Sacramento State College, 1969).

identified as those needed by people with limitations and handicaps so severe that they could not maintain their independence without some supplemental assistance.

Unfortunately, the ambiguity about boundary and definition was not resolved, and by 1968 the boundaries as defined made it difficult to separate the personal social services from the other agencies with the same generalized goals as those embodied in public assistance.[2] These goals are the three *P*'s: preparation (giving hard services to cope with such obstacles as day care and homemaking), participation (organizing consumers to express needs), and protection (the maintenance of equity).

This formulation still left the conception of the new approach mired in goals that were also adopted by other major or basic public programs. Administrative attempts to clear up ambiguities about the program continued until in 1971 the Community Services Administration of HEW produced the GOSS formula: goal-oriented social services. It proposed as the objective of the new services a decreased state of dependency for the individual on a scale that would (1) reduce the need for full institutional care; (2) provide community-based care as an alternative (halfway houses, etc.); (3) encourage the assumption of responsibility for care by the natural family; and (4) encourage maintenance of full independent status without public support. This emphasis was not only on a reduction in economic dependency but on an enhancement of independent self-care on a progressive scale, which was a major turning point in the evolution of federal policy.

The evolution of a program of personal social services can be traced in the volume of federal grants for such purposes. Following the 1962 amendments to the Social Security Act, federal social service expenditures grew between 1963 and 1982 from $194 million to $3.091 billion (see Tables 6.1 and 6.2).[3]

These funds were distributed over a wide range of service activities. The most significant were child foster care, 57%; child care, 16%; homemaker services, 6%; child protection, 5%; employment and training, 8%. Smaller amounts were assigned to support such other services as adoption, information and referral, strengthening family functioning, family planning, housing, health, and protection of adults.

---

[2] See Martin Rein, "Social Services and Economic Independence," in *The Planning and Delivery of Social Services* (Washington, D.C.: National League of Cities, 1969).

[3] See Social and Rehabilitation Service, Office of Financial Management Reports as cited in Paul Mott, *Meeting Human Needs: The Social and Political History of Title XX* (Columbus, Ohio: National Conference on Social Welfare, 1976). Much of the material for this chapter has been drawn from this text. For 1982, see *U.S. Budget, Fiscal Year 1982*, Department of Health and Human Services, IK–67.

TABLE 6.1
Federal Grants for Social Services, 1963–1972, Pre-Title XX[a]

Year	Total Expenditures (dollars)
1963	194,000,000
1964	254,400,000
1965	295,140,000
1966	359,165,000
1967	281,589,000
1968	346,654,000
1969	354,491,000
1970	522,500,000
1971	692,433,000
1972	1,598,215,000
1980	2,691,000,000[a]
1982	3,016,000,000[a]

[a]SOURCE: Social and Rehabilitation Service, Office of Financial Management Reports. Office of Management and Budget, Budget for the Fiscal Year 1982, Human Development Services I-K67 (Washington, D.C.).

Setbacks and Consolidation: 1972–1982

In 1972 the HEW program was confronted with a new Republican administration determined to slow the rate of increase in welfare programs. It had been expected that in 1972 the social services under the existing amendments would involve $4.7 billion of federal aid to the states in the form of matching grants on a 3 to 1 basis. The executive branch through the Office of Management and Budget (OMB) fixed a budgetary maximum of $2.5 billion for such funding. By administrative action, the open-ended program was capped.[4] The federal government's promise to match personal social service state programs without limitation was rescinded.

At this time, the national administration's effort to introduce a new approach to federal–state relationships led to a hope that the concepts of general revenue sharing could be extended and that the complex of federal categorical programs could be simplified by grouping several kinds of programs together in special revenue-sharing blocks. The hope was that this would not only give states and local governments more flexibility in how to utilize federal matching funds but also introduce savings in federal expenditures by reducing presumed overlapping and duplicatory expenditures presumed to exist among current categorical programs.

[4] For a revealing analysis of the dynamics in federal–state relationships that finally led to this limitation, see Martha Derthick, Uncontrollable Spending for the Social Services (Washington, D.C.: Brookings Institution, 1975).

By this means, the administration sought to retain a personal social services presence, while restricting the federal government's involvement. By a combination of administrative regulation and legislative amendment, a new title was finally added to the Social Security Act, Title XX, which provided the 1976 framework for federal support of personal social services. This statutory foundation was secured at the price of introducing an annual appropriation limitation on the amount of money available, but at the time it gave a reasonably firm foundation for continuing federal support to the evolution of a personal social services network.

An Independent or a Subsidiary Personal Social Service: Title XX

Title XX left unclear whether the personal social services commitment would be realized through the creation of an independent, publicly supported personal social services network or whether funds would simply be allocated to a variety of preexisting services (income maintenance, housing, mental health, etc.), each of which could acquire technical and professional personnel to perform functions within its own categorical boundaries.

In order to secure matching funds, states are required to develop plans for the social services but are relatively free to choose what services they wish to offer, where they wish to offer them, and by what means. Certain federal guidelines are proposed, and five acceptable goals are identified: (1) achieving economic self-support or reducing dependency; (2) achieving or maintaining self-sufficiency (as separate from or independent of economic self-support); (3) preventing or remedying neglect, abuse, or exploitation of children and adults unable to protect their own interests, or preserving, rehabilitating, and reuniting families; (4) preventing or reducing inappropriate institutional care by providing for community-based, home-based, or other forms of less intensive care; (5) securing referral or admission for institutional care when other forms are not appropriate and providing services to individuals in institutions.

Services considered appropriate for achieving these goals are not clearly defined, but choices are rooted in the antecedent federally supported programs for the elderly, the blind, the disabled, and children. At least one of the personal services must be provided for each of the goals, and at least three must be directed toward SSI recipients.

At least half of the federal funds must be directed toward recipients of public assistance, SSI, or Medicaid. Certain undertakings are not eligible for federal funding, including medical or remedial care, room and board for more than 6 consecutive months, child day care that does not meet federal standards, generally available educational services, capital expenditures, and cash payments.

The categories of eligibility reflect the persistence of federal policy in trying to reach beyond public assistance recipients. All recipients of cash payments under AFDC or SSI are eligible. In addition, individuals and families not receiving cash payments but having an income not in excess of 115% of their state's median income for a family of like size are also eligible for services at each state's option. Information and referral services and protective functions for children and adults may be offered by states without regard to income criteria.

The election of another Republican administration in 1980 introduced a firm federal policy of restrictive or minimalist government in welfare. Despite efforts to reduce the federal commitment for social programs, budget allocations for Title XX, at least, remained relatively stable between 1980 and 1982, increasing in dollar amount but barely keeping up with such other dynamic forces as inflation, growth in population, the side effects of economic recession that increased the demand for many social services, and the increase in low-wage mothers into the work force, with its accompanying increase in demand for subsidized day care for children.

Table 6.2 shows that federal policy about social services, as expressed and defined in Title XX, has thus far (1982) maintained a base of financial support. Despite political changes in the White House continuing congressional support resulted in a relatively stable support level, with some decline due to inflation. However, budget projections discussed in the following paragraphs threaten this stability.

Title XX and its appropriations do not represent the complete federal commitment to personal social services. Over time, this program was augmented by a number of other federally funded activities identified by their

TABLE 6.2
Grants to the States for Social Services Title XX, 1980–82. (in millions of dollars)[a]

Services	1980	1981	1982
Day care—children	817	886	916
Homemaker	540	580	600
Education, training, and employment	296	321	332
Protective services	341	370	383
Foster care—children	138	149	154
Counseling services	215	233	241
Health related	85	92	96
Residential care and treatment	239	259	268
Family planning	77	84	87
Other	1,315	1,390	1,437
Total costs	4,063	4,364	4,514
Federal share	2,691	2,916	3,016

[a]SOURCE: Office of Management and Budget, Budget for Fiscal Year 1982, Human Development Services Federal Funds I-K67, Washington, D.C.

specific function, not as a personal social service, although all are administered under the Department of Health and Human Services and are
akin to Title XX services. The major other programs and their 1982
estimated budget obligation were:[5]

Administration for Children, Youth and Families (including such programs as Head Start, Child Welfare, Adoptions, Foster Care, Run Away Youth)	$1,336,128,000
Office of Special Education and Rehabilitation Research	1,225,235,000
Rehabilitation Service Administration	1,010,716,000
Administration on Aging	704,356,000
Administration on Developmental Disabilities	61,181,000

If a comprehensive program budget were to be developed, it would also
have to include funds spent on personal social and welfare services by the
Department of Labor, Department of Interior (Indian Affairs), the Veterans
Administration, and the Public Health Services. This range outside of Title
XX that is identified as "social services" indicates how extensive and difficult
to contain is the idea of a unifying concept of personal social services that
would permit inclusion of all activities in one all-encompassing department
of government.

The scale of these programs is not large if one considers the total population. The 1982 administration budget estimates, for example, that 1 million
persons would somehow be touched by rehabilitation services and 332,000
would be "rehabilitated"; 350,000 children are expected to be served by
Head Start programs; 170,000 individuals are expected to be placed in jobs;
431,000 daily meals will be provided to the elderly; and special education
will be given to 265,000 handicapped children.[6] Although these figures are
small when compared to the expenditures and number of persons reached
through the other basic programs of income maintenance, health, and
education, it is reasonably clear that an important beachhead has been established in federal policy, establishing through a 40-year evolution the principle of federal support for attention to the personalized needs of vulnerable
groups, wholly apart from generally distributed welfare services. Mott has
summarized the philosophical foundations for this evolution as follows:

---

[5] U.S. Office of Management and Budget, *Budget for Fiscal Year 1982*, Department of Health
and Human Services (Washington, D.C.: U.S. Government Printing Office, 1982).
[6] U.S. Department of Health, Education, and Welfare, *Fiscal Year Budget for 1977*
(Washington, D.C.: U.S. Government Printing Office, 1977).

1. Government has an obligation to assist society's most vulnerable people to attain the highest possible level of economic and functional independence of which they are capable.
2. The federal government should underwrite a variety of services, locally determined, to improve individual and family functioning through some combination of both public and privately sponsored services.
3. Public service funds should be expended on a priority basis for those with low income, although not exclusively for them.
4. Funds should not be used to substitute for other state or federal support of the primary human services, such as cash assistance, health care, and public education.
5. Use of these services should be voluntary except for crisis-protective intervention, and the shaping of goals should include joint efforts of consumers and service providers.[7]

The first year of operations under the new legislation proved to be a year of widespread confusion and disillusionment. The mandate for personal social services was substantially widened, but the sums of money available were not increased. This passed back to the states the unpleasant task of deciding how to distribute limited funds over a wider spectrum of demands. The planning involved enormous short-term effort to develop statewide plans for federal approval with little time to build up staff for the development of new plans within the new framework. In addition, the phasing in of the program from the federal government's perspective was not at all coordinated with the budget appropriations and planning cycle of state governments, so that many state plans had to be developed without reference to changes in state legislation that would ensue. Finally, the procedures broadened the participation of consumers through public hearings, and this increased the number of special-interest voices legally able to assert claims on available funds. Thus, conflicts between service providers and consumer groups endured in previous categorical programs were introduced again, with new claimants for the same funds.

Aside from these essentially transitional dilemmas, a key policy issue emerged that was not resolved by either the federal legislation or administration. This dilemma is rooted in the ambiguity about the nature of the personal social services outlined at the beginning of this chapter. Should the new program and its policies be used to lay the foundation for a network of tax-supported personal social services throughout the country, or should these funds be used solely to underwrite a variety of services already provided by existing public, private, and proprietary agencies? Should an in-

---

[7] Mott, *Meeting Human Needs*, pp. 49–50.

dependent, personal social services program to provide homemakers or halfway houses be established in a state, or should funds for this purpose be allocated and distributed among correctional institutions and mental health agencies, in order to enable each to develop halfway houses for their categorical populations? If providers of homemaker services for the sick and disabled prefer to concentrate their efforts on relatively short-term services calling for highly skilled nursing, should these funds be used to underwrite their services for eligible populations, even though there is an unmet need and demand for less skilled, long-term homemaker services for disabled persons? If the existing providers choose to concentrate on the short-term services, should the available public funds be used to force them to develop the long-term services or should a tax-supported program be developed for the purpose?

While these policy questions may seem to be matters of turf protection or development, a more serious underlying issue is involved. A rough type of Parkinson's Law can be proposed that established services will consume newly available resources more rapidly than it is possible to expand or develop new services. Put another way, newly available funds are frequently seized upon by existing service providers to meet their operating costs and thus to displace efforts at expanding these services from other sources. If federal funds are available, philanthropic income or local appropriations may be displaced.

The beachhead to which we have alluded provides an opportunity to assure that the personal social services are, over time, available to populations requiring them. But this goal will be realized only if the policy underlying the program is able to work consistently in that direction. Lacking such a consistent direction, it is equally possible that old patterns will be maintained without any change in the nature of the social service system and, therefore, without change in the basic social policy that the legislation has promised.

If we review this evolution in the context of the interplay between societal and public policies, we have an example in which public policy appears to be ahead of the social norms that usually underpin acceptance of public programs. Although there has been no widespread evidence of civic or cultural support for the idea of the government's providing personal social services of the kind we have here considered, still the executive branch—often in collaboration with the Congress—has persistently moved in the direction of establishing just such an addition to the social services. The fact that this policy has grown almost imperceptibly does not diminish its significance. Even when executive policy is reversed, legislative support sometimes assures continuity, as when a Democratic House of Representatives acted between 1980 and 1982. Radical change comes slowly in a check-and-balance system. But once a policy has been achieved, with authorization and appropriation bases, it can survive many attacks.

Controversies over organizational and administrative details can readily obscure the underlying policy issues that confront this subject. Is the definition of goals for the personal social services sufficiently clear to permit steady evolution? What are the effective personal social services necessary to achieve these goals, and how will effectiveness be ascertained for a new and evolving frontier? What is to be the emphasis in evolution: to meet the needs of all persons who confront common problems regardless of social and economic status or to meet the needs of only families with the lowest incomes? A direction for public policy is shaped around such questions as these. A host of other dilemmas can be identified that are matters of administration and operating policy, rather than public policy as we have defined the term.

Integration of the Basic Social Services: New Organizational Approaches

While the major federal effort to incorporate some aspect of the personal social services in national policy has stressed attention to the content of policy, a parallel approach has stressed organizational and structural change. As the number of basic human service programs has increased, more and more concern has been expressed about the absence of any orderly or unified relationship among the programs. The feeling has grown among professionals, legislators, administrators, and the public that the proliferation of agencies and programs has somehow gotten out of control. Perhaps the earliest attempt to deal with the maze of public programs was a commission appointed by Herbert Hoover in 1929 to report on national social trends.[8] In 1948 former President Hoover headed a presidential commission to examine the organization of governmental processes,[9] and in 1959 the Advisory Commission on Intergovernmental Relations was established by act of Congress to conduct several varieties of studies dealing with intergovernmental relationships and trends.

Attempts to rationalize government activities are recurrent themes in policy. Simple logic suggests that like activities ought to be brought together in one accountable administration. But social welfare lacks any simple unifying conception that would make such logic workable. Instead, human needs are most varied, and the interest groups that are activated to meet such needs are also varied, reflecting and expressing different economic interests and influences. The American political process encourages incremental

---

[8] Wesley Mitchell, *Recent Social Trends in the United States* (New York: McGraw-Hill, 1933).
[9] Herbert Hoover, *Report of the U.S. Committee on Organization of the Executive Branch of the Government* (Washington, D.C.: U.S. Government Printing Office, 1949).

change in welfare provision, and each change or addition introduces another administrative or organizational unit to be accommodated in any attempt to rationalize relationships among the parts. Title XX was a way to finance certain kinds of personal services, but it was fueled by a hope on the part of social workers that it could promote a more unified social services system. The welfare structure proved too complex for that, and other approaches continue to be tried to achieve coordination among various welfare activities. If the personal social services approach was one way to achieve a new integration, the major alternative has been based on coordinating independent programs either through a superordinate authority, such as a super umbrella agency, or through fiscal control mechanisms.

By 1966 two concerns riveted attention to the organizational forms for the social services. Despite the rhetoric of the early Nixon years, the major effort appeared to be to control the rate of growth of federal investment in human services, not to reduce or eliminate these services. The concern about total cost was soon linked to a concern about the federal government's apparent dominance in the traditional federal–state–local pattern of relationship. However, attempts to reduce the federal role in a situation as complex as the delivery of human services (which represented by 1968 close to half of the federal budget) were believed to be limited by the inability of state and local governments to take over any significant administrative responsibility. Implementation of the new federalism, which was intended to return policy planning and action responsibilities for human services to the states, thus seemed to require a parallel federal effort to assist the states in restructuring their governmental mechanisms. Federal agencies were to undergo the same type of restructuring to reduce total costs.

This attention to organizational capacity was based on a belief that some type of administrative control had to be exercised over the large numbers of independent programs that had been enacted by the legislature and that such control would result in reduced expenditures, a more efficient use of available money, and better results in the public interest.

Management theory appeared to supply the means to achieve restructuring. On the state level, a variety of presumably related functions and departments were to be consolidated into "super" departments, umbrella agencies, or secretariats, something like the federal model of the Department of Health, Education, and Welfare (HEW). At the level of the federal government, the staff and information capacities of the Office of Management and Budget (OMB) were enlarged to represent the White House views on administrative policy for executing legislated policies and programs. Within HEW (and other executive departments), the Office of the Secretary was likewise enlarged with general planning and policy personnel and greatly increased data systems derived from the department's component parts. It was assumed that through the assessment of information gathered from a variety of agencies and organizations, the umbrella agency and the OMB could achieve a broader perspective about policy than could be held by any one department or bureau whose staff was necessarily concerned with the implementation of a specialized, categorical program mandated in legislation.

Management devices for cost-benefit analysis, program planning, and budgeting were tested and adapted in an effort to assure that the purposes of a variety of federal programs were more clearly articulated, to assure that these articulated purposes and their implementing programs did not contradict each other, and to reduce the presumed duplication and overlapping of expenditures and personnel.

It was felt that only by such a broader perspective and attention to management practices could the whole human services enterprise be made more efficient and be moved in the direction of clear-cut goals, the achievement of which could be tested. Where progress toward achieving goals was slow and unsatisfactory, it was assumed that alternative programs or strategies could be introduced to replace the old ones.

These management concepts proved limited in their success because the operations of government are not as controllable as those of private business. Congress is the basic source of broad policy sanction and if, for whatever reasons—political, economic, or ideological—Congress chooses to mandate categorical programs, the authority of the executive branch to modify how these programs are in fact administered is limited. At best, the executive branch can delay program introduction or reduce its scale by regulation. These difficulties are further complicated when the White House and the Congress are controlled by different parties with competing political agendas. Programs that are seen by the OMB to have a common purpose and, therefore, to be susceptible to rationalization and reorganization may be viewed by Congress to serve the needs of different populations and the interests of different constituencies and, therefore, to be unamenable to consolidation.

The effort to limit or reduce the detail of federal control in the administration of many categorical programs was widely applauded. The breadth and diversity of human organization in the United States is such that detailed administration governing the delivery of services to individuals cannot readily be developed in Washington for uniform application throughout the country. There seemed to be little way to stem the tendency for the federal government to mandate by regulation what child can be examined by what personnel or what individual will be entitled to public assistance in what kind of emergency and under what circumstances. The absurdity of this situation became manifest in numerous ways. Federal support of training programs to develop personnel for the human services had for a long time been carried out by grants to state and private universities, which in turn selected the individuals to be admitted to the training programs. But by 1970, an effort was made to cut back these institutional grants sharply and to replace them by a program that required individual students throughout the country to apply, one by one, to offices in Washington for the procurement of scholarship support to enter professional schools.

Slowly, during the 1970s and early 1980s, the OMB assumed a central planning position for the executive branch, increasing its authority over the planning boundaries within which various departments and agencies were free to function. OMB and White House inner staff became the planning arm for the executive branch, using budget planning and control as the major planning power to push integration. At the state level, in 1968, a federal agency, HUD, made a grant to the Commonwealth of Massachusetts to study reorganization of state government. This was followed by a variety of incentives, encouragement, and pressures from Washington to other state governments to update and improve their capacities to handle more efficiently the flow of funds designed to deal with the social needs of residents. Most of these pressures were in the direction of consolidating government agencies into superagencies. In Massachusetts, for example, over 14 independent state agencies and a large number of institutions, independent boards, advisory councils, and commissions associated with them (which had reported directly to the governor) were consolidated into the Secretariat of Human Services, incorporating all state programs for public assistance, corrections, youth services, veterans' services, rehabilitation, children, mental health, and public health. The resulting new secretariat covered approximately half of the entire state budget and almost two-thirds of all state employees. Even so massive an attempt at consolidation could not be completely logical, since the human services themselves lack a tight logic. In Massachusetts, at least, a parallel yet completely independent Secretariat of Elder Affairs was established with very little money and very little staff, but representing political pressures in that state. Similar anomalies were found in other states.

By 1974, several states, but less than a majority, had carried through some form of reorganization, and the peak of the consolidation effort seemed to have been reached.[10] In these states, varieties of independent agencies were brought together in similar umbrella structures. No clear logic underlay the kinds of agencies brought together, although most of the umbrella agencies did include public assistance, mental health, public health, and youth services.

[10] Examples of this effort are reported in American Society for Public Administration, "Coping with the Demands for Change within Human Services Administration," Summary Report of Conference sponsored by ASPA and the Southeast Institute for Human Resources Development, ed. by Robert Agranoff, June 1976.

The effort to improve organizational capability was extended down to the cities, and many metropolitan areas were also stimulated to create large agencies similar to those of state government. In all these situations, a large number of independent commissions and state boards were brought under the head of one secretariat or commission. The number of senior executives in a governor's or mayor's administration was thus nominally reduced, but the span of control of each executive was broadened by the consolidation process.

These reorganizations were structural, not substantive. The line of authority from administrators of categorical or direct-service agencies now ran, not directly to the governor or a general office of budget, but through an intervening layer of administration. Data systems were introduced to improve the information that this intervening layer of administration could acquire about the broad range of services within its purview. Budgets were usually funneled through the secretariat to legislatures, even though legislatures might, in the end, choose to ignore secretariat recommendations. The staff of the secretariat was in the position to press the various constituent departments to articulate their purposes more clearly and to specify how requests for their programs were intended to achieve their results. This combination of improved data systems collected centrally and the introduction of management by objective program planning was supposed to put the secretary and secretariat staff in a position to influence the general direction of program development in the component departments. It was also hoped that an overall look at what was being expended for what purposes would permit the secretariat to identify duplications, overlappings, and inefficiencies and to reduce waste through a continuous restructuring of how personnel and funds were assigned.

This management concept gives limited attention to two serious deficiencies in the scheme. Most of the objectives of the programs being thus administered are set by legislatures or by compromises and bargaining between governors and legislatures. And the broad purposes of programs in the human services are set for state governments by the federal government. Consequently, efforts to change are limited to goals of efficiency and effectiveness, and sharply conflicting views about what is an effective plan of action usually arise. Lacking real authority to decide what the content of programs should be, the state governments have seen their effort to rationalize the system to some extent neutralized by questions as to what constitutes a more effective way of carrying out a legally sanctioned mandate.

Nonetheless, so large a reconstruction of human service structure as this effort contemplates necessarily takes a long time to evolve. Certain modifications can be noted, although they are not at all universal. At the minimum, one center in state government, a budget office or umbrella secretariat, now at least has the capacity to know something about the system of social welfare programs in which the various departments are involved. It remains to be seen whether more knowledge on a broader front can be absorbed, analyzed, and shaped by policy and planning personnel to produce changes in the system that will be reasonably persuasive in the political controversies through which final public policy is decided.

Legislatures and all political figures necessarily are responsive to the pressures of various constituencies. If resources were unlimited, constituency wants could be mandated without limitation. But since resources are in fact limited, public policy involves hard decisions about how resources are to be distributed among a variety of equally compelling and worthwhile ends. At this stage, it is not at all clear how the purposes of programs can be modified by rational planning, not political, means. For example, it might seem self-evident that if a certain population of the elderly is given the option of living independently without any help or going into an institution that is paid for by public funds, a change in policy and purpose might be clearly indicated. Such a change would involve the argument that available funds should be allotted to individuals in a set of options rather than a single option, a set that would include the possibility of diverting some of these public funds for purchase of supplementary services for delivery to elderly persons in their own homes. Unfortunately, many people do require substantial institutional attention, and funds need somehow to be divided between institutional and noninstitutional supports, but the guidelines along which the division should be drawn are not at all clear. Similarly, expert and professional groups differ substantially about where the line should be drawn. And citizens themselves may disagree. They might agree that individuals should not be "forced" into institutions, but the same individuals may bitterly oppose the maintenance of very disabled persons in neighboring houses. The extent to which rational analysis of information will resolve the disagreements has not yet been fully tested.

On the other hand, there are more limited ways in which this movement to integrate has clearly begun a process of change. There are grave discontinuities in the way in which the existing programs are linked with each other. For example, individuals may be placed in mental hospitals for long periods of time, reach a state of readiness for return to their community, but lack families and homes to which to return. Mental health programs do not have the means or the authority to reconstruct living arrangements; departments of public welfare and other community-based programs have other priorities and are not readily able to prepare homes to receive these individuals. The result is that many persons in institutions remain in a no-man's-land without any means of returning to a community, although they are certainly ready for it. In somewhat similar fashion, a small number of families and individuals have multiple needs that have led to the situation in which numerous staff members from several agencies are in constant touch with a small number of families, each duplicating the work of others. The absurdity of such consequences pushes the search for change.

On such relatively minor fronts, the movement toward organizational restructuring seems to have had an effect. In many communities, service personnel from a variety of agencies are housed in adjacent offices so that eligible persons can sort out their requirements without burdensome traveling to different offices. In a few communities, the work of several related agencies has been closely integrated, with the result that staff members from separate agencies now serve under a common administrator to carry on the functions of all agencies without regard to their previous specialty.

More widespread is the introduction of a case manager, who is assigned core responsibility for any entitled person. The case manager is responsible for obtaining and coordinating any services required to achieve a coherent plan in the person's interests. Coordinating agreements of this kind do not have authority, and in effect, the case manager must depend upon persuasion to secure existing services. Where necessary services are completely unavailable, as in the case of long-term home care, the case manager is relatively powerless.

Some social service departments and some home-care agencies in state government (or subsidized by it) have begun to acquire wider authority and control over resources so that their case managers can act effectively. Examples are seen in area agencies for the aging, which control, through provision or through purchase, a complex of services such as homemakers, chore workers, transportation, nutrition and meals-on-wheels, and adult day care. In a more narrow and less familiar setting, that of health maintenance organizations, staff are in a position to decide what medical setting mix to use for any one patient, choosing between ambulatory medical care, inpatient hospitalization, or a nursing home. In some instances, this authority has significantly shifted medical care from hospital to home and community.

Another approach to the same end of coordination is indirect through reimbursement and grant mechanisms of funding agencies. In health, new attempts being made in 1983–1984 to place a cap or a prospective limit on payment for medical care in hospitals, are expected to force hospitals to move patients into communities in a different pattern than before, with consequent changes in the pattern of home-care services (both medical and social). Since this consequence is not specified by the reimbursement policy, the results are not clearly predictable, but change is certain to follow. This approach does not force coordination; it only hopes coordination will result. Other legislation authorizes demonstration funds and incentives to a few health care agencies along with a charge to experiment with new ways to induce coordination on a voluntary basis (so-called channeling projects).

The best that can be said about the movement toward reorganization is that it seems to express a final acceptance of responsibility by federal as well as state governments for personal social services. Whether the delivery of these services can be made more systematic is being tested in the daily work of agencies that try to absorb reductions in support of the inroads of inflation. The ebb and flow of federal political fortunes keep the personal social services as an established but also continuously endangered entity. Through 1982, the supporters prevailed and kept funding at a sufficient level to assure viability, although a little ground was lost in inflation. However, the administration budget proposals for 1984 represented a continued and determined effort to reduce, if not abolish, federal social welfare efforts. Not having as clear or as powerful a constituent backing as the entitlement programs of Social Security, and other income maintenance programs, the personal social services finally become vulnerable. For example, the social services block grants (Title XX) for 1984 are projected by the O.M.B. to be $2.5 billion, a 15% reduction in absolute dollars, on top of further erosion due to wage inflation and continued increase in demand due to population increase and economic recession. Federal community service programs and community service block grants were scheduled by O.M.B. to be phased out altogether but were saved by Congress with a 10% cut. On the other hand, the Administration on Families, Children and Youth projected a 10% increase over actual expenditures in 1982, and the Administration on Aging grant program to the states increased marginally. At this writing, it appears that a new federalism may slightly increase federal funds directed to the states for their use within a few broad categorical blocks while sharply reducing federally administered programs.

In 1983 state welfare directors, acting through their council in the American Public Welfare Association, kept the coordination ideal alive. The association endorsed a modest version of the case manager solution. This solution was incorporated in legislation introduced into the House of Representatives (H.R. 2536, 1983). It would authorize one-stop delivery of human services under public auspices in a few demonstration areas. One office would be established in each jurisdiction, with workers to give individuals information about benefits they may be entitled to, eligibility requirements, and service location. Standard application forms and procedures for several services would be developed to avoid confusing variety in procedures; a coordinated transportation system between programs and new communication systems among all programs would be matched with unified budgeting, planning, purchasing, and auditing for all participating programs in an effort to weld one system out of independently authorized and funded services.

It remains to be seen whether a policy of coordination, without altering authority and financing pathways, can bring about any more change than that achieved by a long succession of similar efforts in the past. The success of this, or any other effort, will be measured by the extent to which the system itself is altered, not by management techniques in an intractable situation. That requires change in legislative and executive branch authorization, redistributing control over how dollars may be spent, and a more open commitment to a unified or integrated personal service system than has thus far been accepted. The search therefore continues, and is likely to for a long time, to maintain diversity in the service system with minimal controls between the parts.

Confusion between Policy Ends and Policy Means

While the central policy of commitment to the personal social services thus seems to be maintained, despite political changes, the outlook is somewhat less promising if one considers policies in relation to means. Policies have been frustrated by the lack of resources tied to clear outcomes. While the federal and state governments are committed to "doing something" about certain vulnerable populations, the end product of their efforts has not been specified. The clearest example can perhaps be seen in the case of the elderly and the severely disabled. Certainly there is no disagreement that "something should be done" for those persons who lack families and are physically not capable of taking care of all their needs by themselves. But what is it that should be done? We have clearly adopted a policy that assures access to medical treatment for all such individuals. When curative measures have been exhausted and disability remains, we can still fall back on a policy of restoration and rehabilitation. But federal policy on rehabilitation is still quite limited by a primary focus on restoration of economic independence. With minor exceptions and despite a long effort to change the policy, rehabilitation efforts supported by the federal government are intended to restore full physical independence through curative means for economic independence through retraining and restoration of function sufficient to permit employment.

There is still no policy applicable to cases in which reemployment is not possible or continuing attention is required for some irreversible disability. A policy may be developing through current experiments in diverting some Medicaid and Medicare funds to provide for less costly modes of support outside of institutions, but even this more flexible use of medical funds remains based on the expectation and desirability of some ultimate increase in self-care for the individual. Federal policy is ambiguous about responsibility for persons requiring intermittent long-term care or the part-time attention of others. Is the federal policy to rely exclusively upon the families of the disabled, even though the assumption of such caring responsibilities may lead to a breakdown of the families' integrity, or is the policy to supplement the families' capacities to carry the burden? In the case of individuals without families, is the policy to increase the scope of support in their own homes or to rely upon institutions?

The federal government's commitment to the future takes the form of support of various experimental and demonstration programs intended to increase the rate of deinstitutionalization for many previously institutionalized persons—the mentally ill, the chronically ill, and the criminal offender. It remains to be seen whether the results of these experiments, demonstrations, and tests will lead to a clearer public policy about ends and means that can serve as a guide throughout the entire human services system.

Case Examples of Reorganization[11]

The movement toward organizational reform was carried out in the federal government primarily by executive effort, but stimulus through the states was carried out through congressional funding of programs identified as capacity building, such as Services Integration Targets of Opportunity (SITO). Over 50 program grants were received by the states by 1972.

Florida originally attempted to coordinate its programs through legislation in 1969, when 200 independent administrative agencies were consolidated into a loose confederacy of 25 departments under the Department of Health and Rehabilitation Services (DHRS). Nine programs were included: vocational rehabilitation, youth services, aging, retardation, health, family services, mental health, children's medical services, and corrections. Little change was introduced at the delivery end, and some arrangements were provided for administrative coordination horizontally at the level of state departments only. This did not produce any substantial change in patterns of activity.

By 1970 a comprehensive delivery system was initiated in one county with federal support; most of the "integration" was administrative rather than organizational. One county (Palm Beach) sought to develop a common information system, case management for multiproblem families, across-the-board diagnostic services, a computerized client information system, common application and service forms for all departments, local planning councils, and adjacent location of facilities. However, the director of this county program had little authority, and achievements depended almost exclusively upon moral persuasion. The computerized system was not devel-

---

[11] Marshall Kaplan, Herbert Gans, and Alfred Kahn, "Human Resource Services in the States: An Analysis of State Human Resource Agencies and the Allied Services Act of 1972," mimeographed (San Francisco: Research Group, Kaplan, Gans, and Kahn, 1972).

oped, the staff resisted changes, common application forms proved to be burdensome and created more rather than less paperwork, the planning council was a discussion group rather than a decision-making body, and the case management system worked poorly.

By 1974 a state government management and efficiency study produced further recommendations, which led to the 1975 State Reorganization Act. Several alternatives were examined. A completely integrated model had wide support, but it faced objections in the DHRS in that specialized services had reduced visibility; accountability to satisfy state interests was found difficult to establish; county department funding proved less amenable to total integration; and eligibility from federal sources tied to federally funded categorical programs was threatened.

The final reorganization represented one step toward integration. The Office of the Secretary for Health and Rehabilitation Services retained responsibility for public information, legal services, and performance control, the last intended to measure progress toward state-determined objectives. An assistant secretary for operations administered 11 service delivery districts throughout the state. Each district contained a network of DHRS-funded services presumably capable of delivering and controlling medical services, aid to families with dependent children, aging and adult services, dependent and delinquent services, family social services, food stamps, Medicaid eligibility, services for mental health, public health and retardation, vocational rehabilitation, and SSI eligibility. Administrative outlets for these services were located in common offices where possible. Each district was expected to develop a case management unit to identify each client's needs, guide the client to the appropriate services, monitor delivery, arrange for the delivery of supporting services such as transportation, and generally assure that the client's needs, as defined at application, were met.

Parallel to these units is the Office of the Assistant Secretary for Program Planning and Development, which generally supervises the administration of all the services, is responsible for program research, identifies client needs, and develops recommendations for solutions to these needs with priorities. The planning and development office develops policies and standards and provides technical assistance to the district directors. Although maintaining a presumed across-the-board capacity at state government, eight separate categorical program offices under the assistant secretary develop specific plans and standards for children's medical services, mental health, vocational rehabilitation, social and economic services, and health services. These program units are located functionally in the district but have no line of authority.

By the end of 1975, this combination of some central authority, some localized integration, and some regional categorical arrangement for continual development claimed the following results: front-line delivery services were colocated and somewhat unified; unified administration reduced by 440 throughout the state the number of nonservice personnel; district operations plans covered all services, but there was no departmental program throughout the state; a single intake system for all children and youths was set up; personnel and professional influence on the legislature was reduced. Difficulty in mobilizing the state facilities to respond to state or local crises was also reported.

Another quite different example is seen in Minnesota, where administrative reform in the human services began officially in 1972 with the receipt of a SITO grant from the Department of Health, Education, and Welfare. The Minnesota project sought to test a continuing process of program development rather than a reform or reorganization. The Governor's Office for Program Development sought under the grant to build consensus for change among various forces in the human services system. The governor's office maintained a low profile, never calling itself an office for human services reform, for example.

A first step appears to have been the enactment in 1973 of legislation permitting (not mandating) county boards of commissioners to modify their county-wide planning, budgeting, and program for the human services. County commissioners were authorized to replace diverse and independent public boards by consolidated or integrated human services boards consisting of county commissioners, citizen members, and professional personnel, provided that the new boards represented corrections, health, mental health, and social services.

The county boards were to have authority to develop annual integrated budgets and plans for social services, public health, public assistance, mental health, court-related mental retardation, and day activity services for children. Several counties chose reorganization under this option.

Within 2 years, it was ascertained by monitoring state agencies that some single point of entry was necessary at the level of state government to conform to the consolidated, single-entry units developed at the level of county government, so that the county organizations could communicate with a single state office.

In 1975 the state legislature funded a Governor's Office of Human Services, which replaced the preceding Office for Program Development, in order to maintain the process of continuing change. The new state office was given responsibility for monitoring the continued development of the county boards and for analyzing budget, personnel, and program activities in the various county and state agencies and the relationship between these agencies and various regulatory functions that are distributed among state agencies. A host of problems are still being studied, including fragmentation, difficulties in accountability, the inappropriateness of levels of decision making, multiple program relationships, the interrelationship of various flows of funding into the counties, and the absence of single policy points for almost all activities.

It is evident that in Minnesota the difficulties involved in restructuring are still being considered by a process that does not test any specific model other than the county-based consolidated board. The boards are able to exercise some control over independent and diverse programs through the authority to consolidate budget requests into a single county budget for human services.

Attempts to rationalize the human services system have met many obstacles and have produced a resistance to change greater than the forces for change that have thus far been let loose. To illustrate: both federal and state legislatures are reluctant to relinquish the authority inherent in their capacity to authorize and fund categorical programs that have clear visibility; the efforts to make the human services system more responsive to human need by opening decision making to more and more voices has increased rather than consolidated the demands for services, so that a race appears to be under way between the continuous enlargement of demand for more and more activities and anxiety over the increasing cost of meeting the growing demands. The belief prevalent in the early 1970s that reorganization could permit the human services to do more for more people with less has not been proven. In the course of unsettling a basic system of categorical services, some vulnerable populations without strong political support are threatened with loss of help or with being overlooked as newer, more dominant, and salient interests come into play. Mothers who are the heads of single-parent families, while numerous, are less politically powerful than—let us say—spokesmen for the elderly or for the retarded; infants with severe nutritional deficiencies who are severely neglected by disorganized families are at risk of being overlooked until grave damage is done; and disabled adults are frequently overlooked in the rush to provide health services of an acute and episodic nature to all, a development that in turn is threatened by rapidly escalating costs that threaten the economic stability of many communities.

Finally, the various categorical programs that have developed in the past have all evolved with strong supporting constituencies, determined to maintain their present position as regards the distribution of allocated funds. A continuing tug of war remains between these various special categories, and all of them resist any attempt to modify the traditional patterns under which they have functioned.

It cannot be said that a clear-cut policy has yet emerged, other than to argue that the commitment to some level of service delivery is being maintained. Policies of consolidating services by various mechanisms—sometimes by an attempt to merge agencies, sometimes by an attempt to use administrative mechanisms and budget procedures to coordinate programs—have all been tested, and all have been found relatively wanting. What is being set up is a continuing conflict, out of which some public policy other than administrative management alone will evolve in time. The tension between a vastly elaborated network of human services, the stumbling and confusion that results from the lack of a careful relationship between the many components, and the concern over containment in the steady growth in expenditure for the human services may, in time, lead to a public policy concerning the means by which services will be delivered; but this does not yet seem to be on the horizon. The movement toward consolidation of human services has thus far had a relatively brief history, but the resistance to consolidation has proven to be stubborn indeed. [12]

Despite these difficulties, one promising device appears to have emerged, that of the case manager. It is likely that the case management idea is sufficiently useful to survive, regardless of the other forms of service policy that may evolve. To date, the case manager mechanism is primarily limited to handling multiproblem families through one of the three alternative means:

1. The case manager primarily refers applicants according to some plan and monitors the progress of the applicant through various service units.
2. He or she acquires authority over some proportion of all available resources in an area and can authorize payment therefrom for services according to the case manager's plan.
3. A case committee made up of various service agencies operates on all troublesome cases and provides the case manager with guidance in monitoring steps to be taken by the various agency partners.

In 1984 the status of personal social services remains clouded. Federal funding remains at a fixed level, and not all states use all the funds available to them. Federal guidelines are changing almost yearly in response to the practical problems reported by the states. In the states, old programs maneuver against each other to secure some share of Title XX funds. Efforts of reformers to alter the pattern of service delivery away from the old categories are incomplete. Legislation has introduced a mandate to create a new system of personal services, but the resources with which to carry through the change not only are limited but rely upon initiatives to be taken at state and local levels, and at those levels, old patterns have proven stubbornly resistant to change. The absence of a clear federal policy has thus far produced much activity without significant change in program operations.

---

[12] See Harold Orlans, *Human Services Co-ordination* (New York: Pica Press, 1982). This is a summary of regional meetings convened by the National Academy of Public Administration and the National Governors Council.

This continuing state of affairs periodically leads to a demand for a social planning office in the federal government. This was last a reality in the New Deal days of the 1930s when, for a short time, the National Resources Board acted as a strategic planning office for the president. In the 1960s, the War on Poverty reactivated a movement to develop better social indicators or indexes that could guide policy, but this soon failed both because the concept of social indicators was not sufficiently well developed to persuade a reluctant political system and also because the growing volume of data sources covering almost all sectors of welfare in each major department of government served to give planners almost more empirical data than they could manage for planning purposes; in fact, such data were often full of contradictions, and social indicator technology has not been adequate to resolve them. The Office of Management and Budget has, in the meantime, come to function as the center for policy planning in the executive branch, using fiscal more than social measures for choice taking.

Additional Readings

Anderson, Wayne; Frieden, Bernard; and Murphy, Michael. *Managing Human Services.* Washington, D.C.: International City Management Association, 1977.

Axinn, June, and Levin, Herman. *Social Welfare: A History of the American Response to Need.* New York: Harper & Row, 1976.

Kammerman, Sheila, and Kahn, Alfred. *Social Services in the United States.* Philadelphia: Temple University Press, 1976.

Morris, Robert. *Toward a Caring Society.* New York: Columbia University School of Social Work, 1974.

Orlans, Harold. *Human Services Co-Ordination.* New York: Pica Press, 1982.

Turem, J., et al. *The Implementation of Title XX: The First Year's Experience.* Working Paper 0900–08. Washington, D.C.: Urban Institute, 1976.

Children
and the Aged

Dilemmas of Family
Policy

7

Much has been said and written about public policy for the family, but the subject has always been obscured by ambiguity over what constitutes a *family policy* as distinct from a *health* or an *income* policy that serves family needs. Family policy refers to those acts that are intended to strengthen or alter patterns of family life as distinguished from acts that help individuals and so may have an indirect bearing on the family network. The possible negative effects of such policies have been examined, but positive alternatives have not been proposed. For example, some critics believe that present relief policies for mothers and children lead to the breakup of families on the assumption that the male wage earner is encouraged to leave home so that his dependents can qualify for welfare payments more readily. However, the critics offer few alternative programs to provide the necessary aid.

The subject of family policy may be most vividly approached from the point of view of children and the elderly, two groups of individuals dependent upon family ties for affection and care. National effort devoted to the needs of the aged and of children has often been justified on the grounds that it is intended to strengthen family life as much as it is intended to protect dependent individuals. In the following discussion, we will limit consideration of health insurance and income maintenance to the ways they do or do not support a policy for children (or the aged) when they are combined with other specific acts dealing with children's needs, especially their protective or developmental needs.

The aged and children are subsets of all people whose needs have been given special attention. Eligibility by virtue of age represents one practical way to discuss family policy, although the subject could also be approached by considering other family groupings regardless of the age of members: black or Hispanic minority families, single-parent families, the retarded, and so on.

Policy for the Elderly: Social as well as Economic Concerns

Since 1935 and especially since 1965, federal involvement in programs specifically directed at the wants of the elderly has produced funds or services for the following: retirement income through Social Security, minimum assured income in case of permanent disability, medical care through Medicare, supplementary income where the foregoing are not sufficient through supplementary security income programs, special low-cost housing, special nutritional services, special transportation arrangements, special programs for social activity, employment, or constructive activity, alteration of social role, and a larger share in the gross national product. Do these programs add up to a family policy or set of policies toward the elderly in American society?

Following our earlier framework, it would appear that our national approach to the elderly does not violate policy guidelines. The elderly have been considered an especially vulnerable and disadvantaged group on the basis of accumulated evidence that they have much less than average income, more severe health needs than the average, and, because they frequently live apart from their families, grave difficulties in coping with isolation and physical handicaps. The federal government has moved to alleviate some of these pressures and relieve the distresses. The policy approach has been the modest and supplementary role of making special income available for the elderly while relying on the marketplace functioning of our basic institutions. The median income of families with head over 65 was $7298 in 1974 and about $3000 for individuals.[1] Approximately 60% of the aggregate incomes earned by this population were derived from private sources and about 40% from various governmental programs, with 30% of the latter derived from Social Security.[2] But does this financing add up to a line of direction for the use of governmental power? The answer is mixed.

---

[1] U.S. Bureau of the Census, *Demographic Aspects of Aging and the Older Population in the U.S., Current Population Reports,* Special Studies Series, No. 59 (Washington, D.C.: U.S. Government Printing Office, 1976), Table 6–6.

[2] See Matilda W. Riley and Anne Foner, *Aging and Society,* vol. 1 (New York: Russell Sage Foundation, 1968), Chap. 4. In 1974, 52% of retired couples received income from both Social Security and private pensions; 38% received only Social Security payments. See Alan Fox, "Work Status and Income Change," *Social Security Bulletin 39,* no. 12 (December 1976): 15–31.

Clearly, economic status has been improved, as has access to medical care, which will soon be discussed. But public policy for the elderly is especially interesting in that it opened the door to a slight but potentially significant shift in the direction of new societal norms, as well as enlarged public policy. Primarily because of the innovative policy incorporated in the original Social Security legislation, both retirement income and medical care for the elderly are available without means tests, and federal benefits are available to at least 10% of the population regardless of their financial status. This apparent deviation from the long-standing societal policy of using government to intervene only for vulnerable and especially needy groups has been rationalized on the grounds that the aged as a class, not as part of a family, are vulnerable and disadvantaged and warrant this kind of extension. The effect has been that individuals with substantial private incomes draw benefits for retirement and medical expenses as do those with virtually no private resources.

Policy for the elderly is interesting also because it has directed attention to many essentially social problems of the elderly that are not rooted in economic distress. Actions of both Congress, through the Senate Special Committee on Aging, and the executive branch, through the Administration on Aging, have touched many aspects of the life of older persons: Research, experimental programs, and locally initiated activities have been concerned with nutritional status, opportunities for constructive activity, developing useful roles that the elderly can fill once they have been displaced from the labor market, opportunities for gratifying leisure activities, and mechanisms to reduce isolation and loneliness, to name but a few.

This extension in the range of public social policy, so much at variance with past socially sanctioned functions, was justified by the unusual situation that modern society confronts concerning its elderly. In 1880, 3.4% of the American population was over age 65, whereas in 1977, almost 10% was over 65; and by the end of the century, the figure is expected to rise to nearly 15%. The average life expectancy in the population has risen dramatically. In 1900 life expectancy for males was an average of 48.2 years; in 1973 this had increased to 67.6 years. For women the comparable rates were 50.7 years and 75.3 years. This means, not that the species is living longer, but that more individuals are living longer and the proportion of persons over 65, and especially those over 75, has increased dramatically.

This proportionate aging of the population has been accompanied by a phenomenal growth in economic productive capacity and in the mechanical capacity to produce the goods that a population requires. As a result, older persons are decreasingly required for the running of the economy. In contrast with earlier times when the elderly performed a lifelong economic function, today their labor is not required by the economy. This circumstance is most dramatically represented by changes in labor force participation by the elderly. While the participation of persons over age 14 in the labor force has remained at approximately 55% since 1900, the propor- tion over 65 participating in the labor force has declined from 68% in 1900 to 23% in 1975 and appears to be still declining.[3]

At the same time, the American culture has changed. A primary value is now placed upon independent living residences for nuclear families, mean- ing that older persons maintain residences independent of their adult and married children.

The sum effect of these developments has been to create a society con- taining a large group of members who in the past were revered and valued, but who now lack economic and social functions. The lack of definition of their role in turn creates instability and unpredictability in their relation- ships to members of their families and the society in general. In a sense, public policy has been expanded to include some of the responsibilities pre- viously assumed by family relationships. Government programs, whatever their direction or scope, are now concerned with the mobility, social life, recreation, economic security, health, and nutrition of the elderly. At the same time, the potential development of this policy is still constrained by the belief that these wide-ranging needs can best be met through the marketplace.

We must conclude that no guiding directions for government policy have yet emerged concerning roles of the elderly, how their health is to be maintained, or what the balance should be between family or private and governmental support for housing, transportation, and physical care. Only income support has been assumed by the government.

The role of the aged is the one area almost ignored by federal policy, ex- cept in a negative sense. There has been a continuing tendency toward early retirement (i.e., before age 65), much of which can be attributed to liberali- zation in Social Security legislation.[4] Such legislation, for example, permits retirement with some reduction in benefits at age 62 or 60. Other liberaliza- tion has made it possible for persons under 65 who become permanently and totally disabled to begin withdrawing their income benefits as if they had already reached 65. This provision has been heavily utilized by workers in their late 50s and early 60s who become unemployed, find it extraor- dinarily difficult to find competitive employment, and use existing physical handicaps as a means for securing minimum income. The elderly are effec- tively enabled to leave the labor force whether by virtue of their inability to find employment or as a matter of personal preference. This is a direct in- tervention into family relationships. The families of the 80% of the elderly

[3] Riley and Foner, *Aging and Society*, pp. 39–49.
[4] Juanita M. Kreps, "Social Security in the Coming Decade: Questions for a Mature System," *Social Security Bulletin* 39, no. 3 (March 1976): 21–29.

who have families benefit; family incomes are released for the nuclear family, rather than being stretched to cover a three-generation extended family. This is family policy of significance. Minor pressures have developed to reverse this tendency toward early retirement and to widen opportunities for the retired elderly to earn small sums of money through employment without losing retirement benefits. For example, a small-scale program was set up in 1975 to provide short-term employment at limited reimbursement for 149,602 elderly through Retired Senior Voluntary Programs (RSVPs).[5] Such actions are tokens of federal interest, but they do not yet represent a federal commitment to assure that useful and significant roles in the community are made available to the elderly. Whether or not such a federal commitment is required, given the natural choices that individuals have about the use of their leisure time, is untested. To say that a positive federal policy on a role for the elderly is lacking does not mean that this problem has not been recognized in many circles of government. However, recognition has been expressed only in a few demonstrations of interest. In 1978, Congress acted to reinforce an old social norm to meet this issue. It passed legislation making it illegal for employers to terminate a person's employment for reasons of old age alone until age 70. It did not deal with the long-term trend toward voluntary earlier retirement.

A Change in Family Support Policy

In another direction, public policy seems to have been in the vanguard of a change in societal policy. Family members had long been considered responsible for each other, and, in conformity to inherited English poor law constructs, public sources were made accessible only when families were missing or incapable of providing assistance to their members. The Social Security Act provided the elderly with access to independent sources of income. This access reinforced the already apparent tendency for families to separate into nuclear units, living independently although maintaining ties of personal association. By 1965, 57% of all the elderly were living either alone or with their spouses. An additional 11% were living with other persons not related by blood ties. In 17% of the households, older persons and their children lived together, with the older persons as heads of household, and another 11% of the cases lived together with the adult children as heads of household.[6] These trends continue, although the recession of 1979–1983 forced some adult children to return to parental homes for periods of time.

[5] *Action*, Annual Report (Washington, D.C.: U.S. Government Printing Office, 1975), p.1.
[6] Riley and Foner, *Aging and Society*, pp. 168–169. Between 1965 and 1975 this trend continued, although data are compiled differently. In 1975, 15% of men and 37% of women over 65

Studies between 1958 and 1975, however, indicate that this tendency to live apart had not necessarily produced a weakening of family ties. Nearly 50% of the elderly live within 10–30 minutes' journey of some family member, and only 5% live as much as a day's journey apart. More significantly, studies have indicated that affectional ties accompany this physical proximity, measured by frequency of visiting and the like. Schorr reports that, while some older people are isolated from their families, most are part of a family configuration.[7] Upwards of two-thirds of aged parents see their children at least weekly. Studies of middle-class families conclude that the generations have a desire to help one another.[8] Nonetheless, this maintenance of close family ties has been accompanied by a marked shift of financial responsibility for the elderly from family to tax sources. This shift, led by the initial Social Security Act for retirement, has taken place within the basic societal context we have been postulating, since the social security is premised upon individual contribution to an insurance fund with benefits presumably being returned in proportion to contributions made. However, it is important to remember that the Social Security Act does not maintain a sequestered fund. Current contributions by individuals support the present-day aged and constitute a claim by today's workers upon future tax revenues.

The shift in fiscal responsibility from family to state is most clearly seen in state and federal policies governing supplementary assistance payments, first from old age assistance and, more recently, from supplementary security income. Until the enactment of the SSI legislation, policies regarding filial responsibility lay within the jurisdiction of state governments. By 1970 many states made no support demands on adult children, and 21 states, while requiring the contribution as a matter of law, did not make the granting of assistance contingent on that contribution. Since the remaining states that require, at least nominally, some filial contribution if their parents do not have sufficient income also take into account the income level of potential contributing family members, the degree of family responsibility is even

---

lived alone or with nonrelatives, maintaining independent homes as "primary individuals"; 78% of women aged 55–64 years lived alone or only with spouses, as did 60% of women over 75 years of age. For men the corresponding figures are 88% and 84%. See also U.S. Bureau of Census, *Demographic Aspects of Aging,* pp. 47–49; Marvin Sussman, "Family Life of Old People," in *Handbook of Aging and the Social Sciences,* ed. Robert Binstock and Ethel Shanas (New York: Van Nostrand Reinhold, 1976).

[7] Alvin Schorr, *Filial Responsibility in the Modern American Family* (Washington, D.C.: Social Security Administration, U.S. Department of Health, Education, and Welfare, 1960).

[8] See also Ethel Shanas, "Sociological Research Findings about Older People," in *Toward Better Understanding of the Aged* (Council on Social Welfare Education, 1958), p. 52; Gordon F. Streib, "Family Patterns in Retirement," *Journal of Social Issues* 14, no. 2 (1958); Marvin B. Sussman, "Family Continuity," *Marriage and Family Living* 16, no. 2 (May 1954): 112–120.

further reduced. Since most families in the United States have modest incomes and the vast majority of adult children of dependent elderly also have moderate incomes, there are relatively few cases in which there is a sufficient disposable margin of filial income to make feasible a demand that payments be made for the support of parents living elsewhere. On balance, it can be said that the precept that families take care of their dependent family members has been substantially invaded and that as a practical matter families are relieved of this responsibility where aged parents are living independently, except in those relatively few cases where adult children have substantial incomes.

Recognition of this development has been obscured for a long time because of a belief that these benefits are returns on real insurance payments, not social protection. The introduction of public support for the elderly as a class has already altered one dimension of family relationships.

This type of modification of public policy has occurred in other fields. For example, public support for independent living of nuclear families is seen in small programs of specialized housing for the elderly. Federal policy in housing encourages the construction of special accommodations for the elderly living alone, either in public housing, in subsidized low-cost housing, or in special housing developments. In 1956 the Federal Housing Act specifically authorized federal financing for units especially designed for the elderly in low-cost public housing. In 1962 the Senior Citizens Housing Act authorized the insuring and the granting of loans for the housing of elderly in rural communities. One especially interesting program, that of rent supplements, has been mandated for the whole population, but about 25% of the families receiving assistance through rent supplementation in 1969 were elderly.

However, these expressions of public policy concerning the housing of the elderly should not be overvalued. While it was estimated in 1970 that 1.5 million older persons lived in substandard housing[9] or in housing that they could not afford (meaning that they use a disproportionate amount of their income for rent and thus are badly nourished), by 1974 only 331,000 units for the elderly had been constructed to reduce the cost of housing and fewer than 20,000 elderly families received rent supplements. In 1979, 44,000 low-cost public housing units were added—many, not all, for the aged.[10]

The Administration on Aging also supports a variety of other personal service programs for the elderly, but on the basis of reflexive funding. The

[9] U.S. Bureau of Census, *1970 Housing Census, Housing of Senior Citizens*, HC (7)–6 (Washington, D.C.: U.S. Government Printing Office, 1970), Table A–5.

[10] U.S. Department of Housing and Urban Development, *1973 and 1974 HUD Statistical Yearbooks* (Washington, D.C.: U.S. Government Printing Office, 1974).

Congress allocates a fixed sum to the states by formula. The states, either through governmental units or voluntary organizations approved by state units on aging, initiate service proposals that are contributed to by the federal funds when the programs fall within federal guidelines. As a result, specialized programs do exist, such as 2,100 senior citizen centers for socialization, homemakers to enable the disabled elderly to remain in their own homes, friendly visiting programs, and transportation arrangements for the housebound.

This variety of programs represents a direction in policy for the federal government to intervene modestly in the distribution of resources on behalf of the elderly and to reduce reliance on family. This was extended by the amendments to the Older Americans Act in 1973, which provided that 39% of the $99 million appropriated under the act in 1973 must be utilized for the provision of nutritional programs for the elderly. (The funds appropriated increased to $328 million in 1980). In many urban areas, individual and group feeding programs, such as home-delivered meals and meals in senior centers, have resulted. These programs represent a concern on the part of the federal government that the poor elderly receive proper nourishment as a complement to health services. It also represents a readiness to have federal funds used creatively. Nutritional funds made available through senior centers not only strengthen the ability of the group centers to meet the needs of isolated and lonely elderly but also strengthen the desire of the elderly to use those centers. The funds thereby encourage social interaction and, to a degree, counteract the tendency toward isolation on the part of some of the elderly, especially the handicapped.

The sum effect of these actions, both the clear-cut public policies in relation to income and health and the modest demonstration innovations in other social areas, define present public policy for the elderly. The policy is seen in terms of individuals; that is, actions are taken to meet the needs of aged individuals or to relieve family members of many responsibilities. It is still not a family policy—that is, a policy addressed to the well-being of that collectivity called a family.

In 1982, a first step was taken to reverse this policy by phasing in a delay in the age at which older workers can retire at full benefits. This move was induced, not by a concern for family relationships or new roles for the aged, but by economic concern: A growing aged population retiring at an earlier age could no longer be supported comfortably by a proportionately declining adult labor force that had to increase its taxes to make higher retirement payments. At the same time, the criteria for establishing disability were stiffened to make it more difficult to claim benefits. These changes returned the tradition of making policy on fiscal, not family, bases. Inflation over decades also erodes the earnings and savings of elders, and not even cost-of-living adjustments wholly compensate for the resulting loss in real purchasing

power. Also, as more elders live into their 70s and 80s, they become enfeebled and severely disabled, at a period in history when their adult sons
and daughters are both likely to be employed. The cumulative effect has
been to return more responsibilities to families. It also undermines the
modest economic security that recent policy afforded through full cost-of-
living indexing.

Administrative Structure for Federal Policy Shifts

Since this set of policies appears to deviate from the societal constraints, it is
interesting to summarize briefly the sequence of events that led to the present state of affairs. The first evidence of federal policy concerns, other than
those reflected in the Social Security Act of 1935, was the 1961 White House
Conference on Aging, the first of its kind in the United States. The
president's decision to convene the conference may have been related to an
attempt to influence the debate over health insurance for the elderly via an
expansion of social security protection. However, it is not unreasonable to
conclude that the conference also represented an extension of the executive
office concern for the elderly that had its first significant testing in the 1930s
in the debate over economic security. In addressing this conference about
the responsibilities of government for the elderly, former Governor of New
Jersey Robert M. Meyner advanced views that seemed to conform to an interpretation of public policies expressed by the Office of the President: "The
federal system is weakened when the national government does not accept
and fulfill its share of obligations. I hope this conference will set forth fear-
lessly the relative responsibilities of the several levels of government and
make strong recommendations to each for carrying them out." [11] After arguing that governments, both national and state, have an obligation to provide
moral leadership in moving into areas where senior citizens need protection, the governor chose to point out some concrete areas in which federal
as well as state responsibilities needed to be discharged in a consistent direction. Among these were the need to protect the elderly from the special
hazards of injury on the roads and from neglect and abuse in nursing
homes. Beyond reiterating what had already been well established, the fact
that the elderly are often poor and in need of special medical assistance, he
pointed out that the aged are in addition ill housed. He concluded that every
state, with federal assistance, should have an agency to take the lead in carrying out a comprehensive program for the welfare of the aged. Although

[11] *The Nation and Its Older People: Report of the White House Conference on Aging, 1961*
(Washington, D.C.: U.S. Government Printing Office, 1961).

noting that such an agency should provide leadership and coordination, he seemed to imply that the thrust of federal government policy, as well as that of the states, should be consistent responsibility for the development of a comprehensive program concerned with the total welfare of the aged, not only their income and health.

Successive conferences in 1961 and 1971, sponsored and supported by the White House, expanded on these themes. They addressed themselves to a wide range of subjects affecting the religious, morale, housing, health, transportation, and occupational concerns of older persons and proposed relevant federally supported programs in each area. In addition to the conferences, the White House established an interdepartmental committee with a special staff to prod, stimulate, and arouse the major executive departments to give special attention to the needs of the elderly. These efforts were supplemented by the establishment of the Senate Special Committee on Aging, which has over the years produced a series of significant studies and hearings on all aspects of living conditions for the elderly. A similar committee was later created in the House of Representatives.

These activities culminated in 1973 in the enactment of Public Law 98–73, the Older Americans Act, which established the Administration on Aging, a distinctive administrative focus for the interests of the federal government.

By 1980 programs for the aging were funded at the level of $700 million, including $380 million in federal support for 800 nutrition programs to provide 450,000 daily meals 5 days a week in 4900 local sites. In addition, funds were available for the support of a variety of social services administered through 462 area agencies on aging, regional or urban governmental units responsible for contracting with private providers or actually organizing a variety of services for the elderly, including homemaker services, chore workers to maintain properties, transportation, socialization programs in senior citizens centers, legal aid services, and the like. The claim that 7 million individuals were served by these programs needs interpretation; considering the modest sums available to each office, it is likely that much of this servicing consisted of giving information rather than sustained help.

In addition, the Administration on Aging supports special educational programs and training programs to equip professional and paraprofessional service providers with special knowledge about the needs of the elderly so that their services can be more effective. Personnel trained by these funds might be employed in agencies serving only the elderly, such as the area offices on aging, homes for the aged, and senior citizen centers, or in general-purpose agencies serving all ages, such as public assistance, housing, and hospitals.

The scope of the Administration on Aging goes still further. In this field, at least, a consistent evolution and broadening of federal policy continues to take place. Beginning with assurance of income security and the establishment of a comprehensive financial and administrative system for managing income security, the economic bases have been steadily broadened through Medicare to include the hazards of illness and then the wider range of services listed above. The federal government is thus engaged in the lives of the elderly far beyond the guides originally suggested by societal preferences, but the directional nature of this interest is still unclear, for federal support remains in the form of cash payments to individuals left then to rely upon the marketplace of goods-and-services providers. The family purposes that guide the structure of these services are not really clarified by federal policy.

Impact of Federal Policy Enlargement on the Well-Being of the Elderly

The position of the elderly relative to the rest of the population as regards income and access to health services has already been discussed. With two exceptions, it is difficult to identify any effects that these programs have had on the life of the elderly. No clear causal connection can be made regarding extension of life. Some studies, such as those by Carp, indicate that housing does improve the moral of the elderly, but no extensive comparative studies have been completed. [12] The variety of specialized services funded through the Administration on Aging area offices presumably improve the well-being and perhaps the morale of the elderly, since the services are at least utilized and presumably wanted. But whether a change in health, well-being, or morale has resulted has not yet been established.

However, the two exceptions to this general conclusion lead us into the present policy choices that confront the national government. The exceptions are (1) an increase in the ability of the aged to maintain homes apart from younger relatives; and (2) an increase in proprietary nursing home beds for the sick aged. The second of these is clearly on the public agenda. There is no longer much doubt that the enactment of the Social Security protection and the administrative decision to make old age assistance and Social Security payments to vendors of institutional services, especially nursing home operators, has produced a great increase in the number of proprietary nursing home beds available in the United States. Between 1939 and 1970, this number has grown from 25,000 to 1,099,412. [13]

[12] Frances Carp, *A Future for the Aged: Victoria Plaza and Its Residents* (Austin: University of Texas Press, 1966).

[13] U.S. Senate Special Committee on Aging, *Nursing Home Care in the United States: Failure in Public Policy, Introductory Report* (Washington, D.C.: U.S. Government Printing Office, 1974), pp. 20–21.

Part of this increase has undoubtedly been required because the growing number of older persons, especially those over 75, necessarily means an increasing number of persons with severe physical as well as social disabilities that require full-time institutional care. However, the growth of proprietary nursing homes has given rise to the charge that national policy is strongly biased in favor of institutional care for those who are completely capable of managing for themselves. This charge is justified, at least by the fact that Medicare payments for 100 days in a skilled nursing facility and Medicaid payments for indefinite periods of time have until recently been available only for older persons in hospitals or those placed in nursing homes as part of a treatment plan. Neither Medicare nor Medicaid encouraged or permitted the use of equivalent funds to supplement normal Social Security or public assistance benefits to help the individual secure part-time assistance to remain at home, whereas larger sums for full-time attention were made available to those in nursing homes. A succession of studies has indicated that, depending upon the jurisdiction and the scope of alternative services, anywhere between 10 and 40% of nursing home patients are so placed primarily for social reasons. The fact that they are enfeebled does not necessarily mean that they could not have continued longer in their own homes with partial social supports; but until 1976, these have not been readily available. This situation appears to be the consequence of the decision to relate most medical care for the elderly to an economic program, Social Security, and to build both Medicare and Medicaid policies around the controls provided by the medical professions.

By the early 1970s, however, the criticisms about overinstitutionalization and about the quality of care provided in many institutions led to a continuing reexamination of basic national policy. The Medicaid administration undertook to waive its normal limitations on the use of Medicaid funds to permit payment for home-care services outside of institutions on an experimental basis. Medicare administration followed shortly thereafter, authorizing a few test experiments wherein medical funds were used to pay for nonmedical services in an effort to diminish the volume of institutional care.

The legislative branch has introduced legislation designed to provide federal payments for noninstitutional services as part of a major effort to reverse the long-standing tendency to rely upon institutional care when individuals are not wholly capable of managing alone.[14] The policy debate continuing into the 1980s has focused mainly on control of escalating costs.

[14] Examples are bills introduced in the 94th Congress by Representatives Edward I. Koch (H.R. 10324) and Barber B. Conable (H.R. 2268). In the 95th Congress, similar bills were introduced by Representatives Koch (H.R. 452, 453), Conable (H.R. 2029), and Claude Pepper (H.R. 1130).

Numerous experiments have tested the savings from care at home rather than in a nursing home or the savings from reduced hospitalization. A clear policy on long-term care for the chronically sick has not yet emerged because control of all medical costs cannot be induced only by alternative care at home for the elderly—other patients quickly occupy the hospital beds freed up by alternative care arrangements. Nevertheless, numerous alternatives are still being tested by the Health Care Finance Administration and the Congress. [15]

Federal policy has had an observable effect on the ability of older persons to maintain independent households. While early fears that family ties would be loosened as a result have not been realized, a serious new policy issue has risen to the surface. When government assumes any type of financial responsibility for its citizens, responsibilities previously borne entirely by the family, the door is opened to a continuous expansion of this transfer of obligation and responsibility, at least in monetary terms. Should all care in nursing homes be provided without charge to the family under any circumstances of family wealth? Should part-time home-care services be provided for the partially disabled by tax funds, even though those services are in some 75% of all cases still being provided by family members without compensation? Should elders be barred from passing an estate on to their children in order to pay for long-term health or nursing care? Should children be compelled to pay all or part of their parents' medical or nursing care? If the answer is to be yes, how can it be administered? [16]

A major public policy debate is in the making over the appropriate boundary between responsibilities that should be publicly assumed for all citizens and those that properly should be left to family members. The debate is complicated by the fact that 14% of elderly persons lack living relatives or are completely alienated from family members. Where income alone is not sufficient to maintain functional independence because of illness or enfeeblement, alternative social arrangements must be provided. But what of the much larger number with remaining family networks? What are the proper boundaries for the division of responsibility between families and government? It is conceivable that the precedent set in the Social Security legislation will someday be extended to other services considered desirable for the elderly without a means test, with tax support for all persons, regardless of assets. [17]

---

[15] James Callahan and Stanley Wallach, *Reforming the Long Term Care System* (Lexington: Lexington Books, 1981).

[16] James Callahan, Lawrence Diamond, Janet Giele, and Robert Morris, "Responsibility of Families for Their Severely Disabled Elders," *Health Care Financing Review* 1, no. 3 (Winter 1980): 29–48.

[17] Callahan and Wallach, *Reforming the Long Term Care System*.

Another major, unresolved policy issue is that of race. Minority workers not only earn less than whites during their working years but also still die at younger ages, although this differential is rapidly being reduced. The result is that benefits are lower, continuing a lifelong disadvantage. But also, because of early death, a smaller proportion of taxes paid into the system is withdrawn. Average income, counting Social Security and all other transfer incomes, for white males over age 65 was $3463 in 1980; for nonwhite males over 65, it was $2606. This has led to a demand by some minority groups that Social Security payments be adjusted upward for minority beneficiaries to overcome these disadvantages. The intent is to sharply increase the use of Social Security as an income redistribution mechanism, well beyond the modest redistribution that now takes place in favor of low earners, but without regard to race disparity.

These optimistic objectives are justified when it comes to those as clearly vulnerable as the chronically sick, for their needs fall into the basic premises on which America's welfare policy has been based. When it comes to more general income support, a major reversal in policy direction was introduced by the national administration in 1980—to move away from the most advanced parts of Social Security retirement provision. The move was occasioned by an economic recession and a long-term shift in the demographic profile of the nation. As the proportion of middle-year workers declines and the proportion of very old increases, both a product of long-term birth rates, the income produced through Social Security taxes to pay for previously authorized benefits declines as well, at least in the next decade 1985–1995. Actuarial projections indicate that, by the end of the 1980s, annual income from taxes will not be enough to pay out promised benefits; in other words, the system would be bankrupt. After a brief but violent political controversy, a bipartisan congressional committee produced a revision in the system that satisfied both a president who wanted no tax increase and the requirements of the system. Its main features were:

1. To bring all new federal employees and employees of nonprofit organizations into coverage. This will produce more revenue and is consistent with the growing universalism of the system.
2. Tax one-half of Social Security benefits when the adjusted gross taxable income of married couples (including half of Social Security benefits) exceeds $32,999 ($25,000 for individual filers).
3. Increase payroll taxes for both employers and employees.
4. Adjust the tax for self-employment income to make it closer to the combined employer–employee rate.
5. Adjust the cost-of-living allowance to increases in either prices or wages, whichever is lower, in case of an emergency.
6. Improve incentives for workers to delay retirement.

7. Improve benefits for certain surviving spouses.
8. Gradually raise the age at which full retirement benefits are paid from 65 to 67 (by the year 2027).

The thrust of this change is mainly fiscal, but it will have the effect of bringing a major social benefit into the tax system on a crude progressive tax basis and inducing workers to remain in the work force, while reducing other benefits.

Child Protection or Family Policy?

The history of public policy concerning children is less clear than that for the aging, although the history is longer. It is taken as an article of faith that, as a society, we place the highest values on caring and nurturing children as the bulwark of the nation's future. In reality, our policies have, for the most part, relied upon families to provide this nurturing, although we have also built up a surprisingly large number of supplemental services either to protect children who are at risk of neglect or to relieve families of certain pressing obligations.

America has wavered between concern for children, the future of the nation, and leaving family life to families, without direct governmental intrusion. Government has never adopted children's allowances as a way of sharing with parents the costs of raising a family; nor has it adopted programs designed to either increase or retard the birth rate. But, a succession of difficulties in family life has led to specific programs, each with a focused population, a constituency, and a rationale that respects the basic dislike of too much government mixing into family life. These can be clustered into five groups for purposes of considering whether or not the array of ad hoc or specialized services add up to a positive national family policy.

A Floor for Family Income

General income maintenance has been covered in Chapter 3, but specific child-oriented income warrants additional comment. The basic federal program is Aid to Families with Dependent Children (AFDC). This was originally a program to ensure income for children made dependent by absence of a male wage earner due to death, incapacity, or desertion. Over time, however, the program became enmeshed in other moral issues. While no one has publicly advocated that poor children go hungry, the increase in single-parent families, often headed by young black or Hispanic unmarried mothers has produced hostile reactions. The program has always been means tested, but over time it has also been made more and more restrictive both to discourage an increase in family patterns considered deviant from the national norm and to encourage adult recipients to return to work as quickly as possible. Work incentive programs have sought to influence the career patterns of young AFDC mothers by pressing and equipping them for early employment. At the same time, national policy has introduced new incentives for the states (which administer the program) to locate absent fathers and to secure child support payments through legal means wherever the father has moved. The program has become a fragile shield against starvation, where containment or reduction of public expenditure, rather than child or family well-being, is the major criterion for program effectiveness. Despite the disincentives, the program has continued at a significant level. In 1974 it supported 3.2 million families with 7.7 million minor children, and in 1980 the numbers grew to 3.7 million families with 7.4 million children. In 1974 the average family grant was $240.70 a month (supplemented by various in-kind benefits, such as food stamps and medical care), which increased in 1980 to only $280.03 despite substantial price inflation.[18]

The AFDC program, in spite of its restrictive character, remains the major source of economic security for a large proportion of minor children; it enables parents, usually single parents, to keep a family unit together. Over time, the program has been expanded to cover the income needs of parents. Beginning in 1961, eligibility was slowly expanded to include not only families dependent because of the death, absence, or incapacity of the wage earner but also those dependent because of unemployment. The program supports families with children, but hardly in a manner to nurture or enhance child life; the low level of relief payment ensures poor housing and skimpy nutrition without attention to other needs that families and children have to take a social part in the life of their times—clothing, transportation, etc.

The program is supplemented indirectly for some dependent children covered by the old age survivors program of Social Security, who draw modest "insurance" benefits earned by a deceased wage earner.

Health of Families and Children

Health has already been covered in general terms in Chapter 4. A variety of specialized health programs address either maternal or child health. Of all the federal programs, the maternal and child health (MCH) program of the Social Security Act most clearly addresses issues of family health. It is based on the concept that healthy mothers and healthy children assure a healthy

---

[18] Annual Reports of the Social Security Administration and Annual Statistical Supplements to the *Social Security Bulletin*.

foundation for family life and future generations. Since pregnancy and infancy are vulnerable periods, medical care for pregnant women and postnatal medical care for both mother and child constitute a major frontier for prevention of illness. The postnatal period is one when information and education can be unobtrusively introduced into mother–child relationships to strengthen family ties, and the structure for service can be used for early identification of difficulties, either physical or emotional, to facilitate early treatment. The MCH program, administered originally through the Public Health Service and stimulated by studies of the Children's Bureau before its dissolution, funds projects through either state or local health departments. The projects are not universal, as they are in several European states, but mainly reach urban and rural poor, and ethnic minorities in the cities.

A crippled children's program, administered through state agencies, relieves families of some burdens. It takes many forms, working through health departments, private physicians, and hospitals. Its main objective is early identification of crippling conditions that can be treated early medically. Although the program originally concentrated on orthopedic conditions, most projects now funded under the program serve a broad range of severely handicapping conditions.

Beginning in the 1950s, public and professional attention to the retarded, and later to children with other developmentally disabling conditions, led to extensive federal support for special activities to improve conditions of the retarded in institutions and to encourage their retention in, or return to, more normal or mainstream existence in the community, living either with their families or in special community residences.

Family planning has been on the national policy agenda for decades. At first, it was intended to enable families to control and space family size to match family economic and emotional capacities. As family patterns changed and illegitimacy became a way of life for many families, moral issues began to shape the nature of policy. Federal funds have been sanctioned for family planning in income maintenance programs, and Title XX funds give family planning preferential treatment. However, none of this has led to an explicit policy about population—to encourage growth or not. In the 1970s, moral issues about abortion came to dominate the public debate, with protagonists and opponents maneuvering over the use of public funds, over medical practice, and over education intended to interfere in any way with reproduction.

Social Disorganization

Although direct and positive intervention in family life has been resisted, a wide range of special problems have risen to public consciousness that support numerous specialized programs, built up piece by piece. Most of these policies are influenced by the tides of public awareness (and forgetting) of children's troubles, which also stir public concern that "something must be done." The range of such interests and parallel programs is too wide to describe in detail; in 1976, 200 federal programs affecting children were funded. Taken together, they add up to a growing federal involvement in children's needs, which may in time coalesce into a family policy as well. But at present, these actions are minor and experimental. Most policy and programming responsibility to protect children remains with state governments. At the level of the federal government, with the submergence of the Children's Bureau, a national Administration on Families, Children and Youth within the Department of Health and Human Services has become the umbrella for a variety of social services directly affecting children, but it reaches only a few federal programs; others are lodged in the Social Security Administration, Labor Department, Veterans Administration, and Department of Education.

Children who are neglected, abused, or abandoned, or whose behavior is too difficult for families to cope with can come into public care. At the state level, comprehensive departments of social services and departments of institutions or of mental health are the usual administrative base for public care. In 1970, about 500,000 children under age 18 years lived away from relatives, about half in formal or informal foster homes. Another approximately 250,000 lived in institutions.[19]

While a clear federal policy is not easy to trace, it became clear by 1980 that the main thrust of that policy has been to use limited federal tax dollars to encourage community care outside of institutions wherever possible. So-called mainstreaming has characterized policy in mental health, developmental disability, and juvenile delinquency. The conflict about appropriateness of care is not resolved, and both institutional and noninstitutional means are needed and supported. However, the intent of the Mental Health Act, with its support of community mental health centers, clearly pressed for community-level care. The Developmental Disability Act turned to the public school system to assure care for the developmentally disabled in the least restrictive and segregating environments. The latter act guarantees parents the right to a comprehensive assessment of disabled children's needs and arrangement for remedial attention through the schools. State departments of social services, as in Massachusetts, use other federal funds (such as those from Title XX of the Social Security Act) in addition to state funds to provide professional help for families as well as for their children, in an attempt to shore up a family's capacity to care for its children. Even the most difficult cases of child neglect and abuse become the obligation of such departments, whose staff is charged with keeping a child at home if at all possible.

[19] Sheila Kammerman and Alfred Kahn, *Social Services in the United States* (Philadelphia: Temple University Press, 1976) Chap. 4, Table 4–1, p. 215.

In 1972 the Juvenile Delinquency Prevention Act financed a variety of state and locally administered community-based programs for youths in difficulty with the law: community prevention; individual, group, and family counseling and guidance; vocational training; social centers; halfway houses and emergency shelters. As the support of this comprehensive effort waned, parts of it were taken over by a legal assistance program to help the states modernize their legal and criminal justice programs. Other segments became absorbed either by states or by other federal programs, such as Title XX and the Runaway Youth Act. Child abuse and prevention legislation provides federal help to establish information systems about abuse and to support protective programs.

By the 1980s, a wholly new and significant step was taken to alter child care by federal action. Aside from medical care and counseling, the major social device for child care in cases of severe family trouble has been placement in a foster home or an institution. All such programs, whether under voluntary agency or local government auspices, have been premised on continuing work with families and early return of children to their care. The reality has often been otherwise, with little effective work with families and long years of child placement. New federal legislation introduces strong incentives to states to move children in placement into adoption if early return to a natural family is not possible. The incentives include money inducements for adopting families and penalties through the grant-in-aid system for programs that do not reduce the average length of stay in foster care. Ten million dollars was budgeted for 1982 for state use.

The sum of these various developments has been to steadily move the national government more deeply into family policy matters, although the process has proceeded by fits and starts. Still a sense of direction has emerged, although untidily. With the coming of a minimalist government administration, there are clues that the federal role will not be much reduced, although its direction may change. Programs continue to be funded but are not growing; social services are not popular, but federal guidelines, regulations, and conditions attached to reimbursement or grants-in-aid are relied upon instead. A clear and controversial example is the vigorous position taken about financing abortion services, where the government has turned from support to opposition.

Day Care

Day care for children of working parents is a crucial area of family policy that remains unresolved. National administrations continue to be stalemated by two opposing desires: to have all able-bodied adults at work and off public support and at the same time to have children well cared for. The economic facts do not permit all young mothers to work, while the social mores of the times create many single-parent families. A basic national system of child day care would seem to be one reasonable way out of the dilemma, but to date this solution has proven unacceptable. An alternative to providing income to mothers with small children without work require- ment has been equally unacceptable. Basic federal programs, such as Title XX and AFDC (by allowing for costs of day care in calculating eligibility), pro- vide minor backing for the growth of some day care for poor families. The political controversy has been paralleled by a professional one: Should day care be educational in nature—that is, based on child development prin- ciples—or can it be mainly child care or custodial? While the values of a de- velopmental service have been established, it is also costly, and there is an undercurrent of popular belief that it is unnecessary: Small children can be well cared for by any mother, while older children can go to public school.

Budget constraints combine with basic attitudes about family respon- sibility to limit day care growth. In 1973 nearly $2 billion dollars was spent on day care, preschool, and afterschool programs for children, reaching about 33% of children 4 years of age and about 15% of 3-year-olds. In 1970, 4 million children under age 5 years had some day care out of a total child population under age 5 years of 17 million. Half of these had care in their own homes, just over a fourth in someone else's home (family day care), and the balance either in group day care (220,000) or with a mother's care while she was working.[20] To expand a day-care network, whether it is for all children or only for those in poor families, involves a massive increase in financing and a possible displacement of present family care by public tax programs, thus shifting the balance between state and family responsibility in a major way.

Education

The nation's educational system is a final area that the federal government has entered in recent years. Historically, education of the young has been within family and local or state government domains. However, racial dis- crimination and, to a much lesser extent, the increasing incidence of child- hood disability (as discussed earlier) has brought government into educa- tional policy in ways that affect families both directly and indirectly. The most welfare-oriented innovation was the Head Start program. Before 1970, evidence mounted that minority children in poor families did poorly in school and as a result grew into adults who worked in low-paying jobs or had long periods of unemployment as unskilled workers. This was matched with evidence that this cycle was not inevitable, that improvement in learn- ing at the early years had long-term beneficial consequences. In the turbu- lence of the 1960s that characterized race relations, a significant nationally

---

[20] Kammerman and Kahn, *Social Services in the United States*, Chap. 2.

funded program called Head Start was launched to enrich the early education of poor children. In 1980, $700 million was budgeted to reach 414,000
children; this had increased to $950 million for 374,000 children in 1982.
The Developmental Disability Act, already discussed, is another example of
how social welfare policy can be pursued through the schools.

The Reagan administration has sought to use the schools for quite different policy ends. Partly out of a conviction that parents should choose
where to educate their children, but, more likely, to counter the trend
toward desegregation of public schools, various incentives have been proposed to permit families to deduct the costs of private education from their
taxes, which in turn would undermine the fiscal base for public education.
What is significant is that this is more evidence that federal authority in
family matters is not likely to diminish, whatever administration is elected.
What does change is the end to which federal influence is used.

Family Policy

A reasonable conclusion from the foregoing discussion of family policy concerning children and the aged is that the federal government has indeed
moved steadily to enlarge its influence over family life. What is lacking is a
consistent and coherent purpose or direction for the influence to take. Instead, in keeping with the American tradition, specific problems are dealt
with as they arise, the results being shaped by a political battle of ideologies
that does not lead to any general concept of the family in national life.

One viewpoint was enunciated by the White House Conference on Children in 1970:

> *Society* has the ultimate responsibility for the wellbeing and optimum develop-
> ment of all children. The implementation of this responsibility requires that
> child development services such as day care, Head Start and after school pro-
> grams be available . . . to meet the needs of *all* children whose parents or guar-
> dians request, or whose circumstances require, such services . . . and that all
> child development services be completely separated from public assistance
> programs. They must not be developed to lessen public assistance roles (sic)
> but rather as a basic right.[21]

But the realities of the political process have produced a different outcome
to date. In AFDC, income is often below the minimum for decent family life,
and mothers are pressed to work without child care being available. Day-

[21] *White House Conference Report on Children, Report to the President* (Washington, D.C.:
U.S. Government Printing Office, 1971), pp. 286–287.

care policy is unresolved. Additionally, the consequences of family and personal disorganization are dealt with after the troubles arise, through a miscellany of service programs. Health services, especially those to reinforce family health, are not widely developed. Education, as a preparation for adult life, is fought over, but its constructive growth has been obscured by issues of race.

In a negative sense, it might appear that encouraging mothers to enter the labor market, aided by the terribly slow spread of day-care centers, could be interpreted to mean that there is a family policy which further reduces the home obligations of family members. It remains moot whether federal family policy strengthens or weakens the family. It can be argued that freeing women to work leads to freer adults of both sexes and that this in turn produces healthier family relationships. But the counterargument can also be made that this process, encouraged by government action, weakens family ties by encouraging successive changes as adults divorce and remarry or as family care is replaced by impersonal professional day care. If the issue is not resolved by evidence, it is at least reasonable to conclude that federal policy is premised on the first of the two arguments. Unfortunately the motives have been quite different—to reduce public expenditures regardless of the social consequences.

A recent volume reporting the conclusions of a series of conferences comes to rather grim conclusions.[22] Kessen, in reviewing the series, says:

> In the center is the ambiguity of commitment Americans have to children. No longer an economic asset, no longer a comfort in our old age, no longer a continuation of our people in the traditional pattern of our forebears, (we must ask how long a society which exiles its old folks can preserve its continuity with the young), the American child is becoming both in his own life (as a child) and in the lives of his parents, without function.[23]

This is a harsh indictment, but not unreasonable when we consider that parents are encouraged to give up much of the daily care of their children, that children leave home early and set up independent households whether or not they establish families of their own, and that the obligation to care for aged parents is now shifted to public income supports or to nursing homes. Aside from loving each other, what functions do parents and children have for each other in times of trouble (as well as of pleasure)?

At the heart of the matter lies the dilemma of what set of values we can explicate, and whether these should be held and exercised by families privately, or whether government should be expected to intervene actively in family life to further one or another set of values.

---

[22] Nathan Talbot, *Raising Children in America* (Boston: Little, Brown, 1976).
[23] William Kessen, "Ambiguous Commitment," *Science* 193 (July 23, 1976): 310–311.

A common response in the past has been to build up service programs incrementally to take care of discrete difficulties as they arise. But now underlying social trends have challenged many earlier assumptions. Our basic social norms concerning the relative position of government vis-à-vis the family have been overtaken by unanticipated developments in our culture. Families were once the bulwark, and they were treated as sovereign with respect to family needs. Government entered mainly when families, a few in proportion, proved incapable or incompetent to cope with certain stresses. In time, these trends merged with a much more powerful tide, the freeing of individual members of families to realize their aspirations as individuals, not as members of close family units. If we are to acquire a new public family policy, we confront very painful choices. Can we expect the family to function as a unit if family members do not perform clear functions or bear certain responsibilities? And if we extend certain function-relieving services to everyone as a matter of right, do these really strengthen the family as a unit or do they free its members as individuals? And beyond this, do we want government to act on one or the other conception of family function?

Evolution of family or child-care policies has been complicated by changing views about what constitutes a family. Children with only one parent, adults living together without children, communal living groups of unrelated individuals, permanent liasons between individuals of the same sex are all considered families in much modern thinking. How much sustained responsibility such groupings should take for their members vis-à-vis the responsibility government owes to the individuals is not at all clear. This change in public attitude will certainly affect the future evolution of policy concerning the aged, children, and the family as a collectivity.

Despite the turmoil, confusion, and gloomy predictions, the trend as far as the federal government's role is concerned is not dark; it is still growing and evolving. Within the ups and downs of budget financing and economic boom and recession, the government's cumulative role from 1950 to 1980 has been forward looking. The federal government has used its still nascent influence to turn local programs away from segregated institutions, services, and schools and back to community-oriented services and schools. The government is more reluctant to help the poor than the better off, but it has moved to help even the poor in specific programs that ease pressures on families when serious economic, social, or physical threats arise. The help is not universal—it is means tested—but it is there, and it has grown over time, regardless of changes in administration. The national effort to reduce the federal commitment for family life has not yet destroyed this trend, although it has slowed it down. Future elections will decide whether government will continue to help families in crises, or whether a positive policy to nurture children and to shore up family life will mature.

Additional Readings

Butler, Robert. *Why Survive: Being Old in America*. New York: Harper & Row, 1975.

Costin, Lela. *Child Welfare: Policies and Practices*. New York: McGraw-Hill, 1972.

Frankfather, Dwight; Caro, Francis; and Smith, Michael. *Family Care of the Elderly*. Lexington: Lexington Books, 1981.

Kadushin, Alfred. *Child Welfare Services*. 2d ed. New York: Macmillan, 1974.

Kammerman, Sheila, and Kahn, Alfred. *Social Services in the United States*. Philadelphia: Temple University Press, 1976.

Lawton, S. Powell. *Planning and Managing Housing for the Elderly*. New York: Wiley, 1975.

Low, Seth, and Spingler, Pearl. *Child Care Arrangements of Working Mothers*. Children's Bureau Publication 453. Washington, D.C.: U.S. Department of Health, Education, and Welfare, 1968.

Maas, Henry, and Engler, Richard. *Children in Need of Parents*. New York: Columbia University Press, 1959.

Riley, Matilda, and Foner, Anne. *Aging and Society*. Vols. 1 and 2. New York: Russell Sage Foundation, 1969.

Shanas, Ethel, et al. *Old People in Three Industrial Societies*. New York: Atherton, 1968.

Steiner, Gilbert. *The Children's Cause*. Washington, D.C.: Brookings Institution, 1976.

Steiner, Peter, and Dorfman, Robert. *Economic Status of the Aged*. Berkeley: University of California Press, 1957.

Talbot, Nathan. *Raising Children in America*. Boston: Little, Brown, 1976.

Some Policy Alternatives

8

The examples of national policies used in the previous chapters to illustrate the emergence of an American welfare state owe their growth to events of the years between 1930 and 1980. Given the tendency to remember the recent past, most advocates of these policies and their beneficiaries have come to accept them as permanent and natural parts of American society, destined to grow and increase although perhaps slowed down now and again. As we consider the outlook for the future, a sketchy review of history can introduce a valuable corrective in perspective.

The Longer Sweep of Policy Evolution: Before 1930

America's national social welfare is usually dated from 1930, but current policy and the social norms that shape, energize, and also limit its evolution (as discussed in Chapter 2) have a history that started long before that date. In colonial times, most Americans were not only new settlers in a vast continent that they considered almost empty but they were for the most part poor. A few came with a backing of inherited wealth in England, Holland, France, or Spain, but most were religious dissidents or working people trying to make a new life. To relieve the worst of that poverty, they relied on local community cooperation and the skeleton of the English poor laws that laid down a solid framework for local government responsibility to help the poor. Government (local) was a major instrument that citizens used freely.

But in the context of colonial America, the poor meant widows, orphans, stranded sick travelers, and the aged or disabled. These were the clearly helpless in a rough frontier, but there was little provision for unemployment for the able-bodied or the wanderer. The poor, as then defined, were not despised or looked down on as less deserving. Poverty was an accepted part of the human condition. Local responsibility, self-reliance, and attention to a few categories of need were from the beginning the basic elements of caring for each other.

As the next 200 years passed, the national scene was slowly transformed and so were attitudes about welfare. Population grew; immigration brought different cultures that were slowly absorbed; cities replaced rural villages; wealth accumulated; and economic and social classes became separated from each other. Certain religious beliefs also began to dominate; the moralizing attitudes of the well-to-do became widespread, and the able-bodied poor were seen as responsible for their own plight (due to sloth or sinfulness) or poor because this was their destiny in a religion of predestination. The political wars that characterized the seventeenth and eighteenth centuries secured political freedom, but this freedom did not insure economic security. The popular beliefs that all people should be responsible for themselves and their families (except in the few instances of disaster, such as death, illness, and old age) and that the state should interfere as little as possible in human affairs became further solidified.

Despite this underlying world view, public action for the disadvantaged grew and spread, although mainly in local and state governments. Public hospitals and institutions for the mentally ill were established. Tax subsidy was advanced to nonprofit voluntary agencies to help orphaned children and the adult poor, mixing some economic help and moral education. In years of acute economic depression, which recurred with regularity, state and local governments appropriated tax dollars to be distributed as emergency relief, sometimes out of charity and sometimes to head off local violence. So the uses of government enlarged, but slowly and only in crises.

By the end of the nineteenth century, after 200 years in which sharply limited views about welfare prevailed, a slow change set in, starting with the Progressive Era. The new "social scientists" (sociologists, psychologists, and economists)—joined with the more liberal social workers of the period and paralleled the growth of trade unions and of left-wing socialist political thinking. All added new ways of thinking. The Progressive Party, led by a maverick Republican, Theodore Roosevelt, argued for the responsibility of the national government to intervene actively in the economic and social concerns of the nation. National responsibility had already been extended to veterans and their families (after the Civil War) and to merchant seamen, on whom the national trade depended. The industrialization of the economy focused public attention on periodic massive unemployment, on slum housing that bred disease and overcrowding, and on occupational injury. These issues entered into public debate. Several state governments adopted public programs of welfare and income for mothers with dependent children and for the aged, and state laws were passed to protect industrial workers.

Policy change, as permitted by the electorate in an open system of government, was obviously very slow. These 200 years of American history saw a remarkable persistence in a few basic beliefs about public obligation to the disadvantaged that are captured by the norms already discussed. The roots of these attitudes even antedate American history. We can turn to a 2500-year history of beliefs and attitudes in the Western world that reinforce these basic attitudes. From the earliest Christian, Hebrew, Greek, and Roman times, belief in collective obligation to help the poor was limited. But a few exceptions did exist: helping the widowed, orphaned, aged, and sick; family and personal reliance on one's individual efforts; and personal ties of reciprocity between helper and helped in case of charity.

At the height of Greek and Roman civilization, governments of city-states went further and provided food and fuel for the poor as a public obligation, but only if 90% of the population were poor and all citizens (even slaves) were bound together in an intricate network of personal, not public, obligation. From kings and emperors down to slaves, through many classes of citizens, each person was bound to those above and below in obligations to help and to serve. It is true that, during the course of history, a few voices were periodically raised, calling for concern and care for those in distress, including the able-bodied poor, and outside the ties of family or close friendship, but public, collective action remained within the old limits and only supplemented a personal obligation of humane people of means.[1]

The Short-Term in Policy

In the late nineteenth and during the twentieth centuries, major changes began to arise in most Western industrialized nations. What we have now come to call the welfare state began to expand in Germany, England, and Scandinavia. Its main principle was that the national government in industri-

---

[1] The intricate history of caring for others has not been fully explored, except for the emergence of the poor laws in England and for recent American history. Indications about the nature of this history can be found in such books as Robert Bremner, *From the Depths: Discovery of Poverty in America* (New York: New York University Press, 1956); Karl de Schweinitz, *Englands Road to Social Security* (Philadelphia: University of Pennsylvania Press, 1937); A. R. Hands, *Charities in Rome and Greece* (London: Paines and Hudson, 1968); David Rothman, *Discovery of Asylum* (Boston: Little Brown and Co., 1971); Robert Morris, *Why Care for the Stranger*, forthcoming.

alized, urbanized societies has a primary obligation to look after the basic needs of all citizens—for health, housing, income, and the like. It was no longer considered proper to rely on oneself, one's family, or private charity alone, for these could not command the resources that the pressures of a modern economy impose. It is not surprising that this evolution emerged first in the mature economies of western Europe, but it is not often noted that the growth did not result from maturity alone. It was propelled by underlying economic and social forces. A succession of wars made centralized economies dependent on masses of the population for support, and to elicit that support required that something be given to improve the condition of the masses, among whom the poor were once conservatively estimated to number as much as 50%. At the same time, industrialization made possible the mass production of goods to improve life conditions for large numbers of people.

Similar pressures did not build up powerfully in the United States until the 1930s, when a major economic depression caused a crisis comparable to a major war in Europe in the extent of its shock to basic social values and institutions. In the 1930s, the United States began a rapid development of national social policies and programs that soon came to approach, but not to equal, the breadth of welfare provision in northern and western European nations. For the purposes of this analysis, it is important to recall how close the American welfare system, despite this growth, has stayed to the constraining social norms of its long history. If we look only at the post-1930 period, a brief time in the history of welfare ideas, it is easy to see how welfare advocates have come to believe that social provision by a national government will continue to grow and expand. It is only when we take a look at the much longer history sketched above that we realize that continuous growth, although a part of American ideology, is not a guaranteed nor straight path for the future.

Beginning in 1970, and accelerating with the Republican capture of the White House and the Senate in 1980, it has become clear that a slowdown, at least, and possibly a reversal in policy can take place. Some of the outcomes of this shift have been touched on in the previous chapters. What follows is an attempt to look at alternative future courses of evolution in American social policy and in the shape of an American welfare state. Is growth along established paths inevitable? What alternatives exist, either along wholly new pathways or paralleling the old ones?

The search for policy alternatives opens up a cornucopia of possibilities, ranging from the most utopian to the most narrowly technical. Choice among the vast range can be narrowed by deciding upon the time frame to be used. The most utopian alternatives require for their execution a basic change in social values and attitudes and therefore require several generations to bring about the desired changes. An illustration is the view that income should be distributed according to need and not according to ability or any contribution to society's productive capacity. At the other extreme, narrowly technical policies can be put into effect immediately, but although they may have wide rippling effects, they do not change the nature of the problem. An illustration would be the introduction of coinsurance requirements to all health insurance policies as a means of controlling the use of health services and affecting the cost distribution between government and consumer.

This chapter will consider some alternative policies that might reasonably be adopted by governments, given the tempo of history and the underlying social constraints discussed in Chapter 1. In other words, we will be interested in alternatives that move beyond the present structure for human service delivery, but not so far that there is no likelihood of their adoption without a cataclysmic overthrow of present social and public institutional forms. Before considering alternative policies, however, it is worth examining dilemmas policymakers confront in the process of selection.

Conflict of Rights

Many analyses have explored the powerful influence of ignorance, limited vision, and political opposition on the selection of policy alternatives.[2] Less attention has been directed to a more basic difficulty—namely, reconciling conflicting rights. Frequently a perfectly good idea, when translated into policy for action, turns out to remedy one ill at the price of violating another right. For example, in recent years housing policy has attempted to remedy the lack of adequate housing for those with limited income and has been concerned with building neighborhood vitality. Several programs have produced low-cost housing, usually concentrated in areas of the city where the poor tend to live. This, on the surface, seems not unreasonable, for the poor do tend to cluster in neighborhoods with the housing they can afford; the new low-cost housing is seen as a means of strengthening these neighborhoods and improving housing at the same time. Unfortunately, where the programs have been effective, they have produced a situation that by other criteria is seen as undesirable—namely, the concentration of the poor in delimited parts of the city. The fact that income influences population distribution and is also a positive factor in developing neighborly relation-

---

[2] See, for example, Peter Marris and Martin Rein, *The Dilemmas of Reform* (New York: Atherton, 1967); Martin Meyerson and Edward Banfield, *Politics Planning and the Public Interest* (New York: Free Press, 1955); Alan Atschuler, *The City Planning Process* (Ithaca, N.Y.: Cornell University Press, 1965); Daniel Hirshfield, *The Lost Reform* (Cambridge, Mass.: Harvard University Press, 1970).

ships among compatible persons and families is seen by many to be in itself undesirable. The inhabitants of close-knit neighborhoods wish to maintain the character of their neighborhoods, while improving the quality of life in them, but this leads to separation by income class. The awkward situation thus arises that actions that follow the norms of urban social organization produce results deemed undesirable by those seeking to equalize economic and social relationships. In Boston 1976 funds for low-cost housing were slashed for one low-income area that had been quite successful in mobilizing, building, and occupying federally subsidized housing; the reason given for the cuts was that the neighborhood had an overconcentration of low-income families.

Such examples can be multiplied almost indefinitely. We find a strong desire to have accessible to all the highest quality of medical care, as represented by access to complex teaching hospitals, and at the same time a strong desire to have health services close at hand in small neighborhoods, responsive to ethnic and cultural differences. The services made possible by the concentration of medical personnel and technology in large centers cannot be replicated in small hospital units, serving small groups of people. They would be underutilized and the cost of such duplication would be wasteful. Similarly, the services provided by small neighborhood health centers, controlled by indigenous residents cannot be reproduced in a large medical center.

In programs for the elderly, there is a powerful impetus to develop services attuned to their special circumstances: their slower physical pace, the content of their education (so different from present-day education), and their vocational status. Counter to this is the urgent desire to avoid age segregation, much as we seek to avoid race segregation. Senior centers usually separate users from those of other ages, but unsegregated centers usually are unable to meet the needs of the aged while also meeting the needs of teenage youth.

The attempts to seek equity in income maintenance encounter the cross fire of conflicting rights of the very poor, the working poor, and those with higher incomes. The very poor should be assured a decent income without loss of dignity, but the working poor want to have their work efforts rewarded differentially from those who do not work. And those with higher incomes feel they should help only those who help themselves—for example, by working—which leads to the introduction of often undignified and inhumane control procedures.

Recognition of conflicting rights give policymakers a new obligation: to assess the extent to which any policy aimed at redressing a violated right carries with it the likelihood of violating different but related rights. Public policy today demands this more complex level of evaluation and is no longer satisfied by the selection of alternatives simply through power play among political forces.

The search for policy alternatives is therefore more complex than a direct attempt to correct a clear injustice. It involves attention to equally deserving but contradictory rights, awareness of the socially inherited value biases of citizen constituencies, and consideration of the time frame adopted for action. With such a framework in mind, we can turn to some policy alternatives that have been advanced in each of the areas we have undertaken to review.

Overall Policy

Social theorists sometimes argue for adoption of an overall policy within which other actions will be shaped. If this were applied literally to social welfare, it would require that welfare decisions be subsumed within a policy that deals with the entire economy and sociology of the nation. Within that framework, welfare becomes a relatively minor factor as long as its purposes are the care of the dependent and neglected, who constitute a small proportion of the population even though their numbers are large in absolute terms. It is sometimes argued that all social existence is welfare, including the production of material goods, food, recreation and the distribution of all goods among all classes. In that sense, social policy becomes societal policy governing all aspects of existence. It exceeds both the experience and expertness of those concerned with the more narrow definitions of welfare used thus far. Although the narrower experience can give valuable testimony to other policy and political debates, it is not overall experience.

In the broader context, the issues become more than advocacy for more social programs. They involve serious questions about the proportion of a nation's economic and social energy to be cycled through government: How much of it is to be directed to social benefits? How do such decisions affect the capacity of the society to continue to be innovative and productive enough to produce all that its system demands? The disciplines of political economy, not social welfare, must be invoked. There is no empirical basis for judging what portion of the GNP taken up by taxes and recycled through government will begin to undermine the production of the very goods and services and lead to economic castastrophe. This is a judgment argued with passion by those who want less taxes and by those who want more services. Experts in economic and political theory lack concensus and evidence from which to draw any conclusion. Tax revenue as a percentage of the GNP is often used as a measure but can range from 50% in Denmark through over 40% in Germany and Britain and 30% in the United States. But the scale of welfare programs is different in each country. The economies also differ in their capacity to produce jobs, income, and goods (see Tables 8.5 and 8.6). As

a result, overall policy as measured by such gross indexes of public investment is not yet helpful.

Fortunately, there is another sense in which overall policy can be applied to welfare as conventionally defined. If we believe that welfare programs contribute to the well-being of all people indirectly, as well as to
clients directly, then social policy would give attention to much more than
programs and appropriations by government for dependent and needy
groups. Two additional areas are discussed below.

The first is the role of welfare programs in creating jobs, not as public
service employment of last resort, but as part of the base economy. Approximately 400,000 people identify themselves as social workers in the U.S. Census surveys. To these must be added an unknown additional number of
clerks, typists, office workers, transportation and maintenance workers as
well as those who practice in welfare agencies but choose not to identify
themselves as social workers. If schools, prisons, and the like are included,
the numbers of employees rises to some millions, a significant addition to the
work force. They are not treated as welfare beneficiaries, but their dependence on a welfare system for employment has become a standard part
of the national economy. These numbers become the object of attack by
those who wish to reduce public expenditure. But it they were to become
unemployed, they would have to either find employment elsewhere (in an
economy with a growing level of long-term unemployment) or become dependent on the very welfare services that are being cut back. Thus, a larger
analysis of welfare systems as a part of welfare benefits and also of welfare
costs to a society is needed. In like manner, the goods consumed by welfare
recipients must be produced, and their producers also benefit from welfare
directly. Are they to be treated as beneficiaries too?

Such an enlarged framework for welfare analysis permits the analysis
to deal with the realities of what is often called the service society as distinguished from a producer society. However, the viability of a service society
depends on production and distribution of the basic material goods on
which its population depends, so that overall attention has then to be given
to the relationship between material goods and less material services in
creating a satisfying society.

The second example is the role of industry, family, and profit in providing welfare. Most analyses of social welfare treat public or tax-supported
programs and those supported by philanthropy. Recent studies have indicated that this seriously understates the nature and extent of welfare.[3] In
fact, industry has become a major contributor to social welfare in two ways.

[3] See Martin Rein and Lee Rainwater, From Welfare State to Welfare Society (Cambridge,
Mass:. Joint Center for Urban Studies Harvard-MIT, 1980). See also Lester Thurman, The Zero
from Society, and Organization for European Economic Development "Public Expenditure
Trends" June 1978 (Paris: OECD).

It pays, as a part of labor contracts, about a third of its wage bill in social benefits, mainly for health insurance and mainly in the heavily organized basic industries. In addition, some publicly mandated programs place on employers the obligation to finance the programs through payroll taxes. In addition, families and individuals contribute to their own welfare in a still significant way through taxation. Individuals also provide for many services for family members either by in-kind or cash payments. In 1975 the sum of employer and personal contributions to major social programs (such as Social Security and unemployment insurance) as a percentage of the GNP equaled the total of government income transfer payments for the same programs. A 1974 study of the distribution of household economic resources in the United Kingdom found that, in that advanced welfare state, employers contributed 42% to various funds and programs, government another 42%, and households about 15%.

These two examples suggest that not only are welfare policy issues complex but they involve financial support from other institutions in society in addition to government or public tax dollars. The need for a particular service program can be argued, but the decision to act and the method of action chosen will depend on the relationships between any claim made for welfare and the claims made by other elements in society, even when all elements agree upon the existence of a need that warrants public action. Overall policy approaches seek to deal with such matters, but this is an area of policy action into which social welfare has not yet entered, except as one of many contending claimants.[4]

If one moves away from general policies, welfare policy guidelines can be derived from a comparison of the Johnson Great Society years and the later Nixon administration.[5] Despite apparent differences in the rhetoric of political debate, these two periods follow a more or less common path as to the scope of federal responsibility. They were committed to using federal programs to help shape American life, and while there were differences in the rate of growth in federal expenditure for social welfare, a review of the budgets indicates that federal spending to that end expanded during both administrations. The major distinctions were the slower rate of growth under Nixon and the objectives toward which such expenditure was directed. Also, it seemed to be an implicit assumption of the Nixon administration that the federal government's role was to *govern*, not to do—that is, to set guiding rules, but not to administer programs directly. This could explain the persistent efforts to return programs to local author-

---

[4] Martin Rein and Lisa Peattie, *Women's Claims* (Oxford: Oxford University Press, 1983); Martin Rein "Social Policy of the Firm," *Policy Sciences* 14, no. 2 (April 1982).

[5] See Sar Levitan and Robert Taggart, *The Promise of Greatness* (Cambridge, Mass.: Harvard University Press, 1976), which has been drawn upon for this comparison, providing a useful elaboration.

ity, to voluntary agencies, or to the marketplace, albeit with tax support. The Johnson programs also encouraged new volunteer efforts, but public administration was not avoided. Policy alternatives that reflect such strategic differences are not difficult to identify. In health it comes to public management of insurance versus private insurance company management, or support of public hospitals and clinics versus reliance on private physicians. In housing there is a choice between public construction and management of low-cost housing versus private construction with tax subsidy and private ownership and management. In income there is public assistance in some form versus unemployment insurance plus some kind of family or children's allowance.

Johnson's program emphasized the provision of goods, services, and income to the poor and the disadvantaged. The objective was an assault on poverty and improvement of the condition of minorities, especially blacks. It supported community action agencies to give poor consumers a better voice in decisions about programs; legal services, adult education, and neighborhood centers (especially for health) were developed and supported. VISTA, a job corps, a neighborhood youth corps, and other vocational training programs were designed to help the poor improve their economic skills. Head Start and Upward Bound were designed to overcome educational and social disadvantages beginning at the earliest years. Many of these programs sought to change the economic, political, and social bargaining position of the poor.

By contrast, the Nixon administration shifted away from such changes in the socioeconomic arrangements, although it continued to increase expenditures to relieve acute distress. The Nixon program moved away from a primary concern for the poor or very poor and extended its welfare services to the working poor, whose needs did not involve actual physical subsistence. This broadening of the welfare base inevitably reduced the benefits available to the very poorest. Johnson combined socioeconomic change with traditional welfare for the poor. Nixon abandoned the economic change elements, but his broadened relief programs, through the Family Assistance Plan, blurred the conventional boundary between the poor who worked and those who did not.

Johnson worked for a federally administered health insurance and secured passage of Medicare, a federally administered program for the aged. In contrast, Nixon cut funds for hospital construction and for other programs, arguing that the health system needed to be reformed, not expanded. His strategy for reform was a meager program to encourage the development of privately organized health maintenance organizations and a system of physician-organized review of professional services.

In housing the two administrations were less differentiated. The Johnson administration supported the Housing and Urban Development Act of 1965, permitted public housing authorities to lease privately owned dwellings, reduced interest rates on loans to build housing for the poor or aged, and introduced rent supplements for low-income tenants. The Nixon years continued these policies, but funding was markedly reduced.

In other social welfare activities, the two sets of policies differed mainly in priorities. Funds for welfare rose under both administrations. Social expenditures as a share of the total federal budget increased from 26% in 1955 to 33% in 1965 and to 62% in 1974. However, the rate of increase was slowed, as Table 8.1 indicates. (See also Tables 2.1, 2.2, and 2.3.)

The changes in policy from 1964 to 1976 were, of course, a result of complex and contending political forces, but it is reasonable to infer certain policy differences that activated different administrations:

1. Use of the federal government to correct social inequities and to guarantee a minimum standard of welfare for all versus reliance upon private economic processes and slowing the rate of government involvement
2. Commitment to maintain existing programs and to project new ones versus retrenchment or reform of existing systems
3. Belief in constant economic expansion that would produce new income, some of which could be directed to social purposes (the fiscal dividend) without unduly raising taxes versus emphasis on the limits of growth
4. Use of the federal government as an instrument with which to change the private sector (as in the civil rights movement and the

TABLE 8.1
Annual Growth of Federal Social Welfare Expenditures, 1965–1975[a]

Fiscal year	Rate of increase (in percent, based on 1973 dollars)
1965	18
1966	14
1967	10
1968	9
1969	8
1970	15
1971	11
1972	12
1973	5
1974	8

[a]SOURCE: Sar Levitan and Robert Taggart, *The Promise of Greatness* (Cambridge, Mass.: Harvard University Press, 1976), p. 21.

creation of agencies and pathways for services that bypassed traditional state and local organization) versus reliance on voluntary institutions

5. Categorical grant programs aimed at specific problems and populations versus general revenue sharing
6. Belief in taking risks with new experimental strategies to change the
   condition of disadvantaged persons, to "shape civilization," versus
   dependence upon shoring up existing systems, with a hoped-for fil-
   tering down of benefits to the poor

Put another way, one general disposition, akin to a policy direction,
tends to the creation of new agencies, programs, and social institutions to
deal with persisting problems. These problems would be slowly reduced as
a series of purpose-specific programs are created, one after the other. Preexisting programs that overlap the new ones can be either continued or left
to slowly wither away. The counter disposition is to avoid adding still further to the complex of government agencies and instead to rely on efforts to
restructure the ways in which already existing programs and already committed funds are organized.

In many ways, solving problems by restructuring is more difficult than
solving them by creating new programs. Existing organizations and social institutions quite normally fight to maintain themselves. To change them risks
arousing their combined opposition and thus increases the opponents in the
political process through which every policy must make its way. But creating new programs also runs many risks, for the costs of adding new programs may activate other interests or established agencies may feel
threatened by new competition. Whatever the similarity or difference in
political hazard, the policy line for guiding action is clearly quite different:
Different technical tasks are involved in creating new programs, as against
restructuring old ones, and the constellation of political forces is quite different also.

Reversing Policy or Slowing Growth?

With the Republican electoral victory in 1980, belief in the inevitability of
welfare growth was rudely shaken. The new administration brought to office a more clear-cut policy and a more passionate belief in its policy than did
previous conservative administrations. For the first time since the 1930s, it
was the announced policy of the executive branch to remove social welfare
from the national government as rapidly as practical politics permitted. The
boundary of government was defined as stimulating economic growth

through benefits to investors and corporate creators of goods and wealth, which would in turn generate work for all and income for all needs. Voluntary action, especially by corporations, family members, and nonprofit groups, was to be relied upon to meet the many human needs that a "truly needy" population required. Where this failed, government would provide a "safety net" to assure that no truly needy person would suffer, but the definition of need and the level of relief remained subjective and unclear. The administration believed that most people, and especially the able-bodied, could find work if only they tried; efforts to relieve them only delayed their independence.

So sweeping a reversal of policy cannot be easily or quickly acted out. Tables 8.2, 8.3, and 8.4 sum up the effects as of 1982 and 1983. The Congress, not wholly sympathetic with the new vision, saved most of the social programs slated for termination, major cutback, or transfer to state responsibility. Nevertheless, changes were made in 3 years' time (1980–1983) that are radical when compared with past attempts to control the federal social role. Such radical reversals can be pursued by different means:

1. Whole programs can be abolished. Since this requires legislative concurrence, it is not easily achieved.
2. More practical is the slower starvation of unwanted programs by reducing budget requests and appropriations. This can take the form of actual, real dollar cuts or of a denial of increases to compensate for rises in population or in prices.
3. A third approach is to transfer responsibility to the states. In order to avoid obstacles similar to those encountered by (1) above, transfer involves either an accompanying sum of federal dollars, as in a block grant or revenue sharing, or some quid pro quo exchange of obligation. An example of the latter was the Reagan administration's offer to assume the state share of Medicaid costs if the states took over AFDC costs in their entirety.

Any one of these approaches has the policy effect of diminishing the federal role, either in fiscal or in administrative and policymaking responsibility.

Such shifts have thus far been proposed for vulnerable, minor federal social programs that are important to local welfare but do not figure significantly in federal fiscal or management decisions. The major national policy choices involve the so-called entitlement programs—Social Security retirement, disability, Medicare, and the Veterans Administration. It is difficult to conceive of a major retreat from these national commitments, and it has not yet been proposed by even so ideologically committed an administration as that of President Reagan. Instead, steps have been taken to reduce the universalism of such benefits or to constrict the scope of benefits, which is justified as reducing federal tax expenditures and the federal dominance in

TABLE 8.2
Funding Levels in Labor, HHS, and Education Appropriations Bill for Fiscal Year 1984
(in millions of dollars)[a]

	FY 1984		FY 1983
Program	Administration request	Final level	Final level
DEPARTMENT OF LABOR			
Training and employment	3,594	6,419	3,700
Senior Community Service Employment Program (SCSEP)	287.1	317.3	315.2
DEPARTMENT OF HHS			
Social services block grant (Title XX)	2,450	2,675	2,675
Community services block grant	2.9	352.3	384.1
Alcohol, drug abuse, and mental health block grant	340.0	462.0	469.0
Home health demonstration and training	0	5	5
Community health centers	242.0	327.0	360.0
Low-income energy assistance	1,300	1,875	1,975
Administration on aging			
TOTAL	620.8	674.2	671.7
State administration		21.7	21.7
Support services and senior centers (III-B)		240.9	240.9
Congregate meals (III-C)		321.6	319.1
Home-delivered meals		62.0	62.0
Research, training, and demonstrations		22.2	22.2
Maternal and child health block grant	373.0	399.0	317.7
Child welfare services (Title IV-B)	156.0	165.0	156.0
Child abuse prevention and treatment and adoption reform act		16.2	16.2
EDUCATION DEPARTMENT			
Vocational education	492.8	731.3	721.5
Adult education	0	100.0	95.0
Bilingual education	94.5	139.4	110.6
Handicapped education	1,110	1,214	1,199
Rehabilitation services	1,031	1,111	1,450
Guaranteed student loans	2,047	2,257	3,100
Compensatory education for the disadvantaged	3,000	4,700	2,688

[a]SOURCE: Council of Jewish Federations, Washington Office: *News*, December 1983, p. 3.

the economy. Examples are seen in plans to withhold disability payments while appeals are made against administrative denial of benefits on the grounds that some beneficiaries can in fact work despite severe disability. In this instance, the availability of work in a period of high unemployment is not taken into account, only an expert judgment that a handicapped person can do some work. More consistent with welfare state objectives is the proposal to tax retirement benefits when individual or family income rises above a given level.

TABLE 8.3
Block Grants: Estimated Change in Federal Aid, by State, Fiscal Year 1982[a]

HEALTH BLOCK GRANTS

Alcohol, drug abuse, and mental health

Reduced 25–49%
Massachusetts ($7 million)
Mississippi ($3.7 million)
Missouri ($2.1 million)
New York ($21 million)
Ohio ($11 million)
Oklahoma ($2.8 million)
South Dakota ($1.3 million)

Reduced 10–24%
Arizona ($1.7 million)
California ($7.9 million)
Florida ($3 million)
Illinois ($1.8 million)
New Jersey ($4 million)
Washington ($1.1 million)

Level funding
Texas

Maternal and child health
Reduced 25–49%
Arizona ($860,000)
Florida ($1.3 million)
Illinois ($4.4 million)
Mississippi ($1.8 million)

Reduced 10–24%
California ($3.8 million)
Massachusetts ($1.4 million)
Missouri ($1.2 million)
New Jersey ($2 million)
New York ($5 million)
Ohio ($2.1 million)
South Dakota ($200,000)
Texas ($2.7 million)
Washington ($1.1 million)

Reduced less than 10%
Oklahoma ($150,000)

Preventive health
Reduced 50% or more
Oklahoma ($500,000)

Reduced 25–49%
Arizona ($400,000)
Florida ($2.2 million)
Massachusetts ($800,000)
Ohio ($2 million)

Reduced 10–24%
California ($636,000)
Illinois ($200,000)
Missouri ($300,000)
New Jersey ($500,000)
New York ($1 million)
South Dakota ($50,000)
Texas ($540,000)
Washington ($1.1 million)

Reduced less than 10%
Mississippi ($400,000)

OTHER BLOCK GRANTS

Social Services
Reduced 10–24%
Arizona ($3.7 million)
California ($58.2 million)
Florida ($16.8 million)
Illinois ($30 million)
Massachusetts ($19 million)
Missouri ($14 million)
New Jersey ($19 million)
New York ($59 million)
Ohio ($10.5 million)
Oklahoma ($7.2 million)
South Dakota ($1.9 million)
Texas ($17 million)
Washington ($20 million)

Increased funding
Mississippi ($207,000)

Community development—small cities
Increased funding
Arizona ($714,000)
California ($1.4 million)
Florida ($2 million)
Illinois ($1.3 million)
Massachusetts ($4 million)
Mississippi ($3.6 million)
Missouri ($2.7 million)
New Jersey ($1.3 million)
New York ($1.8 million)
Ohio ($4.7 million)
Oklahoma ($2 million)
South Dakota ($940,000)
Texas ($7.3 million)

[a] SOURCE: Richard Nathan and Fred Doolittle, *Consequences of the Cuts* (Princeton, N.J.: Princeton Urban Research Center, 1983), Table 9.

TABLE 8.4
Entitlement Programs: Estimated Change in Federal Aid, by State, Fiscal Year 1982[a]

Aid to Families with Dependent Children	Food stamps
Reduced 10–24%	*Reduced 10–24%*
Florida ($8 million)	California ($60 million)
Massachusetts ($40–45 million)	Massachusetts ($10 million)
Mississippi ($5 million)	New Jersey ($60 million)
Missouri ($15–20 million)	New York ($200 million)
Ohio ($55 million)	Texas ($50–60 million)
Oklahoma ($15–20 million)	*Reduced less than 10%*
Texas ($10–15 million)	Arizona ($3 million)
Reduced less than 10%	Florida ($25 million)
Arizona ($500,000–1 million)	Mississippi ($22 million)
California ($60 million)	Missouri ($1 million)
Illinois ($35–40 million)	Ohio ($20 million)
New Jersey ($15–20 million)	Oklahoma ($6 million)
New York (NA)	South Dakota (NA)
South Dakota ($500,000)	Washington (NA)
Washington ($6–10 million)	**Child nutrition**
Medicaid	*Reduced 25–49%*
Reduced less than 10%	Massachusetts ($21 million)
California ($50 million)	*Reduced 10–24%*
Florida (NA)	Arizona ($3 million)
Illinois ($60 million)	Florida ($34 million)
Massachusetts ($15 million)	New Jersey ($20 million)
Mississippi ($4 million)	South Dakota ($1 million)
Missouri (NA)	Texas ($36 million)
New Jersey ($15 million)	Washington ($10–12 million)
New York ($30 million)	*Reduced less than 10%*
Ohio ($45 million)	California ($20 million)
Oklahoma ($7 million)	Illinois ($1 million)
South Dakota ($1 million)	Mississippi ($6 million)
Texas (NA)	Ohio ($12 million)
Washington ($2–5 million)	Oklahoma ($6 million)
No program	*No significant change*
Arizona	New York

[a]Note: The estimates of losses for Aid to Families with Dependent Children and food stamps cuts are based on estimates of the number of people removed from the rolls as a result of the various changes in eligibility rules. In most states, federal aid in these programs increased because of the recession. The discussion of the Medicaid changes in this section explains the difficulty in calculating the cuts for that program. Child nutrition cuts are based on 1981 compared to 1982 federal aid. SOURCE: Richard Nathan and Fred Doolittle, *Consequences of the Cuts* (Princeton, N.J.: Princeton Urban Research Center, 1983), Table 7.

It can be concluded from these examples that a policy of rapid welfare reversal is likely to take place only within narrow limits. The main rationale is that federal tax funds are better used to reinvigorate the economy, to stimulate industry and commerce, or to defend the nation, whereas funds from state and local governments or private citizen philanthropy are more suitable for social welfare. To this end, the political argument is that the scale of federal expenditures should be reduced or, if that is not persuasive, that the proportion of federal budget funds going for welfare is out of balance with other national obligations and thus undermines national strength. Along either of these lines, the welfare state is not denied, but its reach and scope is kept limited.

A more radical policy strategy is found in the encouragement given by national legislation and regulation to profitmaking enterprises to enter and deliver social services. The first step in this direction was taken early in the life of the Social Security Act when it was decided that such funds could be paid to commercial vendors on behalf of beneficiaries. Vendor payments to proprietary nursing homes by Medicaid contributed to their emergence as dominant providers of long-term care, but in a profitmaking mode. Subsequent policies that guarantee investors in medical institutions a return on investment and cost plus reimbursement of services have further encouraged the corporatization of large sectors of welfare. Medicare payment practices encourage the medical profession to evolve more and more as a business, rather than as a service, since vendors are not precluded from charging patients above the reimbursed fee. Meantime, attempts to contain the increase in health costs chargeable to government have turned the professional, management, and public attention away from the service purposes of health systems toward cost-saving management policies. As a result, most health organizations have begun to adapt their services to assure that full costs are captured from users or third-party payors, even if that means cutting back on services or shifting them to other providers.[6]

The alternative to a reversal of policy has been a slowing down of growth and a restructuring of some welfare arrangements in order to adapt to changing economic conditions. Economic depression imposes cruel choices on policymakers, since the incidence and prevalence of human need rises just at a time when resources may be shrinking. For a time, it is possible to defend existing programs by pointing to other government sectors where savings can be made, as for example in military expenditures. But such savings, where they exist, are temporary expedients.

Depressed economies are seldom ones in which great new initatives can be launched, unless the depression takes on the form of a catastrophe when a total population rallies behind strong initiatives, as it did in the 1930s. Even in such cases, the choice for policymakers is often to make emergency arrangements for relief, not to build new basic structures for society. In the 1980s, no such catastrophe has occurred. Instead, a still small part of the population, perhaps 15%, suffers but with the cushioning effects of limited

[6] Neil Gilbert, *Capitalism and the Welfare State* (New Haven: Yale University Press, 1983).

social programs, and 85% of citizens are reasonably secure. This is not yet a time conducive to major changes.

Whenever the time seems right for a major new movement, as in England after World War II, when its present welfare system was created, and in the United States in the 1930s, there remains a public choice: to move forward or to revert to older patterns of public behavior. American history holds out hope for welfare advocates that, in such periods of crisis, the final choice of the political process will be to enlarge public obligation and extend collective public effort to help those in need, and also to use government to level upward the conditions of life for most citizens.

Some historians, among them William McLoughlin,[7] have identified a trend in America's growing up. In each period, a pervasive sense of unease moved public thought first back to old ideas in a search for security, and when that failed to match the current reality, public support surged forward to create new forms. The last identified period of this kind lasted from 1890 to 1920—a time of rapid industrialization, popular discontent, reaction to widespread poverty, and later the unease of our first involvement in a world war. The period joined a religious-based movement of a Social Gospel and ideas from new socialist ways of examining society. Out of the ferment emerged the Progressive Party and a national demand for major federal involvement in citizen well-being, which reached its peak in the 1930s.

If this pattern holds its force, then the 1970–1980 slowdown in welfare state evolution may be the prelude to a later move ahead. If the welfare concept is enlarged, we can expect that policy focuses may be an expansion of publicly funded entitlements, as in the case of health care or child day care, or emphasis could shift to using national influence to accelerate a more equitable (not necessarily equal) distribution of income across all income classes. Even if these more ambitious aims are not realized, the events of the 1980s suggest that current welfare systems will be reorganized, not necessarily cut back seriously. An example is to begin treating income benefits as real income within the framework of a progressive tax policy, as in the 1983 redesign of Social Security retirement benefits.

The overarching policy directions are thus reduce, expand, or reorganize. The latter has been the effective policy, although the national rhetoric has been otherwise. Expansion may characterize future policy if the experience since 1930 has become sufficiently ingrained in public acceptance to sustain stability.

What will remain unclear is whether the American system will turn over to a national government the power and authority to impose a rationalized system for welfare, or whether the culture of the past will produce an enlargement in social protection through support of many contending and

---

[7] William McLoughlin, *Revivals, Awakenings and Reform* (Chicago: University of Chicago Press, 1978).

competing parties. The latter is most likely, and a continuing tension and competition can be expected between nonprofit community groups, proprietary service organizations, and publicly administered services, all nourished with tax funds, to organize and deliver the content that a mature welfare state requires.

This is the pattern that best fits American preferences, so we can expect legislation and programs that emphasize income assurance, through work or benefits, with which individuals can purchase their wanted or needed services. Regulation to avoid abuse may wax and wane, depending on the amount of abuse that creeps into an open social market system of this kind. The alternative, a throwback to older views of charity, would separate the population into two unequal classes: One, the poorest and most vulnerable, would be served by publicly administered and controlled services using rigorous means testing to limit access, while the bulk of services would flow through a social marketplace of purchases with income earned by those fortunate enough to have it. This is the least likely future.

In the following section, some specific alternatives are outlined.

Specific Program Alternatives

Health

Since the late 1930s, the adopted federal health policies have struggled to find a stable foundation for financing, a structure of service delivery, and professional control. With the exception of Medicare for the aged, our present social as well as adopted policy stance on these issues can be summarized as follows: voluntary insurance for finance, fee-for-service payment, private medical practice based on large hospital complexes, and self-control of professional practice by the professions.

The major policy alternative that has been advanced and fought over for at least 40 years is compulsory health insurance. The details of this struggle have been adequately described in countless articles and books so that the alternative, in its general outlines, is now well defined.[8] With the exception of the Kennedy–Griffiths health security bill and its successor, the Kennedy–Mills national health insurance program (introduced into the Senate in April 1974),[9] all proposals to extend health insurance in the United States

---

[8] See, for example, Daniel Hirshfield, *The Lost Reform;* Theodore Marmor, *The Politics of Medicare* (Chicago: Aldine, 1970); Rosemary Stevens, *American Medicine and the Public Interest* (New Haven: Yale University Press, 1971).

[9] These Kennedy initiatives are intended to act on the medical structure only indirectly, by directing the flow of health insurance premiums, and therefore of income, through a governmental entity, not through the private insurance intermediaries.

promise only to shift the mechanism for paying for medical care. None of them purport to affect the present distribution of medical or health personnel and health facilities nor to alter the way in which health services are delivered. All proposals assume that the present system would function quite well if only the obstacle of financial means were removed—that is, that health service providers and consumers would find each other and be satisfied with what each gives the other.

Compulsory health insurance by federal legislation must be viewed as a minor modification in policy rather than a significant policy alternative. True, the infusion of a compulsory system of insurance coverage will have wide-reaching effects. It will create a large administrative apparatus to collect funds from beneficiaries and distribute them to providers; it may open up access slightly for the poorest but will not necessarily equalize the levels of medical care given the rich and the poor; and it will undoubtedly increase significantly the share of the GNP going to health care and also the price of medical care. Insurance does not, of itself, produce a marketplace in which rising demand can bring forth more services and a reduction in price due to competition. Health services and access to them have been shown to be controlled by the way in which health providers function. The supply of medical personnel cannot be increased readily, and even when it is, the use of the supply is still controlled by providers. Between 1954 and 1974, the number of physicians produced by medical schools doubled, and the ratio of physicians per 100,000 population rose from 149 to 158. But this is exactly the period in which overall medical costs skyrocketed and total medical expenditures rose from 4.5 to 8.2% of the GNP. [10]

The Kennedy–Griffith Bill moved one step beyond this, but only a small step. It provided that the collection of insurance premiums be made by government agencies and that payments of benefits also flow through this agency. In all other proposals, this flow is left to private insurance companies, as is the case with present private and voluntary insurance. This change is not necessarily a guarantee of significant change in policy, given the propensity of all government agencies to fall, in the end, under the control of some producer constituency. As the commerce department is inextricably tied to commercial interests, and the Federal Drug Administration to the drug industry, and the labor department to major unions and manufacturers, so too is it likely that a national health insurance agency would find an unavoidable symbiotic relationship with the health industry. Nonetheless, a government agency presiding over the flow of health-financing funds amounts to an element outside of the health-provider industry that

[10] Alfred Skolnick and Sophie Dales, "Social Welfare Expenditures, 1950–1975," *Social Security Bulletin* 39, no. 1; (January 1976): pp. 3–20. Advisory Commission on Intergovernmental Relations, *Significant Features of Fiscal Federalism 1976* (Washington, D.C.: Advisory Commission on Inter-Governmental Relations, 1976), p. 17.

could, at some future time, use its strategic position as leverage to carry out other health policies that might alter the structure or direction of medical care more fundamentally. This could come about by altering either the rates at which certain procedures are compensated or the conditions for entitlement. It remains a moot question whether or not such a structural change would be a real change, since the use of the imputed "leverage" depends upon the behavior of various political forces. The positive view has been expressed by Senator Edward Kennedy: "We must use the financing mechanism to create strong, new incentives for the reorganization and delivery of health care. . . . I say, give us the lever of national health insurance and together we shall move the medical world. . . ."[11] The opposing view has been expressed by Navarro: "In most countries, experience has shown that the insurance system will adapt itself to the organization of medical care and not vice versa. . . . There. . . is more evidence . . . of the use of insurance programs as leverage against instead of for change in the power structure underlying the delivery system."[12]

To consider a more radical change in policy, we would have to turn to proposals for a national health service, similar to forms adopted in England or the Soviet Union. Under such a system, health services would be provided by government agencies, not by private providers paid by government by some formula. All institutions would be owned by some government unit, although, as in England, actual administration would be delegated to boards or regional authorities with substantial independent operating authority, mainly subject to the policy guidance built into allocations of funds by legislatures. Institution staffs would become civil servants, and other health providers, such as physicians outside of hospitals, would be either employed or as in England, paid under contracts negotiated between representatives of physicians' organizations (such as the local American Medical Societies) and government officials. Such a radical change has never been seriously proposed for policy debate in the United States and may be taken to lie outside the bounds of acceptability to the American electorate, at least for the near future.

At a less global level, policy could be directed at the delivery system structure, whatever the financing mechanism be. National policy could opt for a more total reliance upon the hospital, or medical center, as the hub of all medical care. Under such a policy, all physicians (not only most, as today) would be expected to become a part of a hospital staff organization for purposes of training, professional discipline, and access to other services. The pre- and posthospital attention that any patient requires could be provided

[11] Edward M. Kennedy, "National Health Insurance Proposals: Leverage for Change?" *New York Academy of Medicine Bulletin* 48, no. 1 (January 1972): 152.
[12] Vincente Navarro, "National Health Insurance and the Strategy for Change," *Health and Society* 51, no. 2 (Spring 1973): 224.

or controlled by the medical center through contracts negotiated with ancillary providers. Child and maternal health care would be supervised by the
medical and nursing staff of a hospital, as would admissions and transfers.
Home health services and neighborhood health centers would radiate from
the medical center, and their staffs would be accountable to key staff at the
center. Such integration could be brought about in the same way that tax
funds are distributed for capital construction, as under the Hospital Survey
and Construction Act, by reimbursement policies, since over 42% of health
care is covered by some tax payment, [13] or it could be brought about by control over the distribution of health personnel, in which direction the National Health Manpower and Training Act of 1976 has already moved, but
gingerly.

    A mirror image policy could deemphasize the central role of the hospital
in favor of community- and neighborhood-based delivery systems. Small-
scale experiments in this direction have already been authorized through
funding of neighborhood health centers (originally a part of the War on
Poverty and the Office of Economic Opportunity) and of health maintenance
organizations (HMOs). Taken together, these two modes of service organizations are a counterbalance to the hospital, although they do not replace it.
What is involved in such a policy is systematic tax funding of both capital
and service reimbursement to favor HMOs and neighborhood centers, as
against the hospital. The result, if ever pursued for long, would produce a
less unitary system than that promised by a hospital-centered policy, with
many more separate delivery centers that would be difficult to integrate but
that might be more quickly responsive to variations in consumer needs and
wants.

    The federal authority inherent in the government's paying so much of
the medical bill was used in 1983 in a very characteristic American way, by
avoiding any shadow of comprehensive planning. The central authority was
strengthened by imposing a new system for reimbursing hospitals—the DRG
(diagnostically related groups) system referred to earlier. The plan is clearly
intended to shake up the system by relying on a fiscal device but allowing
providers to respond in their individual best interests as they choose. The
results may be to produce a less service-oriented oligopoly in health, with a
few major centers in each area assembling under their control a large array
of hospital, ambulatory, nursing home, and home-care services. But the
result could equally be a much less centralized system of many more independent providers, each specializing and finding its own way to get paid.

    Finally, the quality of health care can be protected by a shift away from

---

[13] Alfred Skolnick and Sophie Dales, "Social Welfare Expenditures"; *Social Security Bulletin*
40, no. 1 (January 1977): 15.

the present reliance upon each of the professions to police its own members. All the recent measures have continued to rely upon the medical profession not only to police its members' ethical practices but also to control the use they make of hospital and other institutional resources. The entire elaborate structure of professional services review organizations that the Congress mandated to control "abuses" in the use of hospital beds still relies upon groups of physicians and other service providers, such as nurses and social workers, to monitor the use of resources in each hospital. The only significant argument over this approach was with the AMA, which wanted to have its local societies do the monitoring, while the legislation set up outside review groups.

Housing

In the field of housing, many of the conceivable policy options have been tried during the 1960s and 1970s, so that it is difficult to propose one that lies well beyond experience to date. The one that comes to mind is also the farthest removed from an overriding American cultural bias. It is perhaps best expressed in the evolution of English housing policies in recent decades. The British government bears the major, but not necessarily the sole, responsibility for a stock of good and acceptable housing available to all with moderate or average incomes. To carry out this policy, the national treasury makes money available to local governments for building such housing, either by local government directly or by various contractual arrangements entered into locally. The housing is intended for working persons, not for the poor alone, and it is administered by town councils at a low level of rent, to assure that the housing is within the reach of all. Subsidies are relied on to keep rent at reasonable levels. The administration is without stigma; many middle-class families live in council-rented housing, which is designed to blend into the surrounding environment. In some industrial cities, the largest share of rental housing, as distinguished from detached privately owned housing, is owned and managed by local governments. In some working-class areas, as much as 75% of all rental housing is managed as town council housing. But since 1975 a Conservative government has reversed field and begun to sell council housing to private buyers.

An extension of this program was enacted in 1947 in the Town and Country Planning Act to cope with the problem of land speculation, which often produced undesirable housing or housing for the rich, with large profits to the developer, but without producing housing for moderate-income families. Under this legislation, the government recaptured by taxation all the increase in land value that resulted from development and that in the past went to the developer. In effect, when a piece of slum property was developed into luxury housing, the value of the land rose and this difference was taxed 100%. By 1964, after changes in government, a 100% tax was found to be too restrictive and was replaced by a 40% betterment tax.

Short of such measures, the problems of housing have given rise to many less extensive policies, all rooted in the preexisting pattern of private ownership. American policy has tried public construction and management of low-cost housing for the very poor and for the aged. It has offered tax incentives of many kinds to private developers to build housing, given rent supplements to tenants to bridge the gap between low income and high rents, and offered mortgage and other incentives to individuals to enable them to buy private housing. The cumulative effect of such actions has been to assure the construction of a great deal of housing for people with adequate incomes, but it has not succeeded well in producing housing for persons of limited means. Public housing has led to ghettos of poor families, mainly those on relief, while other housing has been priced out of the reach of working low- and moderate-income families. These policies have also been troubled by continuous uncertainty and bureaucratic complexity, as several layers of government are involved at each step of the way. Responsibility is so divided that authority is confused. And when abuses are uncovered, there is a tendency to abandon programs completely on the grounds that they are now tarnished and unworkable. Sharp start-and-stop financing periods alternate with economic ups and downs, so that a steady flow of housing construction cannot be maintained, and the needs of the poorest are overlooked. And housing for higher-income groups is often developed helter-skelter, so that transportation, roads, schools, shopping, and other environmental necessities are underdeveloped.

One alternative to this situation would be the development of a policy line that seeks to rationalize housing construction, rent subsidy, and land-use control into more streamlined development. Stimulus for housing construction is needed, and a national fiscal policy (i.e., on interest rates) is required. But control of land use is a local option, and the application of rent subsidies can also be considered a local responsibility. It is a moot question whether these three should be synchronized by federal government or by local government or by both, as is the case now. To have all three dominated by federal action violates a basic predilection in American life. Perhaps more reasonable would be to leave most responsibility for housing in the hands of the local government, with federal aid but a minimum of federal regulation over administrative details. Wherever located, some central synchronized guidance for these three interlocking facets would represent a real change. A local example of such synchronization is called *linkage*. Some municipalities have begun to withhold zoning and licensing approval until developers accept a special tax per square foot on new commercial and luxury housing construction; the proceeds are used to improve housing in lower-income residential areas and for general neighborhood improvement.

Income Maintenance

The United States already has so complex a variety of income-supplementing programs that the policy alternatives are limited to substituting one general system (nearly impossible) or to harmonizing those that do exist. The problem is complicated by the fact that, by now, income-maintenance policy cannot be tackled in isolation. Wages and wage-related benefits (such as health insurance), plus variations in taxation and access to income-conditioned supplementary income programs must all be taken into account. To illustrate: Higher negotiated wage settlements in industry involve higher prices, which either reduce the value of income programs or require significant increases in benefit payments. But increased benefits mean higher taxes to raise the money, and some of these tax increases are inevitably imposed upon workers since the sums to be raised by taxing only the very wealthy could not be sufficient to meet the benefit increases. But this taxation could reduce worker take-home pay. A large part of the work force already pays an effective tax of at least 30%, counting income tax, Social Security withholding, and the value of the employers' Social Security contribution, which might otherwise be paid to the worker as wages. In Sweden, with a maximum program of income and welfare protection, the blue-collar worker who gets a 5% increase in real income (take-home pay) must get a 32% increase in pay to cover the 5% plus the added taxes.

Added to this maze is the question of access to income-tested benefits, such as food stamps, medical care, and housing allowances. Between 10 and 25% of relief-dependent families were entitled in 1972 to five or more benefits, and a family of four may have income from these benefits averaging $6500 a year. In 1980 this figure rose to over $10,000 in some localities.[14] This is not a large income, but it exceeds that earned by some full-time workers. The result is that either the working poor press for inclusion in these benefits, which increases the expenditure and leads to a further tax increase, or they demand a cut in benefits to those who are not working. Much of this complexity flows from the long-standing American policy that links income programs to work. Virtually all money-assistance programs are contingent on the beneficiary's being in the labor force, holding a job, seeking a job, or being temporarily out of the labor force because of illness or in-

[14] See Joint Economic Committee of the Congress, "How Welfare Benefits are Distributed in Low Income Areas," Studies in Public Welfare, no. 6 (Washington, D.C.: U.S. Government Printing Office, 1973), pp. 86–89.

jury. Complex administrative rules and mechanisms are required to assure that no one receives help who is not simultaneously trying to get work, no matter what the level of unemployment is. Large bureaucracies are necessary to monitor and enforce this linkage.

A basic policy alternative would be one that breaks this work–welfare link. Conditions under which the lack of income alone would be sufficient to generate income entitlement can be specified. The attractiveness of work can then be assumed to be sufficiently strong to draw persons from relief into work when work at reasonable pay is available. Such an approach would need to accept the reality that as much as 20% of the population slides back and forth between work and relief regularly, not because of sloth, but because the economy has many part-time, seasonal, or low-paying jobs that must be filled. Movement between relief and work takes place by the rules of the economy and not because relief administration is able to force people into jobs they do not want to take. Under such a policy of separation, the coordination between work and relief policies can take place at legislative levels, not in program administration. Several approaches to relief policy under such a separation have been advanced.

President Carter's welfare reform proposals of 1977 followed this approach. They separate income programs into two great clusters, one for those out of the labor force and one for those presumed able to work. People in the latter group are helped to find jobs, including public service jobs, and are compensated at a slightly less generous relief rate than that provided people in the former group.

Several policy options have been advanced or are being tried in other countries. To handle the needs of those without work, something akin to a negative income tax or the Family Assistance Plan proposed in the Nixon years could be revived. Under it, all families earning less than a given sum of money would receive a payment sufficient to bring their income up to a predetermined level. Such a program would make more general the policy embedded in the supplementary security income program whereby the aged and disabled, who are presumably out of the labor force, are assured a minimum federal fixed income. Aside from the emotional reaction of some legislators to extending such a guarantee to those on Aid to Families with Dependent Children, mostly black unmarried mothers, the plan was first introduced at too low a national level, $2400 a year. But to raise the minimum level significantly would increase costs greatly and lead to political objections that the tax level would be high. Even if such a negative income tax uses a sliding scale, with benefits dropping as income rises, it is necessary to pitch the final cutoff substantially above the present relief level to avoid the disincentive that now plagues the welfare system—a 100% tax on earnings, every dollar earned while on relief only replacing a relief dollar, without an improvement in income.

This grand design is also flawed because it does not take into account differential needs of families due to illness, disability, age, and the like. Such a policy could produce still another income program, but it cannot replace all existing supplementary programs. Moreover, difficulty of replacement is not limited to family variations. Some current programs, such as unemployment insurance, provide relatively higher benefits, and persons protected by these more generous programs are unlikely to accept a lesser substitute, even if it is more simplified.

A less complex policy involves the federal government's assuming full responsibility for all income maintenance, including the costs of AFDC, general relief, and Medicaid. To work, such a program could not merely underwrite the costs of existing state programs, which vary widely as to eligibility and payment levels. In the end, federalization would involve either a federal income floor, averaged for all states, or the case-by-case fixing of budgets by the federal government, which would be impossible to administer from Washington. A more feasible policy would be the adoption of a federal floor for all relief, especially for AFDC, which the states might supplement if they wished. A reasonable policy would be to separate slowly the responsibilities of state and federal governments and the accompanying control of money that has been associated with our present three-tier partnership, each level of government being involved financially and administratively every step of the way. In this, the federal government would be accountable for maintaining a floor under income in a means-tested program; the states would be free to supplement above the floor if their state culture, financial status, or political alignment called for supplementation and if they could raise the additional funds.

Another approach would be to extend the policy, already in force, of mandating various supplementary allowances, such as food stamps and housing allowances. Such allowances are attached to particular problems and to specific populations with those problems. They have the defect of being very much like relief in kind—the old grocery basket concept of charity—which was abandoned in the 1930s. They have the advantage of permitting a buildup of well-targeted programs to achieve specific aims, not the general income level of all persons, although that may well be the final result. Medicaid, extended to working persons with incomes too low to afford good medical care, can improve attention to health needs. Similar allowances for housing can improve housing conditions. And so on.

Still another approach involves a different kind of partnership between government and the private sector, at least as regards that majority of the population in the labor force at any time. A two-tiered benefit or pension system has been proposed, at least as regards retirement. In it, government protection provides a floor, but labor–management and other industrial contracts add a tier of benefits to the floor. Federal steps to guarantee that private pension plan benefits are vested in workers so that they do not lose protection when they change jobs, and reinsurance in case a company becomes bankrupt, are steps in this direction. Given the pervasiveness of health protection in industrial labor contracts, the two-tiered system could possibly be extended to medical care at least, as well as to retirement.

The United States is fortunate in that it already has in place a great variety of income programs. That they are confusing may be only a small price to pay for taking care of a great many distinctive needs. We are in a position to reexamine all of them to see which provides the most satisfying option for the next stage of development. These programs permit choices in a number of different directions: federalization, partnership, a simplified income floor, decentralization of federal authority, or extension of categorical aids.

To effect any change, one fact of a mature economy must be faced: the increase in the proportion of the work force made chronically unemployed by technological change. This may be a short-term situation, but it is as long as the life of middle-aged adult workers. There is disagreement over longer periods of time. Any income policy should provide long-term income for able-bodied workers made redundant, a step the nation has thus far refused to take.

Aging

The aged already have programs in advance of the rest of the population—retirement income guaranteed, compulsory health insurance, and housing assistance. It is, however, possible to look at national policy for the aged beyond the simple level of income security. The central dilemma of the aged, other than income security, is the role they fill in modern society. At the present time, national policy is based squarely on the premise that persons aged 65 years should be out of the labor force; insurance as well as employment regulations clearly are intended to enforce this view. In fact, liberalization of retirement insurance policies has increasingly encouraged workers to retire even earlier, at age 60 or 62. Labor contracts make it easy for workers to retire at 60 if they wish; and many federal and state military and civil service regulations encourage retirement as early as age 50, after 20–25 years of service.

An alternative policy may be forced into our consciousness by the demographic character of our population. About 10% of the population are over 65. If trends continue, it is expected that the population ratio of the aged will rise 15% in some parts of the country within the next decade or two and to 20% over a longer time span. The health of this population has improved, not so much through medicine as through public health and generally higher income levels, which produce better nutrition and better living conditions. If we add together all dependent persons—that is, children under age 18 and persons over age 65—we find that perhaps half of the population works to produce all the goods for the other half. Thus far, our economy has performed reasonably well, in large part due to increased productivity, mechanization, and high technology, but it is not unreasonable to expect that the rate of productivity increase will slow down. And if we continue to have a larger percentage of persons out of the labor force (the aged and children, as they stay in school longer), then the strains on the economy will begin to show. They have already begun to show in our Social Security system, where these very trends have required a higher and higher level of taxation on the work force, so much so that complaints and creaking in the machinery have already made themselves heard.

A major new policy shift could be taken, which would be consistent with the long-time trend in American attitudes—namely, a relaxation of the current strict retirement regulations. Small steps have already been taken, by permitting nominal earnings after retirement under Social Security. A more significant shift would encourage the continued employment of older persons where they wish to work and where employers wish to employ them, without penalty to either party. Withdrawal of retirement benefits could be phased in relation to the amount of work time, or benefits could be wholly drawn even if work continues in some modified form. Employer taxes could be readjusted to favor continued work, or tax legislation could encourage employers to begin a phased and extended program of retirement, beginning at much earlier years, say, age 50, but continuing to, say, 70 or 75, good health permitting. Such a major shift would probably depend upon a national conviction that the available work force is not large enough for national needs and that it is in the national interest to increase the work force rather than reduce it, as we now do. Such a policy obviously depends on the availability of sufficient jobs for all to be employed, a situation that does not now prevail. In 1982 a Republican government began to delay the age at which any older person can draw retirement benefits.

Alternatively, healthy older people loved to work at many tasks that are now considered valuable, but not economic in the sense of fitting into our goods production economy. Building and maintaining a pleasant environment in city and suburb into which homes and shops can fit; information services to help all of us thread our way through the maze of organization; consumer information and protection services; monitoring the working of chronic illness facilities, such as nursing homes; attention to the social needs of the home-bound disabled or aged—all these come to mind as tasks that older persons with health and interest could perform for our general well-being. They might even be engaged to staff much of our election and cam-

paign processes. Even if additional funds are used to provide modest supplemental salaries to retired persons, their performance of such tasks would do
much to enrich community and national life.

Children

The long history of the United States Children's Bureau has produced,
directly or indirectly, a wide range of services directed at children's needs:
health care and education. However, the bulk of public policy is oriented to
programs that serve families, not children as such, although children are the
intended beneficiaries of many family-oriented programs. One long-
advocated policy is that of children's allowances, intended to relieve families
of economic burdens and thus to improve the condition of child rearing.
Children's allowances would, in effect, be paid to any family with children.
These would not be means tested but could be limited to the second child
and those coming after or to only a few children in the case of very large
families. Such allowances have also been used to either encourage larger
families or discourage too large families, but the long-term results of such incentives are unclear.

   More relevant to today's situation is the issue of day care. With so many
mothers of small children in the work force, either national policy can encourage the evolution of supplements for the mothers' care in the form of
day-care centers or it can try to discourage mothers from working by disincentives to keep them out of the labor force. The latter course seems against
the strong trend of this century, during which the liberation of women from
legal and family constraints has led to a long-term entry into paid employment for women from all economic classes; it is, therefore, unlikely to succeed. Doubt as to its success is increased by the fact that so many mothers
work to bring in a second income as a means of raising family income and
economic well-being. Undoubtedly, this increase in the work force and in
family income has much to do with maintaining purchasing power and with
the continuing consumption of goods, which in turn provides the stimulus
for increased production and for employment of men and women alike.

   Day-care centers, the alternative, seem a much more reasonable policy.
During World War II, this was the national policy, and a national network of
such centers was financed with federal aid. The network was effectively dismantled at the end of the war, although many proprietary centers survived,
largely for families with adequate income. During the late 1960s, a means-
tested measure was taken to revive such a policy, when women on relief
who were able to work were trained and then assured income supplementation to pay for child care where earnings were insufficient. However, this
remained a relief-tainted program. The alternative national policy would be
to support the development of a national network of day-care centers for

children from families of all income levels. Sliding fee scales could assure some equity between those who could pay some of the costs and those who could not. A less discriminating policy would simply develop these centers as a public utility for all mothers needing them.

Some variations on this theme have been tried in a small way. Industry could be encouraged, by tax incentives or subsidy, to provide for day-care for its employees. This option is difficult to execute because of the large number of persons engaged in businesses too small to undertake such programs, even with tax aid. Alternatively, the centers could become a part of the public school system, whereby schools would serve children below present school age. A start in this direction has been taken in the opening of kindergartens, in Head Start, and in other preschool classes in some parts of the country. The costs of local education have recently made it harder for school systems to add a new function, but a national policy could help overcome this difficulty.

A more troublesome question would have to be resolved as part of any such policy. Some proponents see the centers as places to begin early childhood education, while others see them as child-caring centers, with early education secondary. Which emphasis is finally selected determines the nature and intensity of staffing patterns and therefore the costs and personnel requirements.

Directional Alternatives

It may be clear by now that a number of policy options are available as alternatives to those now in effect. Few of them are so far removed from American traditions as to be impossible in the near future. They represent alternative policy options for either major political party. If any are followed, consideration would also have to be given to certain aspects of any policy choice beyond the level of problem-specific or program-specific areas. A few of these have already been touched upon, and we will mention here five more such policy choices.

Work or Welfare?

Social welfare policy has, for the most part, addressed the question: What services should be provided to those without work or independent incomes? It has not often considered the question of work creation as a social policy issue to be addressed by social welfare advocates or social workers. However, there has been a slow increase in chronic unemployment since the 1960s and in the concern that, while the technological change and the new information and service age will create new forms of work and new jobs, it will also create unemployment by making certain industries and jobs redundant. Economic theory considers that such changes create frictional unemployment, which will in time be absorbed by new job opportunities. However, a minority of economists, including those serving the European Economic Community, now fear that more jobs will be lost than will be created. Some studies indicate that about 5% of the U.S. labor force is chronically unemployed for very long periods of time.[15] To this must be added those adults who are outside of the enumerated labor force: the discouraged who have quit looking, mothers of small children who are economically dependent and yet may want to work but lack skills, and the residents of an underground economy who staff many illegal activities as a way to survive outside the usual goods and service producing economy. The people in the last group have dropped out in part because there were no opportunities for them to earn an acceptable income in mainstream work. These various subpopulations are in danger of becoming a permanent underclass to replace the former slave and minority of color underclass.

To the present, this phenomenon has been treated by a carrot-and-stick approach in the public assistance program, by offering relief income coupled with work training. The approach fails to deal with the persistence of chronic unemployment attributed to structural flaws in the base economy. One policy alternative for welfare is to shift the weight of attention from service and income relief provision, to job creation and maintenance. Although the techniques for this lie beyond current social welfare skill, the justification for shifting some if not all attention to work lies in social work's historic knowledge about the eroding effects of unemployment and the way in which that determines the growth of other social problems that the social services must address.

Attention to work creation is justified in that is relies on the basic strengths of citizens to take care of most of their needs if only they have reasonably secure income. Income through valued work is a major preventive approach to welfare. Only when economic needs and wants are met through the efforts of clients, in conditions where they control this large part of their lives without interference, is it possible for social work to know what residual social problems remain that require other forms of service, and only then can social care or treatment be reasonably successful, since the distorting effects of income stress and insecurity will have been removed. A social policy focus on job creation can be advanced either through a restructuring of the work place, as with new forms of shared work, or

---

[15] Michael Sherraden, "Employment Policy and Labor Market Reality," mimeographed (St. Louis: School of Social Work, 1983).

through new cooperative activities, or through public service employment to produce public goods.

An unusual approach to this situation has been advanced, the encouragement of a national system of self-help groups that can produce goods either for their own use or for exchange with others in the economic mainstream. It is postulated that enough able-bodied adults will always be redundant in a mature economy to warrant the development of some organized subeconomy. The two-tier economy would comprise the mainstream, based on money and production for sale, and a secondary economy based on barter and direct exchange.[16]

One example of this remedy has already emerged to provide food for the unemployed using voluntary nonprofit methods. A nonprofit organization called Second Harvest relies almost exclusively on volunteer labor and contributions. It operates through a network of locally controlled bodies that maintain 61 regional food banks, supplied mainly with food contributed by growers or manufacturers—food that in the mainstream of their activity would be allowed to go to waste or be destroyed, although it is perfectly edible food from bankrupt wholesalers, surplus foods from farmers, etc. In 1983 the network was expected to distribute some 100 million pounds of food to charitable organizations that serve infants, children, the elderly, and the unemployed. It is hardly a threat to the basic economy, but it has grown rapidly as an example of a second economy based on either mutual aid or self-help.[17]

Personal Disposable Income versus Government Expenditure

The United States still has some way to go before its governmental income as a percentage of the GNP equals that of other advanced industrial states (see Table 8.5). For example, in 1971 the United States average was lower than that of five European countries, although the American performance is better than many critics of American social policy realize. Data from 1979 indicate a continued increase in this trend, except for the United Kingdom, which was in an extended recession (see Table 8.6). What this means, simply, is that there is a choice between how much money should be left to individuals to spend as they wish and how much they should pay to the government in order to provide for their needs without recourse to the uncertainties of the marketplace. There is clearly a contradiction in citizens' views on this matter, as seen in public opinion polls during the 1976 presi-

[16] Edgar Cahn, "Surplus People: A Modest Proposal," mimeographed personal communication, University of Miami, Law School, 1984.
[17] "Waste Not, Want Not," *The Economist*, November 19, 1983, p. 26.

TABLE 8.5
Tax Revenue as a Percentage of Gross National Product, 1955–1971 (in percents)[a]

Country	Mid-1950s	Late 1960s	1971	Increase 1955–1971
United States	25.4	27.4	27.8	2.4
Great Britain	28.1	34.6	35.7	7.6
West Germany	32.4	33.7	34.5	2.1
Netherlands	28.5	38.7	42.2	13.7
France	32.9	35.8	35.6	2.7
Sweden	29.1	39.6	41.8	12.7

[a]SOURCE: Richard Goode, "The Tax Burden in the U.S. and Other Countries," *Annals of the American Academy of Political and Social Science*, no. 379 (Summer 1968): 85–87; Organization for Economic Cooperation and Development, *Revenue Statistics of OECD Member Countries 1965–1971*, (Paris: OECD, 1973), p. 25.

TABLE 8.6
Total Tax Revenue as Percentage of Gross Domestic Product at Market Prices 1979[a] and 1981.

Country	Percentage–1979	Percentage–1981
Sweden	50.27	36.12
Netherlands	47.42	27.90
Luxembourg	46.17	24.20
Norway	46.06	38.36
Belgium	44.69	31.41
Denmark	44.09	44.29
Austria	41.36	29.14
France	41.16	24.61
Germany	37.34	24.06
Finland	35.03	33.79
United Kingdom	34.02	31.30
Ireland	33.82	33.02
United States	31.32	22.97
New Zealand	31.18	32.78
Switzerland	31.12	20.93
Canada	31.01	30.73
Italy	30.09	21.64
Australia	29.82	—
Greece	27.69	19.13
Portugal	25.82	22.02
Japan	24.77	18.79
Spain	23.27	13.11
Turkey	20.84	18.31

[a]SOURCE: Organization for Economic Cooperation and Development, *Revenue Statistics of OECD Member Countries* (Paris: OECD, 1981), p. 78; and Revenue Statistics of OECD Member Countries 1965–1982 (Paris: OECD, 1983), Table 1.

dential campaign. (A significant majority of citizens polled wanted to have less government and lower taxes, while simultaneously wanting more public action to provide medical care, housing, etc.) Americans want to have as much income as they can get to spend as they wish, but when a crisis arises in health or unemployment, they want a government program to fall back on. [18] Somehow, public policy must find an acceptable mean between these two extremes. One policy tilts in the direction of private income (the American tendency until the recent past) and the other in the direction of more public guarantee.

It is sometimes argued that we can have both of these wishes at the maximum, but here common sense, the attitudes of the citizens as reflected in opinion polls and election results and an examination of economic data indicate that both cannot be secured to the maximum. Even an expropriating level of taxation of wealth or industrial profits would not yield enough funds to provide full government security while maintaining high take-home pay, with little taxation, for workers.

Action to Equalize Income versus Marketplace Rewards

Another related policy choice is between government action to equalize incomes and reliance on the economic marketplace to reward persons according to their contribution to the economy. Programs directed toward other specific problems do create a certain amount of equalization: Minimum wage legislation and income policies determine how low the economic floor can be permitted to drop, and civil rights legislation acts against racial, religious, or other discrimination. But even with these generally equalizing or equity-producing efforts, a wide gap exists between high- and low-income recipients in this society and, for that matter, in all societies, including the socialist and communist. The differences among societies, to the extent they exist, lie in the size of the spread between high and low.

If a policy of giving the same income to everyone in the same condition (i.e., same family composition) is quite unattainable, it is still possible to use social policy to try to smooth out glaring inequities, as we have done historically. A policy designed mainly to raise the income floor for the poorest families relieves distress, but it retains relative poverty—that is, the spread does not diminish since the higher income rises as does the floor. Alternative to this would be a more assertive role by government to redistribute income in a way designed to reduce the spread. We have not really attempted direct control of the spread to date, although we have many examples of floor rais-

[18] See, among numerous studies, Faye Cooke Lomax, *Who Should Be Helped* (Beverly Hills: Sage Library of Social Research, 1979) and Jennifer Hochschield, *What's Fair* (Cambridge, Mass.: Harvard University Press, 1981).

ing. The Family Assistance Plan and Social Security, among others, involve taking funds from all but returning relatively more to the lowest-income families at the expense of higher-income families. The progressive income tax, first enacted in 1916, goes farthest in this kind of redistribution, although its effect has been eroded by the slow addition of many preferences and loopholes that favor moderate- and upper-income families.

Nonetheless, we have seen a slight redistribution among large groups, even though the spread between individuals has not been affected. Between 1964 and 1969, the lowest fifth of the families (in income terms) increased their incomes, while those in the highest fifth decreased theirs, a situation slightly altered between 1969 and 1974. For unrelated individuals, the lowest fifth increased its share in both periods, while the highest fifth decreased its share (see Table 8.7). Since we are dealing in population aggregates, it is worth noting that in these periods the mean number of children per family in the lowest fifth dropped more rapidly than it did among the upper fifth. Also, the growth over the decade in the number of single-parent families was marked, meaning that, for an unknown number of units, a father's separate income could have been calculated along with that of the mother's and children's incomes to combine into a total income for the lower fifth much larger than these figures suggest. Similarly, in this period supplementary benefits in the form of Medicaid, housing allowances, and food stamps were increased. If one estimates that only a third of these in-kind supplements went to the families with the lowest fifth of income,

TABLE 8.7
Percent Income Distribution by Quintiles, 1964–1974[a]

Category	1964	1969	1974	1980[b]
Families				
Lowest fifth	5.1	5.6	5.4	5.1
Second fifth	12.0	12.4	12.0	11.6
Third fifth	17.7	17.7	17.6	17.5
Fourth fifth	24.0	23.7	24.1	24.3
Fifth fifth	41.2	40.6	41.0	41.6
Unrelated individuals				
Lowest fifth	2.5	3.3	4.0	
Second fifth	7.1	7.8	8.9	
Third fifth	12.8	13.8	14.5	
Fourth fifth	24.4	24.3	24.2	
Fifth fifth	53.2	50.9	48.5	

[a]SOURCE: Sar Levitan and Robert Taggart, The Promise of Greatness (Cambridge, Mass.: Harvard University Press, 1976), p. 246. For 1980, Money Income of Households: 1980, U.S. Department of Commerce, Bureau of the Census, Series P-60, No. 132, July 1982.

[b]Families and unrelated individuals.

then their real, as against cash, income would be increased by 40%.[19] All in all, this very slight reduction in income spread suggests that a policy for a more rapid systematic reduction is not wholly unthinkable.

Federal versus State and Local Responsibility

Despite much rhetoric decrying the loss of local authority, the long-term trend until 1980 has been for citizens and local governments to shift more and more responsibility to the federal level. The latest example is the demand by cities and states that the federal government assume full responsibility for public assistance. A reasonable alternative to this trend would be a redistribution of responsibility among the various levels of government. Our history has so intertwined these levels as to make the task very difficult. The trend to centralization required extraordinary convolutions of legalisms to secure federal financial participation without violating the Constitution. As a result, except for Social Security, most welfare programs are nominally state and locally planned, but all levels are involved in funding, and state regulations and procedures must conform to federal rules. To disentangle the web would require the specification of at least some social services as wholly state or local responsibilities and others as wholly federal. This would involve a clean division of fiscal responsibility commensurate with taxing power, so that functions considered to be state or local would be wholly funded by state or local taxes. Some steps have been taken in this direction. Supplementary security income leaves funding and regulation of base income for the aged and handicapped to the federal government. Supplementary payments above the minimum are a state responsibility, although the administrative responsibilities are still rather tangled. Medicare for the aged is wholly a federal obligation, whereas unemployment insurance is administered by the state with federal help. A division of duties vis-à-vis housing has already been discussed. Federalization of AFDC could be traded off against the states' assumption of full responsibility for other personal social services not financial in nature, such as home care or day care for children and the elderly or disabled.

Decentralization, a concept so appealing to American ears, cannot be made real without some such devolution of authority, accountability, and financial burden, but the present situation in state and local taxing power makes their assumption of financial responsibility difficult. All that an alternative policy could work for is a slow untangling of the thread of association and partnership. Not to do so bespeaks a policy of continuation of present policy, which means at least three layers of administrative decision making for each program and confusion about the boundaries of local responsibility.

[19] See Levitan and Taggart, *The Promise of Greatness*, pp. 246–247.

Since the late 1970's various proposals have been advanced, and introduced, to convert preexisting categorical grants into block grants. The basic
premise underlying this approach to reorganization does not necessarily
alter fiscal sharing by the federal government, but in reality the proposals
advanced in the early 1980's all combined block grants with a reduction in
the federal share of funding. The central principle of block grants is simple.
Numerous specialized programs which can be defined to serve a more
generic function are grouped together and the past separate funding au-
thorizations are grouped into a single overall grant. Then this grouped or
"block" grant is allocated to a state agency under rather general guidelines
so that each state is presumably free, or more free than before, to assign
these funds in ways chosen by each state, rather than being limited to functions determined by a federal agency. Such block grants have been authorized for numerous public health programs and for some child welfare programs. The Title XX Social Services legislation is an early example of such
blocking as are some parts of authorization under the Older Americans
Act. No comprehensive assessment has been made of such an approach but
reports of experience indicate that several problems have been encountered:

1. Federal guidelines still accompany the grants and seriously restrict
   the choices that the states can make. Examples are mandating that
   fixed proportions of social service dollars must be used for family
   planning, or that large segments of appropriations for the elderly
   must be used for nutritional programs.
2. Most block proposals are matched by such reductions in federal
   funds that state decisions are determined more by the fiscal difficulty in making up the reductions (a scramble to keep useful projects somehow alive amid pressure by advocates of preexisting categorical projects, for example those serving retarded children, or
   those interested in senior citizen councils) than in developing a rational use of available funds.

Pay-as-You-Go versus Deferred Payment Social Welfare System

Retirement insurance, the bedrock of our current welfare policy, is a good
example of the choice that must be made between a pay-as-you-go and a deferred payment system. At present, persons currently employed pay in
taxes enough to cover the benefits earned by people who are now retired.
But inflation and rising expectations introduce serious tension into the
system. The illusion is maintained that each person has contributed and
therefore has earned his or her benefits; this is true, except that the money
each individual pays in does not pay for his or her own benefits, but for the
benefits of those already retired. This is further complicated by a tendency

for each generation to anticipate its own retirement by increasing the benefit structure while its is working, not realizing, perhaps, that the payments
for the increased benefits are made by the next generation of workers. To
proceed in any other fashion would require that social insurance be recast
in full insurance terms or "funding" payments, meaning that payments
made by workers would be invested in a fund solely for the use of future
payments. Today, amounts in excess of 1 year's payments go into general
funds and are spent for current government operations, as are other kinds
of taxes.

The alternative to this unpleasant procedure is to subject the level of
future retirement payments to whatever future generations of workers will
approve via appropriations from general revenues. This strategy has been
urged by many critics, on the assumption that the political pressure to make
higher rather than lower levels of appropriations will safeguard the rights
of retired workers. In 1983 the Social Security compromise discussed earlier
avoided a major change.

Thus, we see that, at both the general level of policy and the problem-
and program-specific levels, there are real conceptual alternatives. But each
alternative presents policymakers with troublesome choices between valid
claims made by different segments of the citizenry. These tensions tend to
prevent adoption of significant shifts in policy from one administration to
another, but rather encourage slow incremental changes, each building on
the preceding policy concensus. Still, the more powerful alternatives are
there, to be adopted if there is political will and strength.

The Radical Alternatives

In the 1960s, three lines of more radical analysis of social welfare policy
began to emerge in the United States. The alternatives derived from this
analysis have not been advanced as concrete proposals for quick adoption or
even as subjects for contemporary policy debates of national government.
Rather, they represent a radically different way of perceiving the social
problems of the times. One of them is derived from Marxist analyses of
society; others represent a desire to simplify the modern condition and
to create human-scale, face-to-face, self-help forms of social organization to
replace national shaped bureaucracies.[20] In some respects, they purport to

[20] This section touches only slightly on the subject. See such texts as Frances Piven and
Richard Cloward, *Regulating the Poor* (New York: Pantheon Books, 1971); Roy Bailey and Mike
Brake, eds., *Radical Social Work* (New York: Pantheon Books, 1975); Bill Jordan, *Paupers* (Boston:
Routledge & Kegan Paul, 1973); Jeffrey Galper, *Radical Social Work, The Politics of Social Services*
(Englewood Cliffs, N.J.: Prentice-Hall, 1976). For an earlier period, see especially all issues of the
periodical *Social Work Today*.

avoid the awkward choices that are embedded in the conventional alternatives just discussed. A third turns to marketplace solutions.

The best-articulated radical alternatives do not usually deal with specific social or welfare policies, in the sense of guiding principles linked to the execution of specific programs. Instead, these alternatives outline a view about the causes of social and personal difficulties, that they are mainly due to militarism or to distortions of a capitalist society in which exploitation of many by a few is inevitable, no matter how much effort is made to obscure that exploitation by palliative measures of liberal social welfare. This viewpoint argues that social work (or welfare) as now organized is not benign, that what is good for the agency supercedes what is good for the client, that social workers do not run social agencies, and that client problems are not psychological or inherent in their personal defects. Social welfare in America is characterized as a set of institutions that attempt, ineffectually, to resolve contradictions between consumption and production. It is assumed that such contradictions would not arise in a socialist society or that they would be resolved differently.

Case data are presented about the defects in present welfare operations, including the ways in which agency policies injure or neglect clients, the ways in which agency rules coopt workers into anticlient attitudes, and the failure to eliminate income differentials among all classes. From this evidence, the approach concludes that the existing sociopolitical-economic order must be replaced by a socialist society. Therefore, all actions should be directed toward this replacement, or this revolution. Elaboration of this policy stance is often couched in political-strategic terms, not in programmatic terms. The transfer of power and the upending of social control control is seen as the outcome.

Another radical alternative stops short of an explicit political alternative, but it argues the view that clients are claimants on social institutions, not helpless beneficiaries. As such, the policy stance seems to be one of stressing client strength, not weakness. All things must be done that will help clients learn how to express and claim their rights from resistive social agencies. This approach differs from the more articulate Marxist analyses in that it stops at getting agencies to respond to needs (at least as far as the literature goes), whereas the Marxist view sees such demands only as pressures that should ultimately lead to the dissolution of these agencies and their surrounding social structure and the replacement of both agency and society by new socialist forms.

The articulation of such radical alternatives does not fit readily into the framework of analysis used thus far, for at least two reasons. First, and most seriously, the radical analyses enunciate a very general policy stance, the replacement of a capitalist by a socialist society. The explicit character of socialist policies has not yet been presented in terms of specific problems, such as programs for an income system, for the mentally or chronically physically ill, or for the delinquent. If such approaches no longer claim that a socialist society eliminates such human difficulties, neither do they present the skeletal outline of how a program and a policy for such areas would differ from current capitalist approaches.

The concrete discussions to date have focused on two levels only: political strategy to transform society and individual social worker practice within that strategy. Although programmatic and national policy details are not available for review, it is worth noting the kind of practices being urged on social workers. From this point of view, the social worker's function is to instruct clients in the radical or Marxist analysis of their situation so that they may (1) understand their alienation as caused by capitalist exploitation and learn the sociopolitical reality that shapes their lives; (2) build up their self-esteem and resist hegemony (i.e., resist being submerged into the norm); and (3) acquire personal and collective capacities to transform that reality into socialism by practical struggles, which would eliminate the need for social welfare helping institutions.

This is a sketchy summary of a few key arguments, omitting the details that make such analyses provocative. Whatever evaluation of their solutions we may make, they are valuable in a consideration of alternatives in that they force us to confront failures in present policies and programs and to examine the cause of the failures. The case descriptions are poignant and moving as they expose agency behaviors in which desperate human needs are distorted or ignored by staffs caught up in the crazy quilt of programs, regulations, and attitudes.[21] Unfortunately, for the purposes of social policy analysis, a great void still exists between the preamble goal (or policy stance) of building socialism and the case-by-case social worker practice injunctions published by the radical social welfare writers. The preamble goal shares much of the passion and symbolic generality of the U.S. Constitution and Declaration of Independence, while the case critique echoes similar criticisms launched by social workers over the past hundred years. The difference between the more radical and the liberal alternatives lies in underlying causal analysis: Is socialism the essential prerequisite to improvement? If it is, the explicit social welfare content of that alternative, as seen in proposed sectoral policies and programs (not only in attitudes), remains to be articulated.

At the opposite extreme of the alternatives just described is an equally radical proposal offered by the Reagan administration, which was also enunciated in an earlier Nixon administration: to return much of welfare to marketplace-like conditions. Although the rhetoric of this alternative suggests a substantial withdrawal of government from welfare functions, its

[21] See works cited in footnote 20.

reality seems to be more a continuation of large infusions of government funding but through proprietary rather than nonprofit or official agency channels. In housing, tax stimuli are continued, as before, by direct funding or tax credits to developers and builders. In health care, government encourages medical organizations to bid for the privilege of being reimbursed to provide medical care to Medicaid recipients. The focus shifts from quality or access to care to least costly efforts to provide that care. Government regulations or control is reduced. Capping payments to hospitals is introduced to reduce public expenditure, but with full realization that this move triggers major changes in the way health service is delivered for Medicare as well as Medicaid beneficiaries since hospitals must, under the new reimbursement rules, calculate their services on patients whose needs will be least costly. Encouragement is thus given to moving many services, including surgery, out of hospitals into doctors offices and storefront ambulatory care centers. Competition among various provider institutions and agencies is encouraged, in an effort to induce economy.

Unfamiliar as such a policy is, after 50 years of public leadership in welfare, its consequences are not easily predictable. Certainly, patterns of service will be altered as proprietary, nonprofit, and new forms of delivery evolve in competition for public funds that continue to be appropriated. The results conceivably can be greater choice in delivery forms and greater economy, although the results could also be greater concentration of services in national proprietary chains that have capital assets to squeeze smaller agencies out of business, greater selectivity of people to be served (those whose payments are closest to the costs of care), and neglect of those whose conditions are most costly or difficult to handle. The next few years will reveal what the outcomes will be, but in the meantime, it is necessary to recognize the emergence of a new clear policy and the rationale for its emergence.

Additional Readings

The more familiar policy options are discussed in references listed at the end of the preceding chapters. However, there has recently emerged a small body of literature that defines itself as "radical social welfare." The following are a few representative references:

Bailey, Roy, and Brake, Mike. *Radical Social Work.* New York: Pantheon Books, 1975.

Bell, Winfred. *Contemporary Social Welfare.* New York: Macmillan, 1983.

Cloward, Richard, and Piven, Frances. *Regulating the Poor.* New York: Pantheon Books, 1971.

Galper, Jeffrey. *The Politics of Social Services.* Englewood Cliffs, N.J.: Prentice-Hall, 1976.

Nathan, Richard, and Doolitte, Fred. *Consequences of the Cuts: The Effects of the Reagan Domestic Program on State and Local Governments.* Princeton: Princeton University Press, 1983.

Tools of Policy Analysis

Preparing for a Policy Profession

9

Until recent times, science and technology have only indirectly affected the process by which public policy has been shaped; they have not, when directly used by policymakers, affected the setting of goals or the selection of guiding principles. Of course, science and technology have transformed many aspects of contemporary living, and these changes have created problems with which policymakers have had to grapple, using primarily the processes of political exchange and maneuver. The first major federal effort at technical policy planning was the creation in the 1930s of the National Resources Board, which sought to derive from data it assembled new ways to deal with pressing economic, social, and political issues. But it was not until the end of World War II that there emerged a significant scientific interest in the exact tools that might be developed to help governments deal with national concerns. Stimulated by physical and social scientists' concern over nuclear policy, new attention was paid to the social needs of the postwar world, which in time led to the proliferation of federal and state programs for human welfare. This in turn led eventually to the application by business and administrative students of their tools for "scientific" management of large enterprises.[1] Science and business both contributed to the development of social policy planning technique.

[1] For an interesting review of the steady, if slow, march of the U.S. government toward formal planning, see Otis Graham, *Towards a Planned Society* (New York: Oxford University Press, 1976).

The Function of Planning Technology

We have concentrated thus far on tracing patterns of societal norms, public policy, and social policy. If, as argued to this point, various elements of the national government sometimes mount a sustained effort to shift the boundaries of societal norms in order to move in some new direction, then the tools that are available for use in the effort need to be understood. The nature of the means by which change can be effected is the basis of a conflict between what could be called the rational and the political views of the processes of government. The rational view holds that certain techniques can be brought to bear on decision making that will displace political power plays. The political view argues that a democratic society depends upon the continuous expression of citizens' wants in a contest between varying opinions on how to meet these wants. The political view sees the rational approach as too autocratic and technocratic and expresses a lack of confidence in scientific means, while the rational approach sees political mechanisms as too emotional, erratic, and unstable. The truth probably lies somewhere between these extremes. Planning technology does contribute objective input to decision making and leads to more comprehensive approaches to problem solving, whereas political mechanisms invariably lead to more subjective, compromise solutions, since bargaining among competing interest groups lies at the heart of that process. A blend of the two is undoubtedly in the making, and therefore a better understanding of the technical tools now available is necessary.

Discussions of policy tools often mix administrative and management devices with techniques useful in framing policies of a general nature. The following discussion will be limited, to the extent possible, to a few techniques or tools that are especially useful to policymakers who do not wish to rely exclusively on managing political forces to secure action on intuitively derived policies. Such tools are intended to complement political power with empirical evidence and rational analysis.

Policy tools, at their present stage of development, can do little to influence the underlying aims or broadest purposes of government. One party or administration may be committed to government intervention for the well-being of its citizens or for redistribution of income, while another party may be committed to containment of the national state and the undisturbed operation of the marketplace. Such fundamental guides to public action are derived from the backgrounds and histories of persons and institutions that hold these views and are seldom altered by technical devices.

At best, technology may be useful in helping policymakers or political leaders choose the more effective means with which to carry out the underlying purposes. The federal government can be more or less active in welfare by administering programs itself, by fostering administration by other governmental jurisdictions, or by encouraging voluntary efforts. It can act directly by mandating services or indirectly by altering the flow of its funds in one direction or another, without administrative control. It can act to redistribute income by manipulation of tax rates, by control of incomes and prices, or by providing compensatory, in-kind services to some part of the population. These alternative means by which principles of policy are first carried out are another level of guiding principles of policy, not administrative devices, and they can be influenced by technology.

Some technical means now available also serve to influence, albeit slowly, the underlying aims of policy by uncovering needs or potential trouble spots in advance of public awareness. If reliable, such advance knowledge could conceivably affect the underlying aims of political parties. Certainly in the 1930s the economic decline, which was not anticipated, led to a major shift in readiness to accept active federal intervention in hitherto private or local governmental domains. Participation in World War II had a similar effect. Untested is the conclusion that, if these events had been anticipated earlier, the shift in direction could have been introduced sooner. We can assume only that earlier identification of impending disaster might alter the tempo and shape of policy evolution. In 1980 the impact of electronic management information systems and of new medical technology began to transform the health delivery system, making it one area in which the future can be anticipated.

The tools to be considered are those that are believed, at least by their proponents, to be useful in helping policymakers decide the best use of their resources to further the basic purpose of their policies. In this sense, *resources* usually means allocation of funds, but the definition need not be so circumscribed; regulations, reassignment of personnel, and taxation are other resources with which government can effect its ends. The uses and limits of the following mechanisms will be discussed:

1. Assessment of the state of a system: needs identification, systems analysis, opinion polls, advocacy, surveys, social indicators
2. Decision making: program planning and budgeting systems, cost benefit analyses, planning by objective
3. Prediction: demographic projection, simulation, econometric projection
4. Outcome evaluation and research
5. Logical analysis
6. Managing program cuts and crises

Assessment of the State of a System

The oldest and most widely used device for social welfare purposes is needs assessment. It is, however, a mechanism that lacks sharp definition and has a quite primitive technology to draw upon. It is full of the subjective biases that each assessor brings to the data and that alter what the assessor considers a valid need. At its most primitive level, needs assessment takes the form of simply adding up the numbers in a situation perceived as a problem: number of persons with incomes below a given level, number of infant deaths, number of dilapidated houses, and the like. Such evidence may be useful in attracting a policymaker's attention or in mobilizing political support, but it tells little if anything about what should be done, the priority to be assigned to each distress, or the relationships among them.

A somewhat more sophisticated version was developed in Philadelphia in 1956, using the title "needs–resource assessment."[2] Numbers are counted as in the simpler version, but types of difficulty are first classified as to whether they involve the adjustment capacity of individuals or the social, educational, or cultural development of groups in the population. Then each problem is weighted to indicate the proportion of persons affected and the severity of the distress. For example, a rare fatal disease will be weighted more heavily as to severity than one that has transient effects on many thousands, but it will be less heavily weighted as to the proportion of persons affected. To this is added a weighted estimate as to the proven efficacy of programs of intervention to deal with each distress: A serious condition for which there is no known effective remedy will be less heavily weighted than one for which there is a proven remedy. The sum of these calculations is intended to produce a numerical ranking of problems and remedies that can help in the allocation and direction of resources. The process is encumbered by the subjectivity of the weighting, but it at least places in the open the subjective kinds of judgments that are made every day.

A much more sophisticated methodology is that of systems analysis.[3] In its simplified form, this requires that policymakers first enunciate their basic objectives. Data are then assembled about persons, organizations, and programs known to be involved in reaching this objective in any way. It is assumed that these components constitute a system of parts so interrelated that changes in the behavior of one will affect the behavior of the others.

[2] See Health and Welfare Council, Inc., "Needs/Resources Study," mimeographed, 1956; also Joseph Lagy, *Priority Determination Plans*, mimeographed (Vancouver: Community Chests and Councils of Greater Vancouver Area, 1960).

[3] For discussion of this approach see Phillip Boffey, "Systems Analysis," *Science*, November 24, 1967, pp. 1020–1030; Alfred Blumstein, "Systems Analysis and the Criminal Justice System," *Annals of the American Academy of Political and Social Science* 374 (November 1967): 92–100.

These data are organized to show how demand arises where people move through the provider system, how the units handle them, and what happens to them. At its present stage, this device requires a large investment in data gathering so that a population of consumers can be identified and tracked as they move through various provider units. It produces little evidence as to whether the problems of users are solved, but it does give useful insight into whether existing providers are at least receiving and helping persons presenting problems and whether there are bottlenecks or gaps in access. It relies on a conviction that, if service providers receive and retain consumers, then the consumers' needs are being met adequately.

Opinion polls or the accumulation of data about consumer wants through specialized advocacy groups represent another, half technical, half political means of assessing the state of a community or its welfare system. Opinion polls do provide some insight into what citizens and consumers consider important at the time they are polled, but their views about what should be done are strongly biased by the kinds of questions put to them and by the way questions are phrased. Respondents are also limited by what they have experienced, so that the process is unlikely to turn up clues to alternative courses of action. Respondents with unmet medical needs are unlikely to suggest new ways of delivering medical care, although they may express preferences between existing arrangements. More serious than any of these defects is the doubt whether responses of this kind are equated with actions that consumers may take. Except in the electoral process itself, where opinion and votes may be congruent, the match between opinion and action is poor. Respondents may say they "need" a neighborhood health center but may not utilize it if one is established.

Advocacy groups may mobilize evidence about any number of "needs" or consumer wants, but they are inevitably focused on specific problems—the very poor who need income, the disabled with specific handicaps. Although unmet distress can be made more visible, relationships among needs cannot be determined by such means.

A final tool for purposes of assessing the state of a system is a social indicator.[4] Indicators consist of quantitative data that serve as indexes to important conditions in society. Ideally, they provide a picture of both the nature and the state of a system or a society, a picture sufficiently standardized to permit measurement of changes over time. Constructing indicators is difficult because many phenomena about which trend data are desired are not readily quantified. Further, there are biases about statistical data chosen for measurement, and technological and social changes continuously in-

[4] See Raymond Bauer, *Social Indicators* (Cambridge, Mass.: MIT Press, 1966), Chaps. 1, 2; Eleanor Sheldon and Wilbert Moore, *Indicators of Social Change* (New York: Russell Sage Foundation, 1968); and Judith Wins de Neufuille, *Social Indicators and Public Policy* (New York: Elsevier, 1975).

troduce new factors that must be added to fill out the picture but that erode the possibility of measurement over time. Indicators have also been taken by some to imply a statement of policy or a commitment to a particular policy rather than being an objective measure of trends. A rise in divorce can be taken to mean that family life is weakened and that we should reverse the trend, but, equally, it can mean more freedom for women, which should be helped along. Indicators, to be effective, must measure the same phenomenon over a long period of time, so that changes can be identified. But in our present elementary stage of evolution, our understanding changes frequently, so that pressures build to change the bases of what is being measured, in effect eroding the very utility that indicators promised.

Despite these difficulties, indicators are constantly being elaborated and are used by public officials to sense the direction that the past has taken in order to work out the future. A case in point is the indicator of poverty or of employment. Base lines have been developed to measure the long-term movement of employment, but they have had to be reexamined regularly as uncontrolled social forces change the nature of the labor force. For example, if we take into account the entrance of housewives and teenagers into the work force, we seem to be sliding back in our capacity to employ all who want to work. If we were to adhere to earlier criteria about work, we would find that the number of jobs has increased over the years, so that proportionately many more are now employed than were 20, 30, or 50 years ago. Both indicators are correct, but they leave to policymakers the dilemma of deciding if we should be satisfied with trends and keep to past lines or be vastly discouraged and adopt some radically different orientation. Such difficulties need not be discouraging, for they force all of us to consider how we can continuously work for greater perfection in our social order; but they do not give guidance as to what course of action will lead to that end. All these devices, in effect, tell policymakers whence we have come and at what point we have arrived.

Decision Making

Decision-making techniques were first developed in industry and in public administration where the directors of formal or of single-purpose organizations had to make choices affecting the survival of the organization. In time, the principles underlying these administrative processes became elaborated so that they could be applied, at least experimentally, to larger systems, such as the national government or the work of a single government department.

Program planning and budgeting systems (PPBS) represents one of the best publicized attempts to apply a specific systematic process to policy development.[5] The system is simple conceptually, but extraordinarily complex and difficult to use in real situations. Simply put, persons sitting in central policymaking positions, such as in the Office of Management and Budget or the Department of Health, Education, and Welfare, set in motion a long-term process whereby the units accountable to them can organize their allocations and activities in the most efficient manner to achieve broad objectives. For those in the central position, the system also provides continuous feedback of data so that they can know how subordinate units are behaving and if they are moving toward the general objectives laid down by policy. The process forces all, from the top to the bottom of a system, to be more and more explicit about what they are trying to achieve and to synchronize their efforts. To decision makers at the top, it gives data about duplication, contradiction, and omission in the use of resources. It may not of itself create policy, but it provides a better basis for deciding what gets attention. Although subsequently discredited by name, its principles are still used, under other headings.

There are five major steps in PPBS:

1. Appraisal and comparison of various government activities in terms of their contribution to national objectives. For example, Aid to Families with Dependent Children, Social Security for dependents of disabled beneficiaries, and the Veterans Administration all operate vast programs providing funds for children. The system purports to encourage looking at all these in relation to each other and in the context of some objective, be it health or economic security of children.

2. Determination of how given objectives can be obtained with a minimum expenditure of resources. In the example just given, duplications in benefits, gaps in the organization of services, and other inefficiencies can be revealed in examining the relationship of the work of the major agencies. Such examination thus could produce a different pattern of service and expenditure in each agency so that it reinforces the work of the others without duplication.

3. Projection of government activities over an adequate time period. The system assumes that altering programs takes time, since vast bureaucracies cannot function while undergoing rapid change. The lead time in federal appropriations requires at least 3 years between the initial work on an agency budget and the time the budget will be

[5] See David Novick, ed., *Program Budgeting* (Cambridge, Mass.: Harvard University Press, 1965), for a discussion of the original application of the concept; and Robert Mayer, Robert Moroney, and Robert Morris, *Centrally Planned Change* (Urbana: University of Illinois Press, 1974), pp. 163–169, for an assessment of its limitations. Also, Elizabeth Drew, "HEW Grapples with PPBS," *The Public Interest*, no. 3 (Summer 1967).

acted on by the Congress; for practical purposes, a 4- or 5-year lead time is more reasonable.

4. Comparison of the relative contributions of private and public activities to national objectives. The private sector, including business, philanthropic agencies, the family, and informal associations, plays a crucial role in achieving any objective of government. The relationship between the two sectors needs to be thought through.

5. Revision of programs, budgets, and objectives in the light of experience and of changing circumstances.

These steps are clearly conceptual in nature and to become operational require specific and extensive data. Much of the early effort to introduce PPBS was devoted to inserting a new information system into a wide variety of agencies so that information from each could be made compatible with that provided by the rest. This introduced a marked strain in the work of government agencies, since each had to continue old data patterns while trying to add new ones, thus contributing to the exploding volume of paper passing in government operations. Once data systems are installed, complex computerized devices become necessary to absorb, store, and permit rapid retrieval of the data for policy purposes. It is not surprising that the early efforts to introduce this device in the federal government led to enormous strain and some displacement of effort away from program purposes and toward data-assembling almost for its own sake. Less time and energy was left, in the short term, for analyzing or acting on any conclusions that the data suggested.

The PPBS contains another defect characteristic of many technical management processes: a risk of deflecting attention from objectives to process, even after data processes are in place. In HEW, for example, PPBS led to the current emphasis in federal policy on coordination of the work of several agencies. While coordination is clearly necessary, it does not necessarily achieve the objectives for which programs were first installed. The balance between achieving objectives and coordinating activity is little understood, and PPBS has not yet resolved the tension between the two.

Cost-benefit analysis is one aspect of PPBS that antedated it in evolution.[6] It is an economic instrument designed to measure the balance between the costs of a particular course of action and the benefits that may be derived from it. Its great usefulness lies in its capacity to produce a comparison of the relative costs and benefits of several courses of action. For ex-

---

[6] For a discussion of the application of cost-benefit analyses to social programs, see John Hill, "Cost Analysis in Social Work," in *Social Work Research*, ed. Norman Polansky (Chicago: University of Chicago Press, 1960), pp. 223–246.; and Michael Borus, "The Economic Effectiveness of Retraining the Unemployed," in *Retraining the Unemployed*, ed. Gerald G. Somers (Madison: University of Wisconsin Press, 1968) pp. 125–148.

ample, choices can be made between two or more programs, each of which tries to accomplish the same objective. A general program of health education regarding high blood pressure or alcoholism can be weighed against the clinical program, which focuses on a smaller population identified as high risk. Where it is applicable, it is a priceless tool for decision makers.

Unfortunately, its application to large-scale policy choices is limited by some of the same factors that limit the use of PPBS. The costs of any course of action are difficult to ascertain if one wishes to go beyond simple book-keeping. Out-of-pocket costs (for staff, rent, capital construction, and the like) and the value of service benefits can be calculated. But every social program also has a built-in cost known as opportunity cost; that is, given limited resources, following one course of action means that another course cannot be followed and the opportunity to get results from that other course is forgone or lost.

The choice to increase cash income to all the poor may make it impossible for an administrator to reserve funds to pay for specific programs, such as reducing infant mortality by funding pre- and postnatal childbirth clinics. An even clearer example is the choice between improving housing conditions for all low-income persons and trying to prevent tuberculosis by providing health services to a smaller number of vulnerable persons.

Costs may also be external to the program; that is, a program may have side effects that can all too easily be overlooked, but whose costs a policy-maker must take into account. A policy to safeguard the privacy of delinquent children may have the side effect of concealing particular cases whose records show they need attention of some kind. Or a program to produce a great deal of housing quickly may destroy neighborhoods and introduce extra costs of social disorganization.

Closely related to these external costs is the difficulty of measuring the benefits in social programs. We are far from certain that we can prove that social programs deemed by many to be good do in fact influence the lives of their recipients for the better. Even when observation tells us that a course of action must be good, it may be difficult to translate this good into the quantitative terms a cost-benefit analysis requires. Most of this flaw, however, lies not in the tool but in the primitive state of social intervention. We have difficulty in proving that a network of community centers for young people makes much difference in the rate of juvenile delinquency or that social centers for the aged improve the morale of old people. Most evaluative studies reveal that persons not using such services come out about as well as those who do, by any measure of well-being now in use. The same can be said for the widely popular counseling programs. They are believed by all to help those who use them, but this is a highly selective population. When the behavior of large numbers of persons is compared, it has proven difficult to establish that those using counseling get along, in the aggregate, much differently from those who do not. None of this proves that the services are not worthwhile for individuals, but policy choices are concerned with effects on large populations, so that there is still difficulty in applying this tool to programs dealing with human beings and their behavior.

Despite these obvious limitations, the way of thinking that cost-benefit analysis stimulates becomes invaluable. Policymakers and planning staff attuned to such mechanisms can transfer the way of thinking to choices that do not lend themselves readily to absolute quantification. Certainly, all persons intuitively try to balance the costs and gains attached to any important decision. What this technique does is to translate this intuitive process into an open one, so that planners can be more conscious of what is involved in each of several courses of action. Over time, and with more practice, these tools can be improved and made even more technically useful.

Forecasting

In troubled times, everyone wants to know where we are going, but recent experience forces us also to be skeptical as to whether we can ever know. Hope overtakes doubt, and most Americans, while maintaining a strong skepticism, are also willing to suspend disbelief partially. The field of economics, which is considered to have made the greatest progress in forecasting among the social sciences, has been reported as relying on these mechanisms: (1) the loaded deck method (foretelling the future by what has happened in the past); (2) symptomatic techniques (reading clues or straws in the wind); (3) the form book (looking up what someone else has said); (4) the awe of computers (feeding data into a computer and accepting the output of the machine, which in fact reflects the subjective decisions as to input); (5) soothsaying (seers who rely on psychological or experienced insights).[7] If this is what prediction is like in the most developed science, what can we say about the field of social welfare policy?

Despite the foregoing tools, which are closely identified with organization management concepts, forecasting can be said to symbolize the long-term future for policy analysis. If government is ever to go beyond the stage of reacting to recurrent crises and the political pressures of self-interest, if it is ever to escape the heavy burden of acting on yesterday's experience alone, then the capacity to anticipate future events is crucial. There are two elements in this form of prediction: assessing what future states or conditions are likely to be and then anticipating the behavior of institutions and individuals, given those future conditions.

[7] Adapted from Leonard Sills, "The Art of Forecasting Is Ancient, Arcane," *New York Times*, January 3, 1977.

Policy planners approach this set of tools with utmost caution, and properly so. Attempts to anticipate the future have failed many times. Demographers in the 1930s predicted a decline in birth rates, but birth rates exploded in the 1940s, and no one predicted the subsequent falling off 30 years later. The attempts to predict the behavior of the economy or of the stock market have not been successful, although economics is a much better established "science" than is social welfare. The rush of women into the labor force and the prolongation of life for adults who survive childhood diseases or adult respiratory infection was not anticipated.

Despite these disappointments, and with due caution, one may say that human beings and their governments are now in a better position than ever before to anticipate future events under conditions that permit our institutions to get ready for change, rather than be overwhelmed by them. This is not to say that social intelligence or political factions will necessarily act upon advance knowledge, but the potential is in sight.

Three tools are worth noting for this purpose: demographic projection, modeling or simulation, and econometric projection of the relationship between unemployment and inflation (the Phillips Curve). All of these techniques require that certain assumptions be made and held stable, but within these assumptions, certain future events can be predicted with modest assurance.

Demography offers the richest and most fertile field upon which to draw for policy-planning purposes. The behavior of masses of people does change, but not so rapidly in ordinary circumstances that the behavior of the recent past can be ignored. Even changes in childbearing habits are likely to change only from generation to generation. Within certain upper and lower limits, therefore, it is reasonable to project into the next two or three decades the shape of the population in the United States, barring worldwide catastrophe. If we can expect that the proportion of children in the population will grow or remain stable, we can at least anticipate the level of educational facilities that must be maintained and the rate at which youths enter the labor force and demand jobs. At the same time, prolongation of life permits an estimate of the relative aging of a population, the number of years adults are likely to be available for work, and the number of years they must be maintained in the economy after they withdraw from work. Such evidence permits calculation of demand for and use of schools, housing, transportation, and the like. The information does not tell us whether children will want to continue in school for longer or shorter periods of time, or whether adults will want to quit work earlier or stay on longer, or whether adults will continue to live in familiar communities or will want to move on constantly to newer parts of the country. But the data do tell planners enough to warn them when difficulties are likely to confront society. What is needed is a sense of historical continuity on the part of government officials and of citizens so that anticipatory action will be highly valued and permitted in our political process.

This can be illustrated at two ends of the age spectrum. If the number of fertile women of childbearing age is known and if we assume that patterns of childbearing are reasonably stable for one generation, we can anticipate whether in the next generation the demand for primary school buildings and teachers will go up or down. If it is expected to go down, planning and policy can temper the enthusiasm to build new facilities. Buildings can be designed simply and built to last a short time, or they can be built solidly and designed to permit adaptation to other uses when they are not needed for schooling small children. The training of teachers can be organized so that an oversupply does not continue to be trained long after the demand drops off. Even better, training and contracts can be organized so that changes in demand, say from primary to secondary school, can be planned for. By reallocation of human resources, great peaks and troughs of under- and overemployment of teachers can be avoided.

If we can anticipate that the number of aged and retired persons is going to surpass the number of workers (who support those who retire), we can begin rethinking retirement policies and employment and insurance arrangements. In this way, we can avoid being locked into a rigid situation where people are forced out of work when we need human resources or are kept at work when their labor is not needed; and we can, with difficulty, also adjust the comparative benefits of the working and nonworking populations to fit the relative burden to be carried by those of working age. Many options, ranging from modifications of insurance benefits to employment and industrial incentives, can at least be considered.

It is, however, not sufficient to know what future conditions will be; it is also necessary to assess how social institutions will behave. Here we can draw upon the findings of the social sciences and studies of organizational behavior. These studies and findings have not yet been codified, even in primitive form, but some steps have been taken in this direction by Berelson and by Rothman[8] and some evidence is available. None of it is startlingly new, but the information can be used. Thus, we know that bureaucratic organizations are very difficult to move into changed work patterns and that several years must be allowed even if the smallest changes in behavior are to be attempted. Rapid changes usually produce chaos and strong resistance. Labor contracts and civil service introduce rigidities since benefits once acquired cannot be easily changed without countervailing incentives being introduced. Classic examples are found in the tendency of all organizations to

---

[8] See Bernard Berelson and Gary Steiner, *Human Behavior* (New York: Harcourt Brace Jovanovich, 1964); and Jack Rothman, *Planning and Organizing for Social Change* (New York: Columbia University Press, 1974).

elaborate and refine their work when demand slacks off, so that the same number of people do more and more things for fewer and fewer people. The well-known Parkinson's Law is apt: Work expands to fill the time available for its completion. In effect, if there is a fixed work period, the less there is to do, the more time people will take to perform a task.

There is also a tendency for each work function to be subject to more and more professionalization by its workers. All of us prefer to be supervisors or consultants, rather than to be at the bottom of the ladder, doing the hardest work. Some tasks are considered undesirable, and only the most strenuous counter incentives attract workers to such tasks as garbage removal, dishwashing in restaurants, or caring for the physical needs of very old, enfeebled persons. Finally, there is the well-known Murphy's Law (if anything *can* go wrong, it will), which imposes a high barrier to the transfer of any successful experiment to mass application. Success in a social experiment usually depends on the dedication and commitment (and genius) of its first proponents. But when this idea is to be spread widely, it depends for its operation upon quite ordinary people, who usually lack commitment or innovativeness. There are flaws as well as strengths in organization, and both can be anticipated.

These aspects of organizational life were most recently observed in federal efforts to reorganize, simplify, and streamline government operations. Large and small agencies of government and in the private sector each have developed their comfortable patterns of function, satisfying their staffs and their managers and the people who use them. Unsatisfied are the people who do not use these programs and those who wish to change patterns to save money or get different results. PPBS foundered at the level of the federal government, as much as for any reason, because the bureaus and agencies resisted the changes that were being urged upon them from higher authority. The extreme was seen in one state where the state executive office gave up the attempt altogether to modify the pattern of its agencies and converted PPBS into management by objective, only asking that executives identify the objectives they had for their departments and then try to achieve those self-identified objectives as best they could.

This recital of what we have learned about the behavior of organizations is overly pessimistic, but we have also learned what it is that organizations do well and how. It is the challenge of prediction to use this knowledge, not to ignore it, in shaping long-term policies to meet the kinds of problems that demographic analysis indicates can be anticipated. The combination of demography and knowledge of organizations does not deserve to be called a "tool" for policymakers, but the combination of knowledge about future conditions and behavior of organizations at least provides the raw material with which policy staffs can shape their policies more soundly.

In 1976 the Joint Center for Urban Studies, Harvard–MIT, completed a useful exercise in forecasting that suggests direction for the future in this technique, mainly because it illustrated how many hitherto unmanageable social factors can be made specific for forecast use.[9] The objective was to project American housing needs from 1972 to 1980 in a form usable in determining national housing policy. This effort sought in several ways to go beyond a previous major forecast effort by the federal government, that of a blue-ribbon committee chaired by Edgar Kaiser.

1. It separated social deprivation and market demand. It did not assume that inadequacies necessarily had an effect on housing demand.
2. It sharpened the definition of housing deprivation, adding households where the cost of housing was so high as to affect families adversely.
3. It examined a number of specific metropolitan housing markets to estimate the future of each and used these estimates to arrive at a national figure. This stratagem was in contrast to earlier efforts that treated housing as a national market and did not account for local variation.

The forecast used the following units of data, among others: aging of a population over time; mortality rates; new household formation rates, including an allowance for reduction in overcrowded households and the social trend to single-person households; migration rates to and from metropolitan areas; replacement rates for normal losses due to fire and the like; changes in the desire to upgrade housing; rates of occupancy in below-grade housing, including housing too costly for income; and rates of normal construction in the private marketplace. It was also recognized that the impact of some factors was more difficult to estimate, such as a change in the desire to locate in more attractive surroundings and the occurrence and effect of periods of economic recession.

Errors in the resulting estimates could be checked to a limited extent before 1980 by two means. Some data could be simulated for an earlier period and then checked against actual experience, and over the 3 years of the exercise, newest data about housing starts and household formation could be checked with late census bureau reports. The authors found that some errors cancelled each other out, with the result that the final estimate seems more likely to fit the reality than would otherwise be expected. They found that they had overestimated the volume of new housing starts but had been low in their estimates of new households formed, mainly of unattached persons.

[9] Bernard Frieden and Reilly Atkinson, "Forecasting the Nation's Housing Needs," *Working Paper No. 30* (Cambridge: Joint Center for Urban Studies MIT–Harvard, February 1975).

The study, though costly and time consuming, seems to justify the confidence that such projections can be improved as to social policy issues and can be useful in policy planning. Without claiming absolute reliability, the method is probably much more accurate than unsystematic peering into the future intuitively or waiting for massive distortions in housing supply to be discovered after the fact.

A quite sophisticated technique that can help predict future situations is simulation, which involves building quantitative models of social systems. Information is gathered about the variables in a situation and is run through a computer to see what results are produced by any change in any variable. In many ways, this is an effort to reconstruct real-life situations descriptively and then manipulate the pieces to see what results from different combinations. Of course, the reliability of the result depends on gathering sufficient data on the right variables. A simple illustration would be to test by simulation what would happen if the first entry into mental health services were to be shifted from, say, the psychiatric clinic or hospital to the schools or to the police. Would more or different cases be identified? Would more or fewer patients be routed to and accepted by treatment centers? Would different kinds of personnel be able to perform the same tasks and with what different results? To attempt such simulation would require data about many disparate phenomena. How do police or schoolteachers as compared with psychiatric personnel handle mental problems? Where do troubled persons naturally go on their own initiative to get help? To what kinds of initial advice do they listen? How do psychiatric personnel react to referrals from nonmedical sources? The great advantage of the simulation technique is that it avoids even more costly and risky experimentation on human beings. It is analogous to laboratory experimentation in the development of drug therapies before the results are tried on people.

As is true of many other techniques, the costs of simulation are not insignificant. In a well-known case, a model was constructed of the pathways by which all troubled persons found their way to a network of mental health agencies in southern Illinois. This involved laboriously collecting data on all applications and referrals in a large geographic area. Once these data were assembled and the pathways traced, it was discovered that the real point of first contact for most patients was the sheriff's office. With this information in hand, it was possible to simulate changes in agency behavior and client reactions if the sheriff's office were added to the network of mental health agencies. Thus, it was possible to peer into the future, to see what would happen in real life if this step in the mental health network were mandated and made explicitly a part of mental health programming. Simulation has also been used to design a new reimbursement system for hospitals, testing system reaction in advance.

Closely akin to simulation are games, usually designed to test out how organizations and individuals would behave in given situations. The same plan specifies a particular situation and the persons or groups usually involved—for example, agency staff, average citizens, city councillors, legislators, social workers, doctors, and advocates of minorities attempting to get a larger share of resources in the reallocation of funds to meet children's needs. The actors who play the parts of the participants in the situation are briefed on the known and expected patterns of behavior of the persons or groups. The actors are then set to work to solve the game problem. Incentives and rewards and punishments can be built into the game rules, and the way the actors resolve the problem can be taken as a reasonable simulation of what real-life actors would do in a like situation.

Finally, an example of prediction technique can be taken from economics, well in advance of anything yet available for social welfare, but suggestive of a path for future evolution. The econometric projection known as the Phillips Curve is held by many to predict the behavior of the economy as regards employment and inflation. Based on certain analyses of the behavior of several economies, the technique postulates that, in a given set of economic circumstances, an increase in inflation by government action will reduce unemployment, whereas a governmental effort to increase employment beyond certain limits will increase the rate of inflation. In other words, the curve makes explicit the trade-off that policymakers can contemplate between jobs and inflation. Mayer, Moroney, and Morris have proposed an adaptation of this device to social work, wherein it is suggested that the trade-off for policymakers lies in the amount of control that citizens or political figures will accept as related to the seriousness of the social problem confronting them and the evidence that the control will lead to a solution of the problem.[10] The more severe the problem and the more assurance there is that a given course of action will reduce it, the more likely it is that citizens and officials will accept controls necessary to launch a new problem-solving intervention.

From these examples—demographic projection, simulation, prediction of organization behavior—it is reasonable to conclude that social policy personnel do have some tools to help anticipate the future, however limited their accuracy may be. The Phillips Curve precedent also suggests ways in which the available tools could be improved upon.

Outcome Evaluation and Research

The term *evaluation* is used here to mean relatively rigorous scientific efforts to assess the outcomes of social programs in terms of their effect on the per-

---

[10] See R. Mayer, R. Moroney, and R. Morris, *Centrally Planned Change*, for a simplified discussion of the potential application of this curve to social welfare.

sons to whose needs the programs are addressed. This is quite different from customary evaluations of social welfare, which measure success and public acceptance by the number of cases handled or the number of personnel added. Evaluation as used here calls upon the best methods of social science research, and such research requires the time, patience, and deferred rewards that policymakers can seldom afford. Instead of proposing that research is a policy tool, it is here suggested that the results of research enterprises in social welfare constitute a pool of information upon which policy personnel can draw.

Such research does present certain problems to the policymaker that should be recognized at the start. Social science research is still in its relative infancy, and the evaluation of many programs has often been conducted with less than suitable criteria. Even more risky is the tendency of researchers to consider single programs as examples and to criticize the underlying theory of a program on the basis of a few cases. In recent years, program evaluations, especially of large-scale publicly funded experiments, have been publicly funded. One illustration is the evaluation of massive experiments undertaken in educating underprivileged children to overcome the social disadvantage under which many of them labor. The research findings have been almost uniformly disturbing. Head Start was found to have only short-term and transient effects, unless it is extended into later school years, thus transforming the educational system. No changes in school situations or methods had much effect compared to the effect of changes in such nonschool factors as home and friends. Other studies have found little or no change, as measured by children's reading or their work, when resources are increased, when school organization is changed, or when teaching methods are altered. Human resources training programs have been found to have at best marginal effects on future work experience of the trainees when compared with the experience of those not trained by such programs. Large-scale public housing programs have often proven to be collecting points for poverty, crime, and illness. And most careful studies of psychological and emotional counseling fail to find much benefit traceable to the counseling itself.

This discouraging recital might seem to argue that all social programs are without merit. The difficulty lies in the nature of most social science research, which usually is fueled by a desire to probe awkward questions and study subjects for the sake of the intellectual excitement the search affords. Such research usually tries to prove that a given statement is false, not that it is true; proving the null hypothesis is most valued. Given the limited development in research technique applicable to policy questions, the disappointing results may also be attributed to faulty measurements as much as to faulty programs. What these research findings are useful for, despite their limitations, is their warnings about what not to do, about what may be fruitless effort. Such research thus helps clear away the underbrush of an infinite number of bright ideas, leaving to policymakers the opportunity to search out more promising alternatives.

Apart from such uses, evaluation of this character, when conducted skillfully and used delicately, can be used to help correct or improve adopted programs as they evolve. Questionable findings do not have to lead to complete abandonment of programs or policies; they can help to assure that by constant improvement the programs can achieve the desired results in the long run. The political situation makes the adoption of such a view of evaluation difficult for most policymakers, for any criticism of a program is likely to be used by political opponents as a sign of the policymaker's ineptitude.

That this risk is worth taking is seen by some positive results in recent policy research. The Congress has long debated the use of a negative income tax to reform income-maintenance programs. One serious objection, other than its possible cost, has been that it would adversely affect the labor market—that is, that workers once assured of a decent income without work would withdraw from the work force. Careful studies were undertaken under rigorous experimental conditions to measure the effect of introducing a negative income tax to specific populations. The experiments and the evaluations were funded over a long enough period of time to permit reasonable assessment. The findings were interesting, but not astounding. Compared to a control population not receiving the income assurance, a small percentage of the test population was tempted to quit the labor market to enjoy the presumed comforts of marginal income. And only a small percentage of persons did withdraw, mainly women or second wage earners who had entered the labor market to make ends meet for their families, to the neglect of their children.[11] Such a modest finding was not sufficient to overcome political and economic opposition.

Another study used a broader sweep of evaluation than that usually relied upon by social researchers. Levitan and Taggart reexamined the range of programs spawned by the Great Society efforts of the Johnson administration.[12] Whereas most research into such individual programs as Head Start and Model Cities suggested that they had done very little, these authors used different measures: Instead of looking to see whether poverty had been abolished, they noted that, overall, the especially poor and disadvantaged and the black minority benefited in quite measurable ways. They secured much more open access to health services, and they succeeded in getting a more equitable share of these services than before. Their access to better education was measurable, or at least their education was less different from that of middle-class families than was true before the Great

---

[11] Joseph Pechman and M. Timpane, *Work Incentives and Income Guarantees, The New Jersey Income Tax Experiment* (Washington, D.C.: Brookings Institution, 1975).

[12] See Sar Levitan and Robert Taggart, *The Promise of Greatness* (Cambridge, Mass.: Harvard University Press, 1976).

Society spurt. On this kind of measure, income, housing, and the opportunity to share in the decision making of programs affecting their lives (through community action agencies) were all improved. While these gains may not have abolished poverty or even reduced the gap between the poorest and the richest, it could not be said that the programs had no positive effects. Thus, with a shift in the measurements, one could honestly conclude that there were some retrievable gains in certain programs upon which improvements could be grafted in the future.

Logical Analysis

A few words should also be said about a method for policymakers of a quite different order, that of analysis of a situation using intelligence and reflection. Management systems, computer technology, and techniques of data collection and research are only aids to intelligent analysis, not substitutes for it. One of the greatest hindrances to the effective use of intelligent analysis is the haste with which many actions are taken. Policymakers are harassed by overwhelming duties, many of them concerned with insignificant details of travel, meeting many people, and producing or reading quantities of routine documents. Little time is left to reflect on the meaning of experiences and observations or, for that matter, to think over the meaning of research findings, social indicators, and the quantities of data that computers and the mass media make possible. Large quantities of information are useless unless they are reduced to some order and unless there is time to consider intelligently their meaning or significance. Analysis supplies this vital ingredient to policymakers and their staffs. Short of an exposition about the art of reasoning and logic, it is difficult to know what to say generally about the art of analysis, as contrasted to the art of quantifying data. Two examples may help clarify the distinction.

In recent years, policymakers have struggled to chart an acceptable course of action concerning the health of the nation. During this time, the costs of medical care have been inflated beyond all belief, and health or medical services constitute the fastest growing part of the GNP. This has led to numerous complex proposals to contain or control the costs of medical care, ranging from increasing the share the consumer pays for insurance to reduce use, to increasing the tax share, to limiting the use of hospitals, and to mandating what physicians should be paid. In all of this work, few people took the time to look at the health system and the population in relation to each other. Long reflection and examination of old data led many to recognize simultaneously a flaw in the reasoning that governed most efforts at cost control. The flaw was simply a gap between the makeup of the present-day population and the aims of the medical care system.

The medical system is based primarily upon diagnosis and treatment of curable conditions and to a much lesser extent upon prevention of illness. But while our medical technology has become a wonder of complexity, our population has changed. The largest number of health conditions that demand attention are now chronic illness of all kinds, for which current medicine has little or no cure. Some two-thirds of all medical effort, meaning the effort of hospitals, physicians, nurses, and the like, are devoted to such conditions as arteriosclerosis, stroke, spinal cord injury, genetic and birth defects, enfeeblement of old age, heart failure, and renal failure.[13] Most of these conditions remain with patients for as long as they live, often for decades. The conditions are not susceptible to cure or reversal, although sometimes their progress can be retarded. These patients continue to return to hospitals and doctors who can do little for them but who must see them in simple humanity and are paid for it. When self-care gets difficult, the patients are routed into nursing or custodial institutions at a disproportionate rate.

It has taken long reflection to recognize that the traditional health system is out of kilter with the current situation in two respects. The nursing institutions are largely proprietary and are on the borderline between medical care and nonmedical custodial care, but their operations are largely funded by public health tax dollars. And more significant is the almost complete absence of supportive services that could help disabled persons remain with their families or in their own homes with supplemental help, in preference to full-time institutional care. These two gaps seriously disrupt the functioning of the health system, and a disproportionate number of persons who might get along with part-time supplemental care in their own homes are shifted to more costly full-time care in institutions. Only after analysis and reflection were these flaws clearly identified, and then the panoply of data systems could be put to work to secure evidence with which to shape remedies.

Another example can be seen in the unwieldy complexity of government programs that surround citizens at all levels. There are so many programs that even expert professional staffs require still more specialized information experts to help them find what they need in the maze. And the maze depends upon an almost impenetrable accumulation of regulations that bind city, state, and federal government into some kind of partnership, but one in which the responsibilities of each are unclear. Lacking clarity, there has emerged a buck-passing phenomenon in which officials at each level of government are in danger of losing sight of the objective of their welfare programs; instead, they focus on the best ways to reduce their share of

---

[13] Monroe Berkowitz et al., *Public Policy Toward Disability* (New York: Praeger, 1976) and Berkowitz, *Evaluation of the Structure and Functions of Disability Programs* (New Brunswick, N.J.: Bureau of Economic Research, Rutgers University, 1975).

the cost while shifting a greater share to another level of government. The result has been not only to displace the goals of public action but to give rise to a proliferating staffing pattern in which as many or more persons are needed to supervise and monitor the system as are involved in the delivery of the services to the ultimate consumer.

Finally, time to think about the possible short-term consequences of any policy or program can be used to bring together units of knowledge that, when viewed simultaneously, can identify risks and hazards not at first manifest. A useful example is seen in the 1977 proposals of the Carter administration for welfare reform. One proposal was to consider total family income when deciding eligibility for any income supplement to which an individual family member may be eligible. On the surface, this appears to be a logical policy in order to strengthen the sense of family responsibility for its members before public income support is resorted to. On reflection, it becomes clear that such a policy is most likely to encourage individual members of a family to leave home in order to qualify for benefits to which they consider themselves entitled. The experience of the Aid to Families with Dependent Children program comes at once to mind. In that case, the exclusion of families with two parents from entitlement has encouraged desertion by husbands when their earnings prove insufficient to meet family needs.

The dilemmas that ensue are by now widely recognized, but the inappropriate confidence in computer technology and management systems has led to an almost total reliance of government on efforts to increase the amount of data being collected, and at the same time to reorganize the machinery of government, before the purposes to which the machinery is to be put are clearly thought through. While great effort has gone into installing data systems and trying out mechanical devices to clear the confusion, it has only recently become obvious, as a result of reflection and analysis by many, that these are not the first essentials of future policymaking. Analysis has not yet produced useful leads in this area, but the problem is becoming more clearly defined.

Analysis of this kind can be useful at two levels at least. For one thing, it can help policymakers to fine tune policies they have already launched. A program of health insurance can be modified in its particulars to balance more equitably the care needs of the chronically sick and the therapeutic needs of those with curable conditions. And for more complex issues, such as the proper division of accountable responsibility between levels of government, a start can be made to think through governmental relationships that can promise better attention to human needs, rather than to shifting cost burdens.

Analysis of this kind involves an improved welding together of science, values, and human judgment. To quote Hammond and Adelman:

Judgments find their expression in the forming of public policy because it is during that process (of endless debate) that the products of science and technology are integrated or aligned with human values. . . . The key element is human judgment. . . . The fact that an essential element in policy formation remains a mystery has serious consequences. . . . Means must be found to avoid both poor judgments and self-serving judgments. . . . Two general methods have been recognized for these purposes: (1) the adversary method by which scientists with differing judgments are pitted one against the other in front of a judge or a jury, and (2) the search for scientists who have somehow gained a reputation for wisdom in the exercise of their judgments.[14]

These authors go on to propose a third method, whereby the criteria for judgment are rendered somewhat more objective. They are quoted, not so much because their suggestions are necessarily the best possible, but because their concern with the subject brings into public view once again the importance of judgment in the policy process, a quality not replaceable by other tools or techniques.

Managing Program Cuts and Crises

Social welfare and its policies have for 50 years developed methods for managing a growing sector of public life. Beginning with the middle 1970s, the field began to learn how to cope with either a cutback in support or a drop in the rate of growth at a time when demand for services continued to rise. A number of techniques have developed to meet this new situation, most of them based on principles of management drawn from either business or public administration theory. Such methods usually begin with an analysis of the relationship between elimination of resources, potential for recreating new resources, and the strength of resistance to reduction in various service areas. The structure of program authority, especially in the public sector, varies from state to state, as does the structure of the involved citizen interest groups and their capacity to mobilize influence and thus to affect the creation of alternative resources. The scale of resource change plays an important part in the choice of method for managing the change.[15]

The tactics for dealing with retrenchment can be listed as follows:

[14] Kenneth R. Hammond and Leonard Adelman, "Science Values and Human Judgment," *Science*, October 22, 1976, pp. 389–395. (Copyright 1976 by the American Association for the Advancement of Science.)

[15] Charles H. Levine, Irene Rubin, and George Wolochosian, *The Politics of Retirement: How Local Governments Manage Fiscal Stress* (Beverly Hills: Sage Publications, 1981).

1. Program activities can be deferred, scaled down, or eliminated.
2. Services can be transferred to or shared with other agencies not affected by cuts.
3. Projects can be deferred, or tasks in an agency can be deferred while keeping the program alive. Examples are the use of reduced funds to maintain staff, an office, paper, or maintenance work, while reducing the client delivery of services that may be additionally costly. An agency that manages funds for day care by contract with other providers can keep its contracting and monitoring staff on payroll even if there is little money to pay out for day care, while waiting for a new infusion of funds.
4. Productivity can be improved to do more with the limited funds by increasing work loads, streamlining procedures, and incorporating such labor-saving devices as minicomputers and word processors to reduce clerical staff.
5. Changing personnel, using less trained and less expensive staff for more routine functions.
6. Rationing services by setting priorities of need or by instituting a system of user fees.
7. Developing systematic activities to improve the resources or economic base by new fund raising.

Such devices can be grouped into a few general strategies:

1. *Denial strategy,* which relies on borrowing to maintain services, selling off assets, deferring maintenance, and spending surpluses.
2. *Stretching* and *resisting,* by trying to do more with less and avoiding deep cuts or changes; increasing productivity of staff, rationing, reducing the work force by attrition, etc.
3. True *cutting* strategies involve more drastic steps, such as layoffs, closing offices, shifting programs to other agencies, and even terminating some programs altogether. When these drastic measures are resorted to, the strategy involves choosing details that try to smooth out the effects and minimize adverse reaction from interest groups in or out of government.

A shift in national policy that deemphasizes social welfare has brought welfare analysts and administrators to a new appreciation of the techniques of management, which emphasize budget management, fiscal manipulation, personnel management, and accounting and information systems. The incorporation of these techniques in the policy analyst's repertory will both increase the capacity of professional welfare analysts and administrators and also increase their professional stature.

Tools and Professional Policy Careers

This brief review of the technical potential in policymaking serves to show that there is a professional or quasi-professional role in policymaking that, by its existence, confirms that careers for policy personnel do exist in social welfare. It has been long known that policymakers are persons with political skill who acquire positions of influence and power and employ a variety of aides drawn from quite diverse and even nondescript backgrounds. What can be presented convincingly now is that policy careers exist and that it is possible to begin the task of equipping persons for performance of this role rather than relying on the accidents of fortune and influence alone.

By now, policy roles number in the few thousands, less than the several thousands of planning positions and millions of managerial positions that can be identified in American life. Staff to conduct policy analyses are found in, to name the most obvious, state and federal offices of budget; the staffs of mayors, governors, and presidents; the staffs of legislators; planning units in departments of human resources, welfare, or health; and regional planning commissions.

As staff filling these positions acquire a better sense of their functions and of the political milieu in which they operate, they will be ready to learn how to use the rudimentary tools and techniques now available. When the limitations of the latter are recognized, the functionaries will press for and will contribute to the fashioning of better tools for policy analysis. These improvements can come about because they are developed by practitioners of what is still largely an art, and they can then be taught to others. Policy staff can enter into dialogue with scientists of all kinds, to encourage them to develop and bring forward improved tools for testing. In the last analysis, some symbiosis between the scholar, the thinker, and the doer must result. For some time to come, the policy practitioners may be expected to move back and forth between the world of makers of policy and the world of students of policy.

Additional Readings

Aaron, Henry. *On Social Welfare*. Cambridge, Mass.: Abt Books, 1980.

Caro, Francis G. *Readings in Evaluation Research*. 2nd ed. New York: Russell Sage Foundation, 1977.

deNeufville, Judith Innes. *Social Indicators and Public Policy*. Amsterdam and New York: Elsevier, 1975.

Dror, Y. *Ventures in Policy Sciences: Concepts and Applications*. Amsterdam and New York: Elsevier, 1971.

Epstein, Irving, and Tripodi, Tony. *Research Techniques for Program Planning, Monitoring and Evaluation.* New York: Columbia University Press, 1977.

Glennerster, H. *Social Service Budgets and Social Policy.* New York: Harper & Row, 1975.

Kahn, Herman. *The Next 200 years.* New York: Morrow, 1976.

Mishan, E. J. *Cost Benefits Analysis.* London: Allen and Unwin, 1972.

Mishan, E. J. *What Political Economy Is All About.* New York: Cambridge University Press, 1982.

Novick, David. *Program Budgeting.* Cambridge, Mass.: Harvard University Press, 1965.

Rivlin, Alice M. *Systematic Thinking for Social Action.* Washington, D.C.: Brookings Institution, 1971.

Stein, Bruno, and Miller, S. M. *Incentives and Planning in Social Policy.* Chicago: Aldine, 1973.

Wildavsky, Aaron, "Rescuing Policy Analysis from PPBS," *Public Administration Review,* March–April 1969, pp. 189–202.

Williams, Walter. *Social Policy Research and Analysis.* Amsterdam and New York: Elsevier, 1971.

INDEX